Inalienable Possessions

Inalienable
Possessions

The Paradox of
Keeping-While-Giving

Annette B. Weiner

UNIVERSITY OF CALIFORNIA PRESS

Berkeley / *Los Angeles* / *Oxford*

University of California Press
Berkeley and Los Angeles, California

University of California Press
Oxford, England

Copyright © 1992 by The Regents of the University of California

Printed in the United States of America

1 2 3 4 5 6 7 8 9

Library of Congress Cataloging-in-Publication Data
Weiner, Annette B., 1933–
    Inalienable possessions: the paradox of keeping-while-giving /
Annette B. Weiner.
        p.   cm.
    Includes bibliographical references and index.
    ISBN 0–520–07603–6 (alk. paper).
    ISBN 0–520–07604–4 (pbk.: alk. paper)
        1. Ceremonial exchange—Oceania.   2. Women—Oceania—
Economic conditions.   3. Women—Oceania—Social conditions.
4. Economic anthropology—Oceania—Methodology.   I. Title.
GN662.W45   1992
305.42′0995—dc20   91–43580
                                                                        CIP

The paper used in this publication meets the minimum requirements
of American National Standard for Information Sciences—Permanence
of Paper for Printed Library Materials, ANSI Z39.48–1984 ∞

Contents

Illustrations

Figures

Map

Preface

This book is an experiment in a new kind of ethnographic interpretation regarding those critical and perennial problems centered on the norm of reciprocity, the incest taboo, and women's roles in reproduction. The universality of the norm of reciprocity and the incest taboo long have been common parlance in anthropological discourse. Yet the assumptions that underwrite these problem areas were developed a long time ago without recognition of the meaning of women's labor in cloth production or of women's political control over significant reproductive areas of cultural life. In those instances when women did appear in anthropology's most widely acclaimed exchange or kinship theories, they usually were described either as seducers of men or as wives sequestered around the domestic hearth kept busy as the reproducers and nurturers of children. In either case, they were considered peripheral to the theoretical loci of power that resided in men's affairs.

Human and cultural reproduction, however, are sources of power for women as well as men. Since power is always surrounded by contradiction and ambiguity, it must be carefully located in each particular ethnographic case to document how power gives scope but also limits political authority. For example, the rules of behavior that people appear to be following in reciprocal gift exchange or sister exchange are actually surface phenomena constructed out of a deeper social priority that can never solve but only approximate the central issue of social life: keeping-while-giving. How to keep some things out of circulation in

possesion
commoditization
representations

the face of all the pressures to give things to others is the unheralded source of social praxis.

The theoretical thrust of this book is the development of a theory of exchange that follows the paradox of keeping-while-giving into the social and political relations between women and men with foremost attention to their involvement in human and cultural reproduction. The traditional social theories that simply segregate women and men into respective domestic and political spheres and that view men's production as the foundation for political hierarchy are no longer tenable. When women are analytically relegated to the sidelines of history or politics, the emergent view is ethnographically shallow and theoretically distorted.

Whereas major controversies over the meaning and writing of ethnography have arisen in the last decade, little attention has been given to how anthropologists must reinterpret the received ethnographic data that form the basis of the established social theories. The problem is not simply about the ethnographic enterprise but concerns the theoretical concepts rooted in Western history that legitimate the assumptions the ethnographer takes into the field. The other voices that need to be heard are not only local assistants' explanations but those distant and compelling theoretical voices that assume, for example, that inquiries about gifts given are sufficient if they extend to the gifts returned.

Because ethnographic interpretations are subtly framed by these theoretical premises, any comparative analysis faces particular problems. Often the data on gender are meager and comparisons from one society to another cannot be made by simply listing similar social rules or analytical oppositions to prove one's point. The undertaking here involves exploring many different productive and reproductive contexts within any one society while giving as much attention to the sibling roles of women and men as kinship theory has given to their roles as spouses. Searching for the kinds of possessions that people try to keep out of circulation is far more theoretically meaningful than assuming that exchange simply involves the reciprocity of gift giving. Such interpretive efforts also demand close attention to women's production, even when they are as seemingly ephemeral and valueless as banana-leaf bundles, human-hair strings, faded cloth pieces, or old plaited mats.

To chart these new theoretical directions, I draw on a selected number of societies in Oceania that bridge the traditional culture areas of Australia, Melanesia and Polynesia. Comparing such ethnographically diverse societies enables me to show how the same paradoxical concerns of keeping-while-giving mirror similar cultural configurations even when the solutions and the relevant levels of political hierarchy are vastly different from one part of Oceania to another. Although my reinterpretations of ethnographic data are limited to Oceania, the traditional concepts surrounding the norm of reciprocity and the incest taboo are rooted in Western cultural constructions. These constructions have long histories even more knotty than the nineteenth-century classifications that opposed the "primitive world" to "civilization." The conclusions I reach show that keeping-while-giving is not just peculiar to Oceania, but has been an important part of Western economics since the time of ancient Greece. As a generic concept, reciprocal exchanges are only the pawns on the chessboard of culture preserving inalienable possessions and fending off attempts by others to claim them. This approach changes the way we theorize about kinship and politics by centering women and reproduction into the heart of the political process where they ethnographically belong.

This book gestated for ten years, benefiting from my continuing Trobriand fieldwork from 1971–1991. From my very first visit, I became perplexed by how Trobriand women came to devise such an elaborate technology for making wealth out of dried banana leaves. At the same time, I pondered the question that many other anthropologists had raised since Bronislaw Malinowski's 1915 seminal Trobriand fieldwork—Why do Trobrianders have a ranking system of chieftaincy when such a system occurs nowhere else in the area? Did Malinowski cast a Trobriand "paramount chief" so much in the image of a Polynesian ruler that Trobriand leadership seemed significantly different from the politics of Melanesian big men? These questions of hierarchy and origins, however, became even more complicated as they led me into controversies about gender. Although I discovered that Trobriand women made their own wealth that directly affected men's wealth, the response of some of my feminist colleagues was to emphasize that Trobriand women were definitely not chiefs—proof again that, universally, women are always associated with the lesser-valued side of social life. However, this singular opposition left no room for explanations of why women's banana-leaf wealth leveled men's wealth, including chiefs', nor why women had high status, a fact that even Malinowski, although he ignored women's wealth, consistently pointed out.

What finally turned these problems to a social arena beyond the Trobriands was my decision to inquire further into Marcel Mauss's notation in the opening pages of *The Gift* to Samoan fine mats as "feminine property." Interested in finding a point of comparison, I spent four months in Western Samoa, studying the circulation of fine mats. Once I had recognized that banana-leaf bundles and skirts were not a Trobriand anomaly but a particular kind of cloth, then not only Samoan fine mats but the worldwide history of cloth wealth took on significant theoretical importance. My Samoan fieldwork opened up my pursuit of how fabrics were made and used, not just as trade items, but as political and even sacred repositories of wealth. I continued to expand my inquiry and discovered that symbolic meanings that associate the making, circulation and guardianship of cloth with human reproduction and with connections to cosmological phenomena, such as ancestors and gods, were remarkably similar even in totally different parts of the world. And even though women universally were by no means the sole producers of cloth, they were strikingly involved in meaningful stages of cloth production, in the guardianship of certain sacred cloths, and in the general symbolism that calls attention to the power located in human and cultural reproduction.

In developing a more global theoretical approach to these issues, I have published a series of essays over the past ten years. Originally I thought I would bring these essays together in one volume, but I recognized rather quickly that the ideas in the articles had to be taken much further both theoretically and comparatively. Therefore, although I draw on my previously published materials, this work has been substantially revised according to my present thinking.

Many institutions assisted me in my research over the past decade, notably, the John Simon Guggenheim Foundation; the National Endowment for the Humanities; The Institute for Advanced Study, Princeton; the Wenner-Gren Foundation for Anthropological Research; and New York University. I am deeply appreciative of their confidence in my project. I acknowledge the cooperative assistance of the Papua New Guinea government, the Institute of Papua New Guinea Studies, the Milne Bay Provincial Government, the Kiriwina Council of Chiefs and of the many Trobrianders who over the past twenty years contributed their knowledge to my research efforts, especially the late chiefs Vanoi Kekulakula and Waibadi Giyovadala and their successor, Puliasi Daniel, as well as Modiyala Elliot, Bomapota Toitapola, Bunemiga Tonuwabu, Ilewaya Topuleku, and Lepani Watson. I also acknowledge the support of the Prime Minister's Department of Western Samoa and the ethnographic assistance of Dr. Horst Cain, the late

Liki Crichton, the Hon. Nonumalo Leulumwenga, Tuala F. Tiresa Malietoa, Leota Pepe, and Eni Sofara.

In my further research on cloth, I thank Jane Schneider for her efforts in coorganizing the Wenner-Gren conference on cloth with me and in coediting the volume that resulted. I also thank the other participants in the conference whose research confirmed my belief in the pervasive worldwide economic and symbolic uses of cloth. I am grateful to Tom Beidelman and Gillian Feeley-Harnik, my coorganizers of the Wenner-Gren Conference on Divine Rule, along with the other conference participants. This conference helped me view issues of Oceania hierarchy comparatively within Western and non-Western traditions.

Books rarely appear without the support of others who critique one's ideas, offer encouragement or track down obscure references. I deeply appreciate the close reading and the supportive and constructive comments on this manuscript by Michael Fischer, Ivan Karp, Joanna Wychoff, and several anonymous reviewers. My colleagues at New York University, particularly, Tom Beidelman and Fred Myers, were not only unstinting in giving their time and expertise to reading several drafts, but shared field data, gave me innumerable references and always pushed me further along with their encouragement and their ideas. Ann Marie Cantwell, Faye Ginsburg, Bambi Schieffelin, and Constance Sutton lent moral support as well as thoughts from their own research interests. I also thank the graduate students in the joint seminar I held with Fred Myers for their responses to parts of the manuscript. I am indebted to Fitz Poole, Malama Meleisea, and Penelope Schoeffel for sharing their field insights and data with me and to André Iteanu for our many discussions on Orokaiva and Trobriand exchange. My graduate students, Ian Burnett, Deborah Elliston, and Brain Larkin, were enormously helpful with hunting bibliographic references. I thank them as I do Jeanne Wesley who kept the department running when I was submerged in this research.

Finally, my deepest appreciation goes to my wonderful colleague and spouse, William E. Mitchell, whose help and encouragement were vital. Not only did he read and reread, often for a third or fourth time, the many drafts that this manuscript underwent but his critiques always forced me to sharpen my thinking and write with strength. In countless ways I owe him a debt that can only be called—inalienable.

Introduction

*In the little houses the tenant people sifted their belongings
and the belongings of their fathers and of their grandfathers.
Picked over their possessions for the journey to the west. . . .
The men were ruthless because the past had been spoiled, but
the women knew how the past would cry to them in the
coming days. . . .*

    *When everything that could be sold was sold . . . still there
were piles of possessions; . . . .*

    *The women sat among the doomed things, turning them
over and looking past them and back. This book. My father
had it. He liked a book. . . . Got his name in it. And his
pipe—still smells rank. . . . Think we could get this china dog
in? Aunt Sadie brought it from the St. Louis Fair. See?
Wrote right on it. . . . Here's a letter my brother wrote the
day before he died. . . . No, there isn't room.*

    *How can we live without our lives? How will we know it's
us without our past?*

                John Steinbeck, *The Grapes of Wrath*

    This book has its origins in my first ethnographic field-
work in the Trobriand Islands located off the coast of Papua New
Guinea that, early in this century, took on unprecedented anthropological importance through Bronislaw Malinowski's research and personal renown. Malinowski reduced the extensive exchange events he

1

witnessed to a simplified but pioneering classification of "gift" and "counter-gift," theorizing that reciprocity was the basis for social relations in "primitive" societies. My research, beginning sixty years later, revealed dynamic social actions far more socially dense than Malinowski's classic conclusions. While comparing what I found in the Trobriands with analogous situations in more politically hierarchical Polynesian societies, I realized how deeply his assumptions were grounded in nineteenth-century evolutionary beliefs about the communal nature of "primitive" economics.

The "norm of reciprocity" is, in actuality, a theory of economic behavior whose anthropological tenets were shaped centuries earlier. During the rise of capitalism, the give and take of reciprocity took on an almost magical, sacred power among Western economists. In the eighteenth century, Adam Smith and others argued that reciprocal relations operated in the marketplace *sui generis*, keeping the market equitable and stable without external legal controls. A century later, this same belief in reciprocity as a regulatory mechanism was described for "primitive" societies when it was thought that "natives" lived without governing bodies or legal codes. There the gift given and received kept groups socially and politically stable without recourse to government or law. This trust in the motivation behind "primitive" reciprocity persisted so that confidence in how the norm worked in the exchanges of thousands of seemingly inconsequential gifts enabled anthropologists, beginning with Malinowski, to determine fixed, rational criteria for the reciprocal acts they recorded ethnographically. But these criteria, thought to be more scientifically and theoretically sound, also were culture bound so that, over time, it remained even more difficult to perceive how Western economic rationalities were being imposed on theories of other cultures' economic systems.

The acceptance of gender ideologies fundamental to capitalist systems introduced other formidable problems for anthropological theory. Analytical dichotomies, such as stasis/change, nature/culture, and domestic/public, always identified women with the supposedly negative side. Theories grounded in ethnographic descriptions of "gift exchange" among men served to affirm and legitimate men's autonomous control in economic and political pursuits. Women, though physically present, were seen but ignored as active participants in their own right. Even their own productive efforts that supported or enhanced a society's economy were discounted.

In many societies throughout the world, however, women are the producers and, in part or wholly, the controllers of highly valued pos-sessions—a currency of sorts made from "cloth."[1] Intricate symbolic meanings semantically encode sexuality, biological reproduction, and nurturance so that such possessions, as they are exchanged between people, act as the material agents in the reproduction of social relations. Most important, cloth possessions may also act as transcendent trea-sures, historical documents that authenticate and confirm for the living the legacies and powers associated with a group's or an individual's con-nections to ancestors and gods. Historically, women's control over these arenas has accorded them powers associated with magical po-tency, sacred prerogatives, political legitimacy, and life-giving and life-taking social controls.[2] Although Simone de Beauvoir asserted that gender is a "historical situation" and that biological reproduction is sur-rounded by historically constructed (negative) conventions and mean-ings, neither she nor other feminists attend to the political significance of women's complex roles in these cosmological domains. Other ob-jects, however, such as shell, stone, precious metals, or even human bones that are usually associated with men's wealth, contain similar symbolic referents to biological and cosmological phenomena. And in these cases, the ethnographic literature abounds with classifications in which men's actions are privileged because they are connected to the sacred domain whereas women's similar activities are relegated to a pro-fane category.

These interpretive discrepancies illuminate the pervasiveness of Western thought where women's participation in biological reproduc-tion and nurturance are fetishized with negative value. But when the commingling rather than the oppositions between female and male symbol systems is seriously considered, we find that women's control over political and cosmological situations and actions can be beneficent or malevolent, matching the ambiguous potential of men's control and power. This view also reveals the sociopolitical ramifications of how women and men are, at the same time, accorded and deprived of au-thority and power. Men's autonomy is held in check, undermined, supported, confounded, or even, at times, superseded by women's economic presence.

The subject of this book is not women per se but an attempt to cast off some of the most cherished precepts in social theory and, in so doing, establish a new practice for comparative ethnographic descrip-tion and explanation. Ethnographic data cannot be easily pared down to a single semantic marker that encodes reciprocity. Possessions are given, yet not given. Some are kept within the same family for generations with retention not movement, bestowing value. Ironic ambiguities exist in the games people play, in the perverse strategies they employ, and in the complex symbols they use. In practice, kinship is a decisive marker and maker of value, not in terms of genealogical rules or norms of behavior, but because certain basic productive resources express and legitimate social relations and their cosmological antecedents in spite of all the exigencies that create loss. The reproduction of social relations is never automatic, but demands work, resources, energy, and the kind of attention that continually drains resources from more purely political endeavors. Just as a nation's international economic policies are held in check by the powerful demands and strategies of, for example, the country's auto makers, agrofarmers, and oil producers, so too, in local situations, the demands of wives on husbands, sisters on brothers, and one generation on another, tilt production and exchange in directions that limit wider coalitions.

When we acknowledge that so-called secondary domestic values such as biological reproduction and nurturance as well as the "magical" values of cosmologies and gods underwrite economic and political actions, then the traditional public/domestic boundaries break down. Social theory must account for exchange events that acknowledge women's possessions and social actions as much as men's. The division of labor is not simply a dual gender construct, but encompasses the attention and effort that both women and men give to production and to those cosmologies that disguise the unresolvable tensions, problems, and paradoxes that make up social life.

Cosmologies are the cultural resources that societies draw on to reproduce themselves. But these resources are not merely ideologies, located outside the production of material resources. The traditional dichotomy between cosmology or superstructure and the material resources of production and consumption leaves little space to explore the cultural constructions by which the reproduction of the authority vested in ancestors, gods, myths, and magical properties plays a fundamental role in how production, exchange, and kinship are organized. To emphasize and overcome this problem, I use the term *cosmological authentication* to amplify how material resources and social practices link individuals and groups with an authority that transcends present social and political action. Because this authority is lodged in past actions or representations and in sacred or religious domains, to those who draw on it it is a powerful legitimating force. As Thomas O.

Beidelman pointed out a long time ago, "one must understand the cosmology of the people involved so that one has some idea of what they themselves believe that they are doing."[3] Ethnographically, the people involved attest to the primacy and power of cosmological phenomena. For the Swazi, an intrinsic reproductive essence lies at the center of the *Incwala* royal rituals; Australian Aborigines claim that the a priori essentialness of their social life is constituted in The Dreaming; Polynesians consider that the efficacy of procreative power can only be found in the magical potency of *mana*.

Of course, only to follow Polynesians' explanations is to elevate cosmology to a level of first principles, returning us to the Durkheimian position that all social life comes into being through the sacred, cosmological domain. For Emil Durkheim, the maintenance of the sacred—totemism as the case in point—was unambiguous, generating social solidarity that resulted in a homogeneous order. Like the norm of reciprocity, Durkheim believed that the sacred domain functioned as a totality never needing external control. A traditional Marxist position equally circumscribes cosmological phenomena as unproblematic because the sacred domain supports ideologies that function only to mystify and disguise domination and subversion. How then can we account for the symbolic and material complexities prefigured by distinctions and discriminations associated with gender when historically women have held claims to authority through their power over cosmological authentication? First, we must acknowledge that cosmologies act directly on social life mediating and, at the same time, fomenting society's most unresolvable problems. Second, we must see how power is constituted through rights and accesses to these cosmological authentications that give value to certain kinds of possessions which are fundamental to the organization of exchange. And third, because through exchange the cosmological domain becomes a significant source of power, its ambiguity and precariousness create difference, not homogeneity.

Unfortunately, much of the history of anthropological theory has been a search for universals, a positivist approach that would discover rules of descent, the incest taboo, totemism, or reciprocity and then elevate these norms to a privileged position. Yet it is the paradoxes of social life that contain the seeds of first principles—those duplicities and ambiguities that create tensions that can only be ameliorated and never resolved. Exchange acts fuel these tensions because all exchange is predicated on a universal paradox—how to *keep-while-giving*. In the closing paragraph of *The Elementary Structures of Kinship,* Claude Lévi-Strauss describes a universal dream expressed in an Andaman Island myth which tells of "a world in which one might keep to oneself" and escape from the "law of exchange."[4] Turning his back on Durkheim's primacy of myth and ritual to project his own scientifically determined structural model, Lévi-Strauss dismisses this myth as fantasy—and so undercuts the very precept by which exchange value is determined.

The Paradox of Keeping-While-Giving

Some things, like most commodities, are easy to give. But there are other possessions that are imbued with the intrinsic and ineffable identities of their owners which are not easy to give away. Ideally, these inalienable possessions are kept by their owners from one generation to the next within the closed context of family, descent group, or dynasty. The loss of such an inalienable possession diminishes the self and by extension, the group to which the person belongs. Yet it is not always this way. Theft, physical decay, the failure of memory, and political maneuvers are among the irrevocable forces that work to separate an inalienable possession from its owner. We all are familiar with the crowns of queens and kings—the signs and symbols of authority and power—or antique furniture and paintings that proclaim a family's distinguished ancestry. From environmental concerns for the future of the world's rain forests to the political controversies generated over the return of the Parthenon's Elgin marbles to Greece, certain things assume a subjective value that place them above exchange value. When a Maori chief brandishes a sacred cloak she is showing that she is more than herself—that she *is* her ancestors. This is the power of cosmological authentication. The chief incorporates her ancestors' fame, their rank, and their authority unto herself; her guardianship of the cloak accords her that right. In a similar way, a noted Japanese Noh performer told me that when he dons the Noh mask of *Okina,* he becomes not *like* the god, but *is* the god.

Gregory Bateson long ago saw the problems inherent in a functional or structural theory of reciprocity. His formulation of schismogenesis based on his Iatmul fieldwork was an attempt to find the "governor" that prevented the constant giving and receiving in an exchange or ritual event from spinning out of control.[5] In fact, inalienable possessions that groups and individuals hold dear to them act as that governor. Inalienable possessions do not just control the dimensions of giving, but their historicities retain for the future, memories, either fabricated or not, of the past. Not always attainable, keeping some things transcendent and out of circulation in the face of all the pressures to give them to others is a burden, a responsibility, and at best, a skillful achievement.

Even though permanence for all time is an impossibility, individuals and groups work with exacting care to recreate the past for the present so that what they do in the present affects the future. As the Spanish philosopher, Miguel de Unamuno y Jugo, observed, "reason builds on such irrationalities."[6] Unamuno believed that human beings "live in memory and by memory" and that the basis of social life was "the effort of our memory to persist . . . to transform itself into our future" even in the face of our foreboding of death.[7] Sigmund Freud, of course, had a much more pessimistic view of how the unconscious urge toward death directs human actions. More recently, contra Freud, Ernest Becker argues that the very fear of death haunts us from birth, motivating us toward acts of heroism that give us "a feeling of primary value, of cosmic specialness, of ultimate usefulness to creation, of unshakable meaning."[8] Examples of heroic ventures through which individuals strive for immortality in efforts to deny death fill the pages of people's histories. These acts of "heroism" manifest themselves in behaviors as diverse as the enactment of a first birth ritual, the building of a pyramid, the recitation of a genealogy, the naming of a college dormitory, or the carving of a totem pole.

The motivation for keeping-while-giving is grounded in such heroic dynamics—the need to secure permanence in a serial world that is always subject to loss and decay. Enormous energy and intensity are expended in efforts to transmute or transcend the effects of deterioration and degeneration and/or to foster the conditions of growth and regeneration. Therefore, attention to regenerating or recreating the past is neither random nor inconsequential. Historical consciousness is promoted; change is disguised. Situations of political revolution or rebellion, where hierarchy is so developed that one segment of the society revolts, appear to be exceptions. Yet when the victors claim leadership, they immediately constitute their legitimation through the creation of symbols that stand for the past. Consider how the leaders of the T'ang dynasty used regalia from earlier times to fabricate their genealogical connections to former rulers.[9] In much the same way, Joseph Stalin used V. I. Lenin's body to create an inalienable monument that helped legitimate his legal right to rule,[10] whereas following the revolution, all heirs to the Tzar were shot, their buried bodies exhumed, their bones burned, crushed, and scattered to prevent any relic from ever reemerging as the rallying point for a counterrevolution.

Even small groups expend enormous efforts and resources, for example, to convince a younger generation to beware of loss, to preserve relationships, and to guard sacred possessions. In Ian Dunlop's fascinating films on Baruya male initiation, young men, dressed in thick layers of women's fibrous skirts which scratch their legs, are told by the older men that the skirts scratch them as a reminder never to forget the women; their task as adults is always to protect them.[11] Later, in what is the most self-reflexive part of the film, the Baruya men uncover an ancient stone axe blade. Turning to the anthropologist, Maurice Godelier, the Baruya leader says that they have kept this most precious possession secret from him all the years that he has lived with them. Now they reveal it and in so doing, disclose their true social identities. Unlike other possessions, the axe blade embodies their ancestors' histories. Such moments capture the determination to defeat change by substituting an icon of permanence even if manifested in a Baruyan axe blade, an Australian sacred ancestral *tjurunga* stone, or a Maori ruler's woven cloak.

The paradox inherent in the processes of keeping-while-giving creates an illusion of conservatism, of refashioning the same things, of status quo. Although possessions, through their iconographies and histories, are the material expressions of "keeping," the most that such possessions accomplish is to bring a vision of permanence into a social world that is always in the process of change. The effort to make memory persist, as irrational as the combat against loss can be, is fundamental to change. The problems inherent in "keeping" nurture the seeds of change.

THE PARADOX OF PERMANENCE
AND LOSS

Anthropologists have labored long over the question of change in human societies. Lévi-Strauss, for example, subverted the issue by defining entropy as the hidden "purpose" of culture crystallized in his image of the "primitive" *bricoleur* continually refabricating different versions of the same thing—what Robert Murphy terms "Zen

Marxism." Marshall Sahlins, recognizing that change must be accommodated in any dynamic structuralist theory, shows change as the central feature of how the cultural order reproduces itself. But in his examples of Polynesians' reactions to Western contact, Sahlins is not completely disengaged from his earlier evolutionary framework. Following Lévi-Strauss's metaphorical distinction between "hot" and "cool" societies, Sahlins maintains that differences in social complexity can be equated with a society's responsiveness to stasis or change. Implicit for Sahlins (and much more explicit for Lévi-Strauss) is that some groups, such as Australian Aborigines, are closed to change, merely replicating the same things through time. In "ranking" societies where history is more formalized and rank accommodated through lengthy genealogies, Sahlins shows much more dynamically that "the cultural order reproduces itself in and as change."[12]

In the first volume of *Capital: A Critique of Political Economy*, Marx emphasizes how continuity in the conditions of production cannot be achieved without the necessary conditions for reproduction, thereby underscoring how change stands as a constant threat to reproducing surplus value. For example, in the long-term maintenance of relations between capitalists and wage-laborers, both parties must deal with dislocating circumstances, such as external immigration policies and markets for raw materials and internal conditions of the housing and training of workers. Even wars, famine, and public opinion were among the events that Marx enumerated.[13] To minimize change, to respond to shifting situations rapidly, to prevent workers from controlling their own destinies are some of the social conditions that must be attended to so that change can be incorporated into the reproduction of the relations of production.

The opposition between change and stasis when applied to a division between "egalitarian" and "ranking" societies obscures the more fundamental problem that Marx identified. In reproducing kinship relations and political alliances in small-scale societies, change also is a condition that must be worked against. How these societies reproduce the past for the future in and through loss is the key question. In one sense, an inalienable possession acts as a stabilizing force against change because its presence authenticates cosmological origins, kinship, and political histories. Yet the possession may be the very symbol of change as those in the top ranks of a society may combat change by reconstructing or fabricating genealogies or sacred chronicles in order to identify themselves with the possessions of earlier leaders or dynasties. In other circumstances, those further down may well fight for change, invoking connections to other, more obscure symbols.[14] In Gandhi's struggle for India's national independence, he invoked the hand spinning of a traditional cloth called *khadi,* what Nehru later called Gandhi's "livery of freedom."[15] Both the act of spinning and the wearing of khadi elicited a complex symbolism, reasserting women's traditional productive domain and uniting women and men against the economic tyranny of Manchester's manufactured cottons and the political hegemony of British rule. When we take such possessions as a serious subject of study, teasing apart their histories and how their subjective value is constituted, we find that such possessions, as they move in time and space, become the carriers of more information and greater authority than other kinds of things. Control over their meanings and transmission from one generation to the next accords authority to their owners.

The power generated by this authority reveals a further ambiguity in the nature of inalienable possessions. Because each inalienable possession is subjectively unique, its ownership confirms difference rather than equivalence. Exchange does not produce a homogeneous totality, but rather is an arena where heterogeneity is determined. Although individuals or groups negotiate with each other on many levels in each exchange encounter, the ownership of an inalienable possession establishes and signifies marked differences between the parties to the exchange. The possession not only authenticates the authority of its owner, but affects all other transactions even if it is not being exchanged. For the possession exists in another person's mind as a possible future claim and potential source of power. If I possess a sacred cloth, in Walter Benjamin's terms, its "aura" extends to my other possessions as well because my social identity, rank, or status is legitimated by my possession of one sacred object.[16] Such ownership gives me authority that operates in other transactions so that my ability "to keep" empowers my ability to attract. In other words, things exchanged are about things kept.

The paradoxical tension created by keeping-while-giving exists at the root of all attempts to defeat loss. To overcome the destructiveness of loss, individuals and groups devise myriad ways of disguising the impermanence of social life. But these are not benign efforts to counterbalance death. They are grounded in exchange arenas where difference in the present is affirmed whereas difference in the past is disguised. These are the dynamics in which inalienable possessions are empowered to act as the source of difference and hierarchy. The strategies and negotiations surrounding inalienable possessions acknowledge the complementarity, the domination, and the subversive tactics that, taken together, show the extent or limitations in transforming difference into rank and hierarchy.

In this way, inalienable possessions are the representation of how social identities are reconstituted through time. The reproduction of kinship is legitimated in each generation through the transmission of inalienable possessions, be they land rights, material objects, or mythic knowledge. These possessions then are the most potent force in the effort to subvert change, while at the same time they stand as the corpus of change. Among Australian Aboriginal groups, The Dreaming provides the means through which parts of ceremonies, sacred names, songs, and body designs are given to others, creating a strong sense of relatedness among dispersed, widely distant groups of people.[17] But some individuals attain more sacred knowledge than others, so that even with a strong egalitarian ethos, difference enters into each encounter. Whatever exchanges occur between elders and younger kin are influenced by the fact that elders hold the inalienable possessions—sacred stones, ceremonies, totemic designs, and names—giving them authority because others desire what they have. In this way, the Aboriginal cosmology is a fertile source of inalienable possessions that are guarded, inherited, sometimes lost, and at times, conceived anew. In general, cosmologies are active forces in social life that, in mediating systems of meaning, also entail material or verbal objectifications that actively become the agents or instruments of change.

Thus the bricoleur mystifies change in order to create and participate in change. Birth, decay, and death are the natural phenomena and the wellspring out of which difference emerges. Inalienable possessions are powerful because they represent and encompass these primary sources making difference a potential threat and a tangible reality. But even though inalienable possessions are dominant politically, they are not simply under the control of men. Women, too, are centrally involved in their production and guardianship as well as their cosmological authentication. Maori cloaks, woven by women, symbolize women's rights to ancestral prerogatives and the legitimization of rank for women and men. Australian Aboriginal hairstrings, an important component of ceremonial life, are often produced and exchanged by women. The list of such involvement by women in production and exchange is lengthy, yet ignored in exchange theories. At the core of the paradoxical tensions over keeping-while-giving is the problem of gender.

THE PARADOX OF REPRODUCTION
AND GENDER

Great strides have been made over the past twenty years in the anthropology of gender, but it still remains difficult to overcome functionalist or structuralist theories that claim to govern social practice from above while associating gender with categorical definitions or single symbolic systems grounded in ranked oppositional patterns. What generates such a long historical attachment to these theoretical positions is that, to date, studies of gender have been uncritical in their acceptance of the primacy of a norm of reciprocity. Exchange theories reveal strongly entrenched gender biases because the relevant subject matter remains what males exchange between one another. For me, my first question in the Trobriands was, would Malinowski have ignored Trobriand women's banana-leaf wealth if men had produced and exchanged it? Subsequently, I saw the same bias repeated in other societies, most notably in relation to the multiplicity of symbols, possessions, and exchange events associated with sexuality and reproduction.

In the 1960s, John Murra argued that Peruvian fabrics provided the economic basis as tribute and treasure for the rise of Inka civilization. But even with this example of cloth produced by women, the production and accumulation of such wealth has never been considered an essential resource in theories of political evolution.[18] In cases where fabrics are manufactured wholly or largely by men, cloth still is considered by anthropologists as a subsidiary resource, a soft object whose symbolic meanings relate to cosmology, ancestors, birth and death, and the woman's side of things. Against the hard currencies of gold, silver, or shells that anthropologists usually define as encapsulating individual heroic exploits, clan political prestige, or the groom's side in marriage, cloth wealth, like the economic presence of women, fades in analytical importance. But the recent volume of essays, *Cloth and Human Experience,* shows how politically vital cloth can be in cultures ranging from chieftaincies to large-scale class societies, as such possessions provide repositories of wealth to be kept as well as to be given away.[19] Although on a global scale and over several centuries women played a larger role than men in cloth production, any universalizing between gender and hard and soft wealth excludes how much men are involved with and dependent upon cloth treasures. Similarly, women's symbolic and social involvement in the circulation and guardianship of hard substances, such as jade, shells, or even ancestral bones, at times intersects with men's political actions.

The analysis of cloth reveals more than the complex interweaving of gender and production. For inalienable possessions, both soft and hard, evoke widespread, common symbolism associated with human reproduction and the cultural reproduction of the kin group, be it family, clan, or dynasty, accomplished primarily through keeping-while-giving. Cultural reproduction also includes the cosmological authentication of inalienable possessions through which the presence of ancestors or gods legitimates divinity, chieftaincy, or eldership. These processes reveal how sexuality and reproduction are intimately part of social practice, played out in a range of social actions surrounding the rituals of death, marriage, birth, inheritance and the transmission of ancestral authority. Over a decade ago, Pierre Bourdieu argued, contra Lévi-Strauss, that marriage patterns did not follow formal, structural rules, but rather grew out of complex strategies, part of an "entire system of biological, cultural, and social reproduction."[20] Yet rarely are the cultural rituals and meanings associated with human reproduction or cosmological authentication brought into economic consideration. Although Friedrich Engels noted that biological reproduction provided the basis for the social relations of production, he never pursued this point to show how the political relations of biological reproduction have changed over time, shaping Western social and political histories.[21] In fact, even among many feminists, the irreversible fact that women give birth has long been viewed as the proof of biology as destiny, that women's bodies de facto relegate them to homes, childcare, and domination by men. Although in Western traditions, men have organized ways to relegate biological reproduction and women to a private domain while they controlled the public institutions that legitimated primogeniture, kinship, and kingship, the negative value accorded biological reproduction is by no means universal.[22]

Anthropologists, however, in their analyses of non-Western traditions, followed similar Western priorities, segmenting rituals surrounding pregnancy and birth that connected these events to ancestors and gods into the less essential part of dual categories—the natural, private, and profane side of social life. It was Malinowski with his Trobriand data who documented the reciprocal exchange of women between two matrilineages, but it was Lévi-Strauss who shifted the paradigm to show that women are only one among a panoply of objects exchanged between brothers-in-law. His model purports to define the invariant rules that all societies use in the organization of kin and affinal relations by showing how control over women's reproduction signals the transformation from nature to culture. Lévi-Strauss, however, argues that women occupy a special place among "objects" because, in their movement between men, they embody and conflate both nature and culture. Even though he raises women to this analytical level of objectification, Lévi-Strauss still denies women motivation and access to their own resources and strategies.

Surprisingly, the structural implications of a woman as a sexual object gained strong support even among feminists. In the 1970s, with the beginning of concentrated research interest in gender, Lévi-Strauss's ideas were elaborated, for example, in Sherry Ortner's claims that women's universal subordination results not from biology per se, but from a society's cultural constructions that surround biological reproduction. In these constructions, women's roles in reproduction (i.e., nature) are ranked far lower than men's cultural accomplishments.[23] Gayle Rubin, also following Lévi-Strauss's theory of marriage exchange, argued that the oppression of women was psychologically embedded in the way individuals are conscripted into particular systems of exchange relations that are organized by men.[24] Ortner and Rubin attempted to challenge biological determinism by relying on structural and psychological analyses. In divergent ways, however, they both were trapped by the essentialism in Lévi-Strauss's theory of reciprocal marriage exchange that objectified women's sexuality without acknowledging how their sexuality became a source of their own strategy and manipulation through keeping rather than giving.

More recently, Marilyn Strathern's book, *The Gender of the Gift*, proceeds from the same assumptions about the norm of reciprocity. Strathern presumes to move beyond positivist theory by beginning with indigenous notions of personal identity and then showing the types of social relations that are their concomitants. She uses the terms "detachability" and "transformation" to discuss exchange events, but the processes she describes still are tied to a Lévi-Straussian model of reciprocal exchange. Therefore, objects are merely the reflections of their transactors' embeddedness in social relations, and the value of an object remains only a consequence of the identity of the exchanger.[25]

Being grounded in the a priori essentialism of the norm of reciprocity, Strathern's argument cannot account for the temporal aspects of the movements of persons and possessions and the cultural configurations that limit or expand the reproduction or dissipation of social and political relationships through time. All social values are existential rather than, as Strathern claims, intrinsic. Social value must be created and re-created to prevent or overcome dissipation and loss. The movements of persons and possessions through time and space are bound by, and to, the temporality of birth and death as well as production and decay, bringing into dramatic relief the problem with such dogmatic Western convictions that a woman's sexuality and her role in reproduction make her into a property that must be exchanged and controlled by men.

These assumptions and fears have a long and complex history in Western political theory most dramatically spelled out by Rousseau, to whom Lévi-Strauss acknowledges a large debt. The novel *Emile*, for example, brilliantly expresses Rousseau's deep obsession with the magnitude and primordial need of men to ensure their own paternity, given the universality of the incest taboo.[26] When Emile cruelly rejects the woman he loves because she is carrying another man's child, he proves that a woman's entire life is utterly dependent upon and driven by her ability to conceive. Therefore, sexuality and human reproduction are collapsed into a single entity that defines a woman's primary presence in social life. It is this view that Lévi-Strauss scientifically objectifies in his theory of reciprocal marriage exchange, thereby conflating sexuality and human reproduction. As a consequence, he ignores the culturally reproductive domains in which social, economic, and, even in some cases, sexual intimacies between sisters and brothers are maintained even when they marry outside their own natal group.

In general, kinship studies are still defined by these cultural constructions in Western sciences as anthropologists treat sibling incest as ideological, mythical, or extraordinary. Despite Lévi-Strauss's elegant sociological theory of marriage exchange, the incest taboo does not simply transform biology into culture nor does marriage replace a consanguineous set of relations with a sociological set of alliances. One central problem is that beliefs in the logical priority of the norm of reciprocity define the rules of marriage exchange as an equivalence between one man's gift of his sister for the return gift of another man's sister. Another problem is that women's kinship roles are defined by collapsing the multiplicity of their reproductive exchange domains into biological reproduction despite the fact that a sister and a wife are not equivalent. A further problem emerges from excluding the multiple identities of women and men as both spouses and siblings so that even cultural reproduction is viewed analytically as an automatic, functional process.

The intimate relationship between brother and sister, rather than the incest taboo, is the elementary kinship principle. First, sexuality and reproduction are culturally divisible into significant elements and foci of action and control, in which women after they marry play substantial exchange roles as sisters.[27] Second, sibling intimacy is key to the cosmological authentication of intergenerational histories while reproducing social difference. Sibling intimacy reproduces social identities, rights to cosmological and material resources within the siblings' natal family, lineage, or clan. But since women and men typically draw on different cultural resources and constituencies, exchange between siblings makes difference essential to these reproductive processes. Marriage, in providing additional resources to sister-brother siblings, further enhances the power of their intimacy and gives them resources from other social groups. Overall, the social and political complexities that involve local practices of sibling intimacy vary widely from one society to another. But these ethnographic diversities mask the common kinship principle of siblings who, after they marry other spouses, reproduce by exchanging with each other and/or their respective children in order to authenticate intergenerational stability while exercising and enhancing the power of difference.

The transformation of difference into rank and hierarchy is bound up with how women and men, as wives and husbands and especially as sisters and brothers, play out these multiple culturally reproductive roles. This is what kinship is all about. Proscriptive rules ignore the social and political dimensions of sibling intimacy even when its presence in Western history is significant. Robin Fox asserts that all cultures follow the one Biblical commandment, "Go forth and multiply." Yet God's rules emanating from the Garden of Eden approved of sibling incest and marriage not only for the obvious reasons with Adam's and Eve's family, but even later, among Noah's family. Medieval nobility depended upon sibling marriages to increase their power, thereby grossly abusing the law of the Catholic church when the Pope tried to limit marriage to the seventh degree of consanguinity. But in establishing religious orders, the Catholic church itself depended upon the value of sibling incest by having women enter into "spiritual marriage" with their "brothers"—the residents of monasteries close by.[28] Since many siblings from wealthy families entered these communities, often sisters were "married" to their own blood brothers. In other parts of the world, Polynesian chiefs and kings did not command allegiance and submission without the cosmological powers of their sisters. In many cases, these women themselves became well-known chiefs and queens. Brother-sister incest existed as a portentous political option either as an actual genealogically correct marriage or as the prerogative of the first sister and brother clan ancestors. Sister-brother incest is at once sacred and profane, politically dynamic and rigorously disguised, the ultimate solution to legitimacy and the most feared compromise. Reductionist rules of its prohibition linked as they are to the rules of reciprocity can never expose the vast reproductive power in sibling intimacy even in societies where sibling incest is rigorously taboo. The sibling taboo is bound up with the same paradoxical dynamics and motivations that haunt and shape the problem of keeping-while-giving.

Reconfiguring Exchange Theory

This book is an anthropological experiment—a new way to conceptualize exchange processes and values which accommodates the place of gender in social theory and leads to a reconceptualization of how difference is transformed into rank and hierarchy. I call these chapters experiments because they represent an alternative mode of ethnographic description and explanation. This mode is based on the paradoxical nature of social life, focusing on the ambiguities and heterogeneities in exchange rather than upon normative and homogeneous characteristics. My experiment is to reexamine classic anthropological exchange theories and the ethnographies that validated these theories to demystify the ahistorical essentialism in the norm of reciprocity which has masked the political dynamics and gender-based power constituted through keeping-while-giving.

In the first chapter, I trace the problems I inherited in my own Trobriand fieldwork from Malinowski's projection of the norm of reciprocity as the underlying principle in all "primitive" social relations. I show how the norm of reciprocity developed as a Western cultural construction and how its use was transformed to fit different Western and "primitive" economic situations, whereas the most ancient and powerful economic classification, inalienable and alienable possessions, was ignored. This historical discussion sets the stage for chapter 2, where I take Marcel Mauss's *The Gift* and reanalyze the most controversial theoretical text on "primitive" exchange and the Maori ethnography that provided Mauss with the answer to the problem of why a gift given elicits a return. Although Lévi-Strauss believes that Mauss's ethnographic entanglement in the Maori point of view limited his ability to develop a structural model of exchange, it is precisely the dense

Maori ethnographic descriptions that reveal the priority that the Maori themselves accord inalienable possessions. Women's production of cloth, some of which becomes inalienable because it is imbued with *mana*, the procreative power that women acquire, is central to these priorities. The guardianship of inalienable possessions such as these transforms difference into rank.

With this reinterpretation of Maori exchange and gender in mind, in chapter 3 I first examine the elementary principles in Lévi-Strauss's theory of marriage exchange to show that although actual sibling incest may be culturally disavowed it remains intransigent and politically vital. Turning to Polynesia, where questions regarding political hierarchy have long been argued, I take up these issues by reanalyzing ethnographic data from three societies, Samoa, ancient Hawaii, and the Trobriands, which differ politically in terms of rank and hierarchy. My selection is ethnographically arbitrary, based solely on my having done fieldwork in the Trobriands and Western Samoa; I then draw on the Hawaiian material because it represents the most elaborated Polynesian political hierarchy. In each case, whether sibling incest is overtly practiced, disguised, or latent, the reproductive power in brother-sister intimacy gives women as sisters an impressive domain of authority and power. The variation in the political extent of that domain among these three societies correlates with the way inalienable possessions are used to substantiate difference through the authentication of sacred origins and genealogies.

My aims in chapter 4 are twofold: first, to reexamine exchange in a range of societies without the formal establishment of ranking and hierarchy, from foraging groups to egalitarian and big-man societies, and to show how ownership of inalienable possessions still generates difference that establishes a degree of political autonomy for women and men. Second, to draw on data from diverse societies where descent is reckoned patrilineally to show how, even in these cases, men's and women's autonomy is dependent upon the bonds of brother-sister intimacy. Keeping to the general Pacific area, I take my examples from several Australian Aboriginal groups and from the Bimin-Kuskusmin and Melpa peoples of Papua New Guinea.[29] My comparisons show how the development of hierarchy is limited by the authentication and circumscription of inalienable possessions as well as by the way the roles of men as brothers conflict with their roles as spouses.

These comparisons continue into chapter 5 where I take up the most historically celebrated ethnographic example of exchange: the *kula*, an inter-island network of partners living on other Massim Islands with whom Trobriand Islanders exchange elaborately decorated armshells for necklaces. Although in one way the return to the Trobriands recycles back to the incipient nature of Trobriand hierarchy in relation to the Polynesian examples discussed in chapter 3, the Trobriands also represent the most complex ranking system in relation to the more egalitarian examples in chapter 4. What we find is that in the other kula areas of the Massim, kula activity provides a context for chiefly authority where actual ranking and chiefs do not exist. In these situations, ranking is sustained briefly yet ultimately defeated because the shells are inalienable only for a limited time. But within that time period, exchange is subverted, keeping is paramount and difference is politically flaunted. In the Trobriands, where difference is transformed into rank, brother-sister intimacy, materially expressed through exchanges of women's cloth wealth, provides the economic and cosmological resources that matter.

In chapter 6, I summarize my arguments to show the cultural effort it takes to reconfigure the loss of sisters, the loss of inalienable possessions, and the loss of cosmological authentication not just because of death or decay but because of their value to other groups. Local solutions remain disjunctive and incomplete, skewing gender relations in various ways that, in some cases, give women political power and possibilities. In other situations, women may have status in some domains while they are subordinated in others. Where subordination does occur, as wives, for example, women's willingness to be dominated may be because as sisters they achieve a level of authority that ultimately is important for their own children. A simple set of essentialist norms or classifications cannot encompass these multiple possibilities. The very terms *reciprocity, reproduction,* and *incest* have long complicated Western histories that deny their cultural neutrality and reflect Western assumptions about authority, power, and the political domain. By showing that keeping-while-giving is fundamental to the establishment of difference, I also show how power is lodged at the center of how women and men produce, guard, and authenticate inalienable possessions. For even when the possession itself is not present in an exchange, the fact of its ownership and the potential of its irrevocable loss confirms the presence of difference between one person or group and others. Out of this difference negotiated in exchange over what is not exchanged, power is generated and, under certain circumstances in which women are vital, transforms difference into hierarchy.

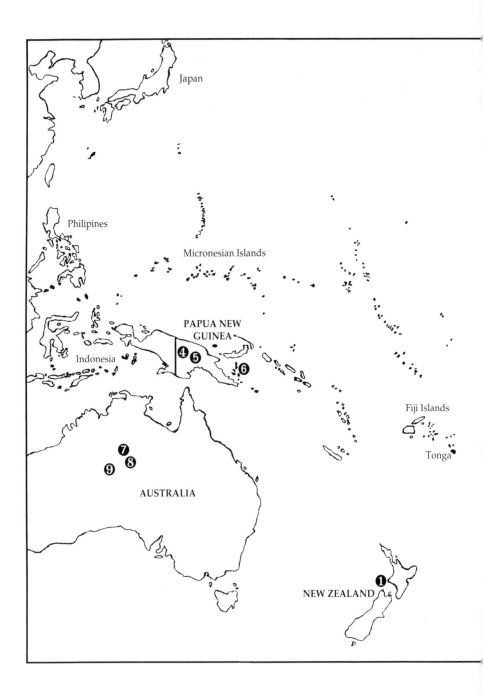

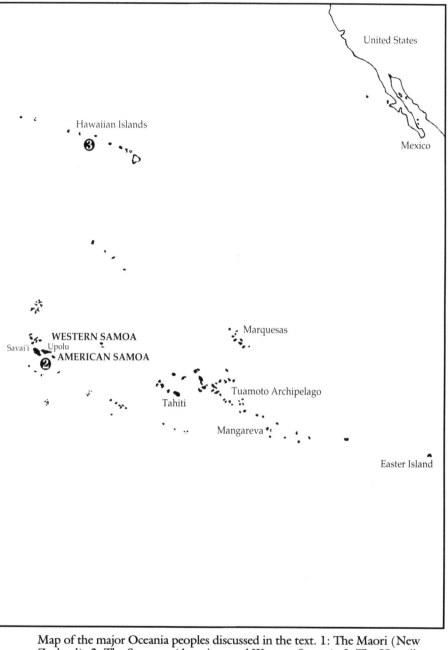

United States

Mexico

Hawaiian Islands
❸

WESTERN SAMOA
Savai'i Upolu
❷ AMERICAN SAMOA

Marquesas

Tahiti

Tuamoto Archipelago

Mangareva

Easter Island

Map of the major Oceania peoples discussed in the text. 1: The Maori (New Zealand); 2: The Samoans (American and Western Samoa); 3: The Hawaiians (USA); 4: The Bimin-Kuskusmin (Papua New Guinea); 5: The Melpa (Papua New Guinea); 6: The Trobrianders (Papua New Guinea); 7: The Warlpiri (Australia); 8: The Aranda (Australia); 9: The Pintupi (Australia).

CHAPTER 1

Inalienable Possessions: The Forgotten Dimension

King Agamemnon rose, holding a staff which Hephaestus himself had made. Hephaestus gave it to Zeus . . . and Zeus to Hermes. . . . The Lord Hermes presented it to Pelops . . . and Pelops passed it on to Atreus. . . . When Atreus died, he left it to Thyestes . . . and he in his turn bequeathed it to Agamemnon, to be held in token of his empire.

Homer, *The Iliad*

The ceremony for the inauguration of a king or queen . . . of Ra'iatea. . . . was a time of the greatest moment . . . and greatest of all the work was the concatenating of a new lappet to the . . . feather girdle . . . the royal insignia in which the monarch of either sex was invested. . . . The sacred needle was never taken out of the work, which was intended to continue forever, a new lappet being added for each successive reign.

Teuira Henry, *Ancient Tahiti*

When anthropologists embark on extensive fieldwork, it is not just they, as Malinowski once said, who will "make" the cultures they study but they, too, are fashioned intellectually through what they learn. Like parents who nurture and socialize their children with their own beliefs and world views, "informants" turn their ethnographers in particular directions. The similarity stops there, however, because ethnographers do not record informants' words as though on a tabula rasa, but as modified by their own theories and perceptions honed on the issues and arguments of previous anthropological discourses. How to get beneath what historically we, as anthropologists, take most for granted and, in its stead, hear what our field interpreters are actually saying is a major problem.

In my own case, I first went to the Trobriand Islands prepared to follow Malinowski's and others' precept that reciprocity is the basis of social relations. In *Argonauts of the Western Pacific,* Malinowski wrote that the critical part of exchange is the return side—the "equivalent counter-gift" that balances the exchange.[1] So I dutifully asked in each instance about the return gift, but the answers I received failed to fit Malinowski's typologies. What I also found perplexing was how such enormous energy expended in ritual preoccupations and economic pursuits could be reduced to what Malinowski described as "ceremonial gift" and "counter-gift." I asked myself how an elaborate exchange system like kula, in which men voyage to other islands in elaborately decorated canoes, as in figure 1, to exchange ornate shell necklaces for decorated armshells, could function only to ensure that the exchange of an armshell for a necklace previously given would eventually take place. Could the linear events of giving and receiving really be the prime movers in the integration of these small-scale social systems, as Malinowski believed?

The most striking cause for reformulation for me was the Trobriand word *mapula,* a term around which many theoretical arguments have developed.[2] Malinowski originally defined mapula as "repayment, equivalent" and as "the general term for return gifts, retributions, economic as well as otherwise."[3] He drew these conclusions, in part from the nineteenth-century views he still held about the autonomy of reciprocity, which then seemed ethnographically confirmed by Trobrianders' statements, such as "This is the mapula for what he has done."[4] To Malinowski, such comments indicated that mapula was the return side of a gift previously given, proof that reciprocity was the basis of "primitive" social relations. But Trobrianders also said that mapula was used for the small things, such as fish, tobacco, and rice, which a man gives his wife and children. Malinowski saw no actual returns for these gifts and so decided that they ran counter "to the general rule that all gifts require repayment." Instead of tracing out these discrepancies to see where they led, Malinowski decided that such differences were merely ethnographic inconsistencies "explained away by the natives" to accommodate the priority of the norm of reciprocity.[5] Although Trobrianders called these small gifts mapula, Malinowski, anticipating negative processes, called them "pure gifts"—a classification lacking a corresponding Kiriwina term.[6]

The problem of mapula did not end there. Marcel Mauss regarded the mapula payments that a man makes to his wife as "one of the most important acts noted by Malinowski."[7] What captured Mauss's imagination was that such gifts were not merely used for the exchange of goods and services, but formed the underpinnings of alliance relationships. This led Mauss to question Malinowski's category of pure gifts wondering if any gift would be given without some expected return.[8] Malinowski responded to Mauss's criticism in a later publication, *Crime and Custom in Savage Society,* by recanting his definition of pure gifts and affirming that no gifts were ever free. He admitted that his mistake was a failure to take "a sufficiently long view of the chain of transactions" over time because "in the long run the mapula exchanges balance."[9] Thus, the solution for Malinowski was a simple reclassification of mapula from pure gift to one in which "the mutual services balance."[10]

The Legacy of Mapula

Initially, I too fell victim to the legacy of mapula. But although I accepted Malinowski's original definition, I was discovering many differences between what my informants were telling me and what Malinowski had written. The problem with mapula was that, a priori, I adopted its original Malinowskian definition and then proceeded to take its meaning for granted. In the beginning of my fieldwork, mapula was so much part of my own working vocabulary that I remained deaf to what my informants were really telling me. Only when I returned to the Trobriands at a later time was I prepared to listen when my interpreter said:

If my father gives me [mapula] a coconut palm and several years later a strong wind comes and knocks down the palm, my father will give me another one. If I go to the trade store and buy a kerosene lamp and later the lamp breaks do you think Mr. Holland will give me back my money? Mapula is not the same as *gimwali* [to buy and sell]. If anything ever happens to that coconut palm my father will always replace it [mapula]. When my father dies, his brothers will come and give me money and take the palm back. If they do not do this, I continue to use the palm until I die. Then someone from my father's matrilineage must come and make a payment for the palm tree. If no one comes, the palm is lost to them and my own matrilineal relatives will get the palm.

Clearly, mapula represents one set in a complex series of transactions denoting more than Malinowski's gloss of "repayment, equivalent." As I now understand it, some things, although given to others for a time, ultimately are inalienable possessions. At issue is not how one gift elicits a return, but rather which possessions the members of a group are able to keep through generations, even if they must loan them for a time to others. In the Trobriand case, land, names, magic texts, and body and house decorations are among the possessions that belong to members of individual matrilineages. Often these possessions are on loan to people born into other matrilineages, a prominent way of temporarily making kin of non-kin. Later, these inalienable possessions must be reclaimed, often by people in the next generation who had nothing to do with the original giving. Sometimes these possessions are lost to the owning group who may not have the wealth to reclaim them. So although the circulation of inalienable possessions permits the reproduction of an expanded network of kin through time, such acts always carry the potential for loss and the chance of betrayal.

How could Malinowski with all of his ethnographic sensitivity miss this central feature of Trobriand exchange? The answer is to be found in the conflict between his ethnographic data and how he believed "communal" exchange should operate. The problem Malinowski faced as an anthropologist writing early in this century was how to define the Trobrianders' "primitive" economics, which was radically different from a Western market economy even though, as he wrote so passionately in *Argonauts of the Western Pacific,* their exchange system involved rational principles. Yet for all his functional precision, Malinowski leaves us, as Mauss first noted, without any evidence for the motivations and sanctions behind Trobriand exchange.[11] In the case of kula, why did one armshell elicit a return necklace? In *Crime and Custom* Malinowski set out to tackle Mauss's question and, at the same time, to overturn Mauss's own answer to the problem. Avoiding any reference to Mauss's conclusion that the "spirit" embedded in the gift elicited its return, he forcefully argued that Trobrianders were driven by *custom* to interact with one another through a constant give and take. Custom alone, without Mauss's "spirit of the gift," provided the legal force that motivated reciprocal returns.

The controversy over mapula, however, continued. Lévi-Strauss, chiding Malinowski for trying to create a functional reason for the mapula gifts from husbands to wives and children where none was needed, wrote that:

The lack of reciprocity which seems to characterize these services in the Trobriand Islands, as in most human societies, is the mere counterpart of a universal fact, that the relationship of reciprocity which is the basis of marriage is not established between men and women, but between men by means of women, who are merely the occasion of this relationship.[12]

Lévi-Strauss enlarged upon Mauss's implications of mapula as alliance building and showed how women serve as one among the many counters exchanged in societies. In Lévi-Strauss's hands, mapula became exaggerated as a symbol of the economic and political subordination of women because a woman was merely "a sign and a value" of men's reciprocal obligations to one another.[13] By pointing out that Mauss's (and Malinowski's) mistake was to assume that reciprocity necessitated an extrinsic, energizing force, Lévi-Strauss claims that exchange must be conceptualized as a whole, an inherent synthesis that needs no external acceleration.[14] In *The Elementary Structures of Kinship,* he reduces hundreds of individual gifts and counter-gifts to rigorously defined cycles of reciprocal marriage exchanges, each of which correlates with a particular type of social structure. Whereas Malinowski is committed to the pragmatic view that custom exerted the operational pressure to make Trobrianders "give for the sake of giving," Lévi-Strauss is committed to the structural view that behind diverse ethnographic facts, the same reciprocal logic exists in peoples' "passion for the gift."[15] Even though Lévi-Strauss argues that reciprocity theoretically needs no energizing force, in fact, this passion is over women's sexuality—the external motivation in the creation of elementary structures of kinship.

Are these simply two diverse theoretical positions that explain the same phenomenon, or is there a universal motivation for reciprocal acts that has not yet been fully disclosed? The answer is not ethnographic nor even theoretical, but historical. Although the norm of reciprocity as the fundamental principle of "primitive" social life was not formalized until the end of the nineteenth century, confidence in the underlying motivation for these norms derived from Western economic history.

The Norm of Reciprocity in Western History

Beginning with Thomas Hobbes's observations that individuals give up part of their autonomy in return for protection, the notion in political philosophy of a norm of reciprocity as a fundamental principle in human society entered into these speculations to justify the rise of a free-market economy without state interventions. John Locke's seventeenth-century view of private property set out in the second treatise[16] and, in the next century, Adam Smith's notion of the "invisible hand" that keeps the market secure from external controls,[17] are only two among many philosophical theories of the times in which the norm of reciprocity was fundamental to how the market could operate autonomously.

Reciprocity was elevated to a moving force in these discussions. If reciprocity was natural to economic endeavors, then the give and take of market interests eventually would balance out, regardless of individual greed or misappropriation. The Scots economist, Sir James Steuart, who predated Durkheim by more than a century, proclaimed that the economic ties that linked people through the division of labor as producers of different commodities were the "cement binding society together." If any adjustments were needed, a "statesman" would only have to create "reciprocal wants" by "*gently*" loading the opposite scale.[18] Reciprocity continued to hold this privileged place because it remained the key to the market's stability which, at best, needed only slight encouragement.[19] Adam Smith sustained the most powerful argument for the absence of external intervention precisely because Smith believed, even more than Steuart, that the reciprocal give and take of the marketplace would accommodate its own adjustments without need for even gentle control. His philosophy was that when people enter into reciprocal exchange they become better people.[20]

This trust, however, in the moral role of reciprocity in a market economy did not originate with the rise of capitalism but arose almost whole cloth from the way authority and even sacredness were embedded in reciprocal exchange throughout the Middle Ages. Many scholars have long depicted the emergence of capitalism as a swift revolutionary transformation from the Middle Ages.[21] Louis Dumont, for example, echoing Marx, writes that "relations between men" were replaced by "relations between men and things,"[22] accentuating how capitalist commodity production fundamentally altered medieval social relations. But this medieval political hierarchy also was authenticated through relations between people and things. Much as the magic hand of reciprocity that stabilized the capitalist market also authenticated the relations of dominance, the ideology of a norm of reciprocity similarly was used to sanctify the dominant political hierarchies of medieval social life.

For example, as early as the tenth century when the system of taxation on which the Roman Empire was built had disappeared, princes were forced to rely on their landed estates or "domains" to provide economic support.[23] The historian John Baldwin shows how these domains enabled the nobility to hold monopolies over mills, wineries, roads, markets, marriages, and even ecclesiastical rights. Through the ownership of landed property everyone, from divine kings and lords to peasants, merchants, and monks, was held together through what historians call gifts of patronage and charity. These gifts were reciprocal but the value and the social relations they forged can only be analyzed in relation to what it meant to keep inalienable property. The moral force behind the ownership of inalienable estates was authenticated by the status of nobility or the sacredness of the Catholic church and this cosmological authentication radiated over all the owners' other exchanges. In this way, social difference was affirmed even as these exchange events were clothed in the moral ethic that the norm of reciprocity made men into better men. This ethic continued into the fourteenth century where the norm of reciprocity became part of a new "urban ideology."[24] As more private money was needed by nobles to finance speculative ventures and wars, the medieval sin of engaging in usury was displaced by the growing respectability of merchants' and bankers' activities that the Catholic church, reversing itself, came to sanction. Consequently, men of finance now became the great patrons of urban charity.[25] Like the earlier example from the Middle Ages, these gifts to friars and their newly expanding urban religious communities were reciprocal as wealthy merchants gave up vast amounts of money in return for religious so-called gifts and sacred protection. But the motivation for the merchants' benevolence was predicated on the Church's sanctification of their rights to lend money and profit.

Beliefs in the inherent morality of the norm of reciprocity had a long history in the West. The norm of reciprocity acted as the *modus vivendi,* authenticating the authority and autonomy of aristocrats, the Catholic church, and later, wealthy industrialists. By the nineteenth century, however, the negative realities of unchecked capitalist development began to unmask in human terms the seemingly inherent morality of reciprocity, to expose the underlying conditions of economic and political domination. Alarm in many quarters was expressed over capitalists' economic policies with the growing recognition, most strongly stated by Marx, that reciprocity in the division of labor alienated, rather than benefited, most human beings. For Marx, the eighteenth-century contrasts between "savagery" and "civilization," codified in Lewis Henry Morgan's evolutionary theories, dramatized the alienation associated with Western inhuman market systems when compared with the cohesiveness found in kinship-based "primitive" societies. Ferdinand Tönnies's distinction between *Gemeinschaft* and *Gesellschaft* and Henry Sumner Maine's opposition between "status" and "contract" similarly underscored the strong communal nature of "primitive" societies where the freedom to give and take existed without the social inequalities imposed by capitalism.

For these early theorists, there was little knowledge other than missionaries' and travelers' sketchy accounts of how economics actually worked in "primitive" societies. But these projected images of reciprocity as the basis for an equitable economics in which Western society had originally participated were widely agreed upon. At the same time, oppositions such as "savagery" and "civilization" confirmed popular opinions that "primitives" knew nothing of individual ownership. Colonial interests had long depended upon this claim, summed up by the distinguished nineteenth-century lawyer, Sir William Blackstone, who described how "'no man's goods' of the primitive world became the private property of individuals in the world of history."[26] Thus, by the end of the nineteenth century, the economic world of the "primitive," then vibrantly alive but still a subject only of armchair study, was viewed as both the antithesis and alter ego of Western *Homo oeconomicus.*

It was Durkheim who drew together the threads of these two diverse views in the most comprehensive manner. Although his classification of "mechanical" and "organic solidarity" was based on the accepted evolutionary differences between "primitive" and civilized Western societies, he acknowledged and even built on their similarities. In both cases, reciprocity serves as the "social cement" in the division of labor; individuals are linked to each other through the exchange of goods and services. But Durkheim, trying to set forth what the underlying motivation for reciprocity must be, pushed further. He describes how exchange involves an intensive bonding more formidable than mere economic relations. Social cohesiveness occurs because one person is always dependent on another to achieve a feeling of completeness. In this way, a social and moral order is established sui generis.[27] Later, in *The Elementary Forms of the Religious Life,* Durkheim shifts to an ethnographic approach to show how in "archaic" societies this social and moral order comes into being through the sacred domain. In the heightened intensity of ritual activity, the overwhelming sense of communal participation enables each person to feel completed through the presence of others and at the same time, to feel consecrated and encompassed by a higher sacred order.[28] Even though Durkheim developed his thesis through his reading of Australian ethnography that described Aboriginal ceremonial life, we see here the reemergence of centuries-old Western convictions about the morality and sanctity of reciprocity. Durkheim's theory (expanded by Mauss) that archaic societies revealed the core principles around which a future, more equitable Western economics could function identified religion (in the archaic not the modern sense) as the evolutionary process through which the transformation from "primitive" to modern society took place. At the end of *The Elementary Forms of the Religious Life,* both his personal politics and his sociology are encapsulated in the statement that beyond the individual there is society—"a system of active forces"—embracing the effervescence of representations and practices—the very ideas and activities that science and modern economics exclude.[29]

Malinowski, strongly committed to a utilitarian methodology, sharply rejected Durkheim's economic and religious theories, calling them metaphysical because they were not based on proper empirical evidence. Yet Malinowski, despite his extensive fieldwork, never resolved for himself whether Trobrianders (and by extension, all "primitives") represented the alter ego or the antithesis of Western *Homo oeconomicus*. Although he set out to prove that Trobrianders were more like us than the popular images of "savages" led Europeans to believe, he had grave problems translating his Trobriand ethnographic data into Western rational terms. Trobrianders did not just grow yams for food; they painted and elaborately displayed them and sometimes even let them rot. Trobriand necklaces and armshells were so ostentatiously decorated they had no use-value (see fig. 2). Why then did these islanders, whose physical environment put them at risk for food resources, let their crops rot and face the dangers of overseas voyages merely to gain such nonutilitarian objects?[30] After five hundred pages of describing the intricacies of kula exchanges, Malinowski could discover no reasonable native justification for these events other than that Trobrianders' desire to "give for the sake of giving."[31] Caught between the reality that Trobrianders did have a notion of ownership and property similar to Western concepts and the awareness that they followed culturally dissimilar rules and beliefs, Malinowski opted for what had become an accepted way to describe reciprocal exchange—as either ceremonial or utilitarian. Although this dichotomy mirrors Durkheim's sacred/profane oppositions, Malinowski refused to equate "ceremonial" with the theoretical implications Durkheim accorded the "sacred." But in elevating custom to the motivating force in reciprocity, Malinowski wrote how custom is "obeyed for its own sake" because of the "awe of traditional command and a sentimental attachment to it."[32] For Malinowski, too, reciprocity was imbued with a morality that drew on legal, economic, sociological, magical, and supernatural forces and pervaded every aspect of "primitive" life.[33]

If Malinowski had looked to other, much older economic principles in Western history, Trobriand mapula and other seemingly irrational actions might not have been so troublesome. Expunged from consideration was what Maine called the most ancient and important obstacle to the free circulation of objects: the classification of all property into "immovables" and "movables."[34] So significant was this schematic division throughout the Western world that it was the central feature in property law from Roman times through the Middle Ages into the Enlightenment and was still debated in Maine's time.[35] In fact, its origin in the West can be traced back to the ancient Greeks, where livestock was considered movable, whereas things stored in chests (usually cloth possessions) and land were immovable.[36] Although this early Greek usage aptly reflects the relative mobility or nonmobility of the things themselves, later Roman laws included as immovables other possessions such as slaves, oxen, precious metal implements, and jewels.

Never a rigid dichotomy, possessions shifted from one classification to the other at various historical times and places while the classifications themselves were variously supported or subverted by different laws and assimilated and partially destroyed with the rise of capitalism. Despite these historical shifts, the conviction prevailed that possessions belonging irrevocably to a patriline or a clan were of higher value than those things that could be freely exchanged because they were not inheritable. If we place the example of Trobriand mapula against even a partial Western history of inalienable possessions, we see that although vastly different in scope, mapula represents an intricate, but by no means unusual, solution to keeping things for all time. I use the words *inalienable* and *alienable* in place of the Western classification, in part, to show its much wider universality and also to emphasize that portability is not the issue at all. What makes a possession inalienable is its exclusive and cumulative identity with a particular series of owners through time. Its history is authenticated by fictive or true genealogies, origin myths, sacred ancestors, and gods. In this way, inalienable possessions are transcendent treasures to be guarded against all the exigencies that might force their loss.

Inalienable Possessions in Western History

Georg Simmel wrote that during the Middle Ages landed property "was—*cum grano salis*—something incomparable: it was value as such, the immovable ground above and beyond which real economic activity was carried on."[37] Whereas other alienable properties are exchanged against each other, inalienable possessions are symbolic repositories of genealogies and historical events, their unique, subjective identity gives them absolute value placing them above the exchangeability of one thing for another. In fact, throughout medieval times, keeping inalienable possessions intact was so vital that landed estates were protected by extensive legal codes, decreeing that blood kin had the right to repurchase land that had once passed from the hereditary line. Because of the economic and political power controlled and contained by keeping what Maine called the "higher dignity" of inalienable possessions, diverse strategies and negotiations evolved that demonstrate historically the political advantages in owning inalienable possessions and the dependency that tied alienable things to inalienable possessions.

In eleventh-century France, we find an example that appears to break the rule of keeping possessions inalienable while, in reality, the example proves the rule. For about two hundred years, French nobility regularly gave up portions of their inalienable landed property to monasteries and convents to consecrate special saints. Held in trust by monks, these portions of inalienable land were elevated to a spiritual domain, where ownership would remain eternal and uncontested (although generations later, occasionally heirs did try to repossess these properties).

In contrast, alienable property remained inappropriate for such bequests, even though the transfer of inalienable land was extremely complex, requiring a *laudatio parentum,* the signature of each person who would have inherited rights to that parcel of land and thereafter agreed to renounce any legal claims.[38] But these offerings were not merely charity. The historian Stephen D. White documents the returns these wealthy benefactors gained in the opulent hospitality and spiritual privileges and prayers bestowed upon them by the members of the religious community. In addition, the monks gave their lay supporters material goods, such as jewelry, fine dishes, clothing, farm animals, wine, and money. White argues that these returns cannot be thought of as commodities for they were not merely exchanges of one value for another. Like granting burial rights or places in an abbey, the return "gifts" were only made to those who signed away their legal rights in the *laudatio parentum.* The kinds of objects returned to members of this consenting group were ranked according to each person's status.[39] Thus within a large, relatively undifferentiated kin group, rank and status were continually being affirmed or redefined by a sacred order whose authority was ideologically uncontested. Death, however, provides the most significant key to understanding the social and political implications in these exchanges. In giving up some inalienable possessions, the nobility was granted salvation at death with future rights after death to "heavenly inheritances" as they entered God's kingdom to recreate the status features of medieval social life.[40] In life, those who gave over landed property to the Catholic church insured God's legitimation over the rest of their property, both inalienable and alienable, adding the cosmological authentication of the Catholic church to the aristocratic legitimacy of their rank. These acts then enhanced their political authority vested in their rank not only for one generation but for the heirs of those who signed the document. Their descendants drew on the same spiritual relationships that served to sanction their own political authority and the enduring dominance of their rank.[41]

The factor that makes the authority vested in these inalienable possessions a higher value than other kinds of things is that their authentication is dependent upon the histories of ancestors, divine rulers, and God. So pervasive was the source of this authority that in the Enlightenment, philosophers modeled their claims for individual liberty and private property after the way inalienable possessions authenticated the rank and status of their owners. Reading John Locke, for example, we see how precisely this relationship carries over into his major thesis that "every Man has a *Property* in his own *Person*" created out of "the

Labour of his Body, and the *Work* of his Hands."[42] As Peter Laslett points out, Locke did not define property only in terms of material possessions, but more broadly as "'Lives, Liberties and Estates'" recognizing the tangible way in which inalienable possessions are part of the person.[43] In fact, Locke's beliefs that property was inherently part of yet separate from the person, are similar to views that in the twentieth century Marcel Mauss espoused as the foundation of primitive exchange. In Locke we observe a dramatic projection of traditional inherent rights in inalienable possessions toward all private property secured from other encumbrances by the State's protection.

Yet the presence of inalienable possessions was not displaced by capitalism nor was the power of these possessions ignored by financiers and industrialists. The eighteenth and nineteenth centuries are full of examples in which the *nouveau riche* bought their way into marriages with women whose impoverished aristocratic families gained liquid capital while the children of these marriages would inherit titles and inalienable properties.[44] Capitalism only served to heighten the dependency on the connections between alienable and inalienable possessions. Even a short visit to the New York homes of J. Pierpont Morgan or Henry Clay Frick, now museums, or an hour spent wandering among the ornate nineteenth-century porcelains, jewels, furniture, and portraits filling the vast rooms of the D'Orsay Museum in Paris brilliantly pinpoints how Western capitalists increasingly aped the nobility in their zealous acquisition of symbolic markers that not only acknowledged an intimacy with the latest fashions but claimed the honor and renown generated by the ownership of inalienable possessions. The rich spawned by industrialization combed the world to fill their palace-like mansions with precious works of art once the renowned properties of the ruling nobles and ecclesiastics.[45]

The activity would not have surprised Smith for although his writings proclaim the great benefits of capitalism, he too recognized the political necessity for protecting inalienable possessions.[46] While early on in *The Wealth of Nations,* Smith advances the political value of market exchange, in later chapters he pronounces shock at the way nobles now seek "trinkets and baubles" from merchants, pursuing these acquisitions to the degree that they are forced to give up their own estates. Such acts Smith condemned as "folly"—the selling of "their birthright." For only

the gratification of the most childish, the meanest and the most sordid of all vanities they gradually bartered their whole power and authority and became as insignificant as any substantial burgher or tradesman in a city.[47]

The authority and esteem embedded in inalienable wealth was far greater than its exchange value. It was fame and honor, rather than pure economics, that Smith recognized as the fundamental impetus for pursuits of wealth. By giving up their inalienable landed property and possessions, not for salvation in heaven, but in order to afford the newest luxuries and fashions, the nobility was in danger of diminishing, or even losing, the strength of their political authority. Thus in the midst of capitalist expansion, the political power of inalienable wealth was starkly revealed. As the economist Albert Hirschman shows, by holding that noneconomic motives such as renown and power act as the basic stimuli for economic pursuits, Smith could then maintain that it was people's fears of losing this authority and honor that would keep their passions in check and force them to alter any unfair practices in the marketplace, resulting in the best interests for society as a whole.

What fundamentally triggered these fears, however, was the fact that landed property was ceasing to be the primary and most powerful means of generating great wealth and was being replaced by speculative capital. Yet capital alone without nobility created pressing political problems. As Adam Ferguson pointed out, if heirs of aristocratic families were threatened with poverty in an era of economic affluence, they would accept promises of any strong government to prevent these real or imagined dangers.[48] Not only were the intimate relations between persons and inalienable possessions transformed into beliefs about private property and private enterprise, but actual reliance on inalienable possessions continued to spark hopes and fears over what would happen if alienable possessions totally replaced inalienable possessions and what would happen if they did not.[49]

The Culture of Inalienable Possessions

In general, all personal possessions invoke an intimate connection with their owners, symbolizing personal experience that, even though private or secret, adds value to the person's social identity. Both Mauss and Simmel recognized that the boundaries between persons and things are not rigidly separate just as Thorstein Veblen showed even more explicitly how ownership of certain things both reveals and expands a person's status and personality. But there are possessions in which prestigious origins, successions, or an edifying authority connected to the past like gods, divine right, ancestors, or high status make these particular possessions different from other things even of the same kind. In societies with complex political hierarchies, precious possessions such as gold crowns, jewelry, feathered cloaks or fine silks may accumulate historical significance that make their economic and aesthetic values *absolute* and transcendent above all similar things. Each object differs in value even from other objects of the same class that in some instances may circulate as common currency in exchange. In this way, certain possessions become subjectively unique removing them from ordinary social exchange as they attain absolute value rather than exchange value.[50] The paradox, of course, is that such possessions, from time to time, are exchanged, lost in warfare, destroyed by rivals, sold, or are unclaimed, thus undermining the ability of rulers or families to keep intact the material symbol that legitimates their rank, status, or uniqueness.

The rituals in which a monarch is crowned or a Polynesian chief is invested with divinity are built around the moment when such a historically significant possession authenticates the act of coronation by conferring authority.[51] At the most sacred moment during the coronation of Elizabeth II, her earthly robes and crown were removed and replaced by a plain, white linen tunic, resembling "both a winding sheet that binds the dead and a swaddling cloth that wraps the newborn."[52] Only then was she dressed in other sacred regalia, each piece of which also was historically significant, and served to transform her body from something "natural into the body politic."[53]

Lords and queens, however, are not the only benefactors of the power that inalienable possessions wield, nor are tunics and robes the only objects that confer authority. Scattered in the ethnographic literature are examples of myths, genealogies, ancestral names, songs, and the knowledge of dances intrinsic to a group's identity that, taken together as oral traditions, form one basic category of inalienable possessions. Similarly, guardianship and reverence for human bones, sacred stones, woven fabrics, ceramics, and shells, as well as gems and jade comprise a second category, that of material objects. Of course, words and objects are not always mutually exclusive, for objects may have oral histories transmitted with their ownership and myths may be related to geographical landmarks, giving material authenticity to words.[54]

Because inalienable possessions succeed their owners through time, transferability is essential to their preservation. In many societies, oral traditions have great longevity and, especially among groups where durable objects are scarce, texts as inalienable possessions are guarded and carefully transmitted from one generation to the next.[55] But words can be altered and reframed; what one person says can be paraphrased by another resulting in vastly different meanings. Some people forget or deliberately tamper with parts of texts whereas others may die before the entire corpus of their knowledge is given to their successors. In the same way, an object's origins can be disguised or relocated in someone else's genealogy, but ideally objects and words remain unchanging. Although the passage of time may encrust an object with patina or contribute to its fraying, these alterations heighten rather than diminish the object's value. As an icon, an object can be admired and venerated long after its immediate historical relevancy has ceased as the many possessions that fill museums illustrate. Therefore, objects do retain some priority over oral texts, a point ironically made by Jonathan Swift in *Gulliver's Travels* when speech was outlawed and the "Sages," like "Pedlars" unpacked their sacks and conversed amongst one another with things.

Of all objects, however, food is the most ineffectual inalienable possession because its biological function is to release energy rather than store it. Therefore, in its use to humans, food changes, deteriorates, or perishes.[56] So significant is this loss to those without extensive durable things that, in some cases, attempts are made to transform food into more permanent words or things. Among the Warrira of the Papuan coast, the genealogical histories of taro plants are sacred inalienable knowledge,[57] whereas on Goodenough, one of the Massim Islands, strings tied around long yams presented in competitive exchanges are kept hidden for many years, publicly revealed only in sudden political confrontations so as to prompt memories about past events.[58]

Landed property is another category of inalienable possessions as the examples from the Middle Ages show.[59] But even centuries later, Veblen, who is best known for his ideas concerning conspicuous consumption, recognized how land acts as the primary "standard of wealth," with estates acquired from ancestors even more honorific than those gotten through one's own acquisition.[60] Throughout American society, land still is used as a measure of a family's history and prestige.[61] During the 1970s, while doing fieldwork in a small Texas town, a few of my wealthy informants impressed upon me that among the elite, the accumulation of money could never substitute for extensive land holdings even if the land itself was economically unproductive. Nonprofitable acres were often bought so that a person's heirs would be unable to sell off or subdivide the property. Today, almost one-third of the land mass of Britain is owned by titled families. As Ilse Hayden points out, the aristocracy remains wealthy today, despite the public's impression that they are on the verge of ruin. An important measure of that wealth is in landownership.[62] These attitudes toward land would come as no surprise to ancient Athenians who believed that the sale of land was not only an offense against their children's inheritance but against their ancestors because the dead were buried on such land. Furthermore, loss of land inevitably led to the loss of aristocratic status because, as Smith was to warn the aristocracy centuries later, without land, one was forced to become a trader, artisan or laborer—all degrading occupations and, for the ancient Greeks, prohibiting them from the right to vote.[63]

This predicament of nobles losing their birthright by giving up their landed property, thereby reducing themselves to ordinary merchants and traders, is replicated with many other examples where class and capital are not at issue. A Trobriand chief who loses part of his land because he lacks the wealth to reclaim it will lose much of his power; his successor must work hard to reclaim these losses. The work associated with the guardianship of inalienable possessions is consuming, even dangerous. The Aranda sacred tjurunga stones, which embody each person's ancestor, are so valued as inalienable possessions that if a man were to accidentally drop or chip one, he would be killed by his own kin.[64] As glorified as an inalienable possession may be at one point in time, its successive owners may destroy it, lose it in battle, or tarnish what it stands for. Tahitian royalty visited by James Cook in the eighteenth century had an ingenious solution to such problems (as cited in the opening quotation). When the feathered segment was woven onto the royal girdle each time a new ruler was inaugurated, the needle used was carved from a human bone. The placement of the feathers read as a hieroglyph revealing the names of former rulers, and the needle remained in the garment as it was expected to continue forever.[65]

The work necessary to produce social identities in things and people is a tremendous burden, creating a political dependency on inalienable possessions. But at the same time, these possessions become vehicles for political autonomy. The right to control inalienable possessions can be used as the means to effect control over others. As fourteenth-century lords controlled vassals and serfs through the temporary disposition of their landed estates as patronage, so too an Aranda leader assumes full authority over the loans of tjurunga stones to other clans.

The other members of his group, by according him unprecedented authority over their most precious possessions, give up part of their own autonomy and bind themselves more closely to him than to anyone else. Through such control of inalienable possessions, authority emerges creating potential nodes of centralization that in particular circumstances sustain rank and political hierarchy. The basic dilemmas surrounding these loci of power and the challenges to the priorities of keeping possessions out of circulation appear in various local guises and forms throughout human history, revealing how the motivation for reciprocity is centered not in the gift per se, but in the authority vested in keeping inalienable possessions. Ownership of these possessions makes the authentication of difference rather than the balance of equivalence the fundamental feature of exchange.

The Constitution of Difference in Exchange

Durkheim's search for the universal motivation behind the norm of reciprocity led him to his most significant conclusion—its locus in the sacred domain. In the drama of Aboriginal ritual, Durkheim found the kind of communal abandonment, frenzy, and freedom that generates not only religious feeling but the communal origins of social life. Similarly, Mauss in his readings of the seasonal shifts in the ritual life of the Eskimo showed how reciprocity is authenticated through the vitality of ritual practices that, although encompassing some profane elements, are consecrated within the sacred domain. In fact, Durkheim believed that the formalization of the sacred as the source of equality for "primitive" societies could become a powerful evolutionary tool for a future modern world in which ritual and religious sentiments would bind people together into more equitable social communities.[66]

Although both Durkheim and Mauss hinted at the importance of their work on "primitive" exchange for problems of modernity, it was left to others to transfer their findings more firmly in this direction. Among the members of the Surrealist movement working toward these goals, such as Michel Leiris, Georges Bataille, and Roger Caillois, it was Bataille who attempted to reformulate Durkheim's and Mauss's theories on "primitive" exchange into revolutionary ideas about the reorganization of Western society.[67] Bataille's interests were not to analyze "primitive" exchange, but to construct a way to reproduce the resanctification of commodities and community in Western society. I turn briefly to his work because his theory of expenditure, though hardly complete or ethnographically accurate, was the first to turn the norm of reciprocity on its head and situate political power at the center of the sacred.[68]

Taking his lead from descriptions of Northwest Coast potlatch disbursements of wealth and Aztec sacrifice, Bataille claimed that these ritual expenditures brought about communal integration through a transcendent experience that prefigures death for all participants. Therefore, society achieves a moral union, not simply through Durkheim's perception of the sacred as shared symbolic reaffirmation, but through a political economy of expenditure. Because capitalism, Bataille argued, was founded on utilitarian needs for production, gone were the medieval ritual displays of wealth that brought people together in religious communion. Now people publicly conserved their wealth and produced commodities in the name of the common good when what was needed was complete expenditure in the way a Kwakiutl chief distributes everything he has. Unfortunately, Bataille was unaware that Kwakiutl chiefs schemed to keep their most renowned cloaks and coppers out of exchange, conserving them by expending so much else. What Bataille neglected to account for was that when an extremely valuable copper was given to a rival chief at a potlatch, only a piece of the metal was broken off. The chief's strategy was that at a later potlatch he would be able to reclaim the metal and rivet it back onto the original (as fig. 3 shows), thereby elevating the fame and value of the original. But he did recognize that the Maussian contradiction between generosity and gain was not the issue. It was the *things* exchanged that were special; potlatch objects were marked with ambivalence (and therefore, power) because they could be destroyed.

Bataille shows us that to destroy a valued possession is to violate it, to cause its death. What he ignores is that to keep the possession while meeting the demands of expenditure and display is to firmly entrench one's difference. It is in the potential threat of violence and destruction that power emerges, transfixed at the center of keeping-while-giving. The "totality" of reciprocity as defined by Mauss is actually an unbounded arena where combative forces are subtly or aggressively engaged. The expressions of passion or disinterestedness in an exchange are the result of strategies played out on this ground of opposing forces because exchange events invoke the consciousness that another possession can never be the same as my possession. Even the knowledge that an inalienable possession is hidden away confirms the presence of difference in social identities. In each exchange, participants remain aware of what is not being exchanged and their actions are directed not only to the immediate events but to these events in relation to the ownership of inalienable possessions and the power they differentiate. The seemingly linear aspects of reciprocal give and take are merely overt attempts to become part of, to participate in, or conversely, to snare, what is not part of that exchange. Difference denies the concept of a homogeneous circumstance in which the gift given merely elicits a reciprocal return without thought of an inalienable possession's radiating presence, its political energy, and the danger of its irreversible loss.

What stabilizes but cannot preempt the opposing forces set into motion by difference lies in the source of an inalienable possession's authentication. An inalienable possession's uniqueness is inseparable from its place within traditions passed down from generation to generation. But these traditions are not unchangeable, immovable beliefs. As Benjamin noted, even though a fourth-century B.C. statue of Venus meant one thing to ancient Greeks and quite another to the clerics of the Middle Ages, both were confronted by its uniqueness.[69] This absolute value accommodates the movements of inalienable possessions through time and space, even as these possessions attract new meanings, fictitious memories, altered genealogies, and imagined ancestors. What gives these possessions their fame and power is their authentication through an authority perceived to be outside the present. Connections to ancestors, gods, sacred sites, the legitimating force of divine rulers, or ideologies such as the reciprocal freedom of the marketplace authenticate the authority that an inalienable possession attains. Through this legitimating force a possession becomes unique, rising above the flux of other things that can easily be exchanged. What this apparent stability disguises is how hierarchy resides at the very core of reciprocal exchange.

The Anthropological Dilemma

Although Durkheim, like Mauss, recognized that the sacred was also profane, Durkheim saw these dualities overcome in sacred rituals that regenerated social solidarity and created a homogeneous social order. Bataille, on the other hand, saw that the heterogeneity of the sacred was the source of political power because it retained rather than mediated difference, using violence, sacrifice, and expenditure as resources for the construction of a hierarchical order.[70] But modern anthropology, so deeply entrenched in perceptions about "primitive" societies, held to the nineteenth-century view of the norm of reciprocity. Even when Mauss described the ambivalence generated by the gift—at once desirable and disinterested, dangerous and social, the source of sacrifice and acquisition—he still avowed that, ultimately, reciprocity neutralized power. At the end of *Essai sur le don,* he returned to this theme when he argued that if reciprocal give and take were reintroduced into capitalist relations, a more egalitarian form of modernity would result. Even when anthropologists, such as Marshall Sahlins, tried to uncover less esoteric and more rational motivations for reciprocity, they still could not integrate the concept of gain with the Maussian (and Hobbesian) belief that exchange made enemies into friends. Lévi-Strauss circumvented the problem entirely by rejecting the consecrating power of ritual as merely surface phenomenon, arguing that the gift was a sign, a convention of language so deeply engrained in the human mind that reciprocity occurs without the need for external motivation. It was only in dreams that the Andaman Islanders found their mythical world where they could keep and never have to give.

Had Malinowski gone to the Trobriands in the sixteenth, or even in the seventeenth or eighteenth centuries, *Argonauts of the Western Pacific* would have been a different book, and the anthropology of exchange would have had a different trajectory. Generations of anthropologists, not looking back far enough into Western economic history, follow Malinowski and continue to discriminate between ceremonial and utilitarian gifts and countergifts. They continue to take for granted, as did Smith and others, that there is an innate, mystical, or natural autonomy in the workings of reciprocity. What motivates reciprocity is its reverse—the desire to keep something back from the pressures of give and take. This something is a possession that speaks to and for an individual's or a group's social identity and, in so doing, affirms the difference between one person or group and another. Because the ownership of inalienable possessions establishes difference, ownership attracts other kinds of wealth. When a Trobriander keeps a famous kula shell, other players seek him out, bestowing upon him other bounty in an attempt to make him into a partner, just as feudal lords through the authority vested in their estates attracted merchants, peasants, and monks. It is not accidental that inalienable possessions represent the oldest economic classification in the world.

CHAPTER 2

Reconfiguring Exchange Theory: The Maori Hau

As much as Phaiakian men are expert beyond all others
For driving a fast ship on the open sea, so their women
Are skilled in weaving and dowered with wisdom bestowed by
  Athene,
To be expert in beautiful work . . .

Homer, The Odyssey

The works of women are symbolic.
We sew, prick our fingers, dull our sight,
Producing what? A pair of slippers, sir,
To put on when you're weary—or a stool
To stumble over and vex you . . . "curse that
stool!"

Elizabeth Barrett Browning, Aurora Leigh

In *Argonauts of the Western Pacific* Malinowski is painstakingly forthright about his dilemma over how to interpret Trobrianders' kula behavior. In every chapter, he searches for behavioral analogies that a Western audience will understand then immediately undoes the point by reemphasizing the exoticness of kula exchanges. Looking back on his work more than half a century later, these particular conundrums stand out because his analogies with Western economics were remarkably sensitive even when his reversals were wide of the mark.[1] Early on in *Argonauts,* Malinowski briefly muses over the

similarity between kula shells and the historical significance attributed
to the crown jewels he once saw in Edinburgh Castle. He writes how
suddenly he realized that "however ugly, useless, and . . . valueless an
object may be, if it has figured in historical scenes and passed through
the hands of historic persons, . . . [it is] therefore an unfailing vehicle
of important sentimental associations."[2] Still he remains convinced that
kula shells are "too well decorated and too clumsy for use."[3] Despite
the intense emotions that surround the acquisition of kula shells that
Malinowski himself reported, he believes there can be no question of
political drama associated with these "long, thin red strings, and big,
white, worn-out objects, clumsy to sight and greasy to touch"[4] because
they are not "convertible wealth" or "instruments of power."[5] Yet, at
the end of *Argonauts*, he writes how exhilarating it is for a Trobriander
to possess a kula shell, how one might be placed on a dying man "to
inspire with life; and . . . to prepare for death."[6] Again and again
Malinowski comments that kula shells are valued differently than Western wealth. Because they represent ideas about wealth and value that
to the Trobrianders are emotionally so meaningful, he is certain that
ethnographers will discover similar examples in other parts of the
"primitive" world.[7]

　　Marcel Mauss took up this challenge by sifting through reports on
"primitive" life and finding a common thread that linked these data to
Malinowski's kula examples.[8] As a result, anthropology's most famous
and controversial text on reciprocity, *Essai sur le don*, was published in
1925, three years after *Argonauts of the Western Pacific*. The main initia-
tive in Mauss's essay is to discover what Malinowski failed to find—the
underlying motivation that makes one gift given elicit a return. Unlike
Malinowski, Mauss recognizes the symbolic and political meanings in
kula shells, taking us beyond Malinowski's attention to their "sentimental associations." In turning to Polynesian sources, Mauss locates a text
in which a Maori elder describes the concept of *hau* as the "vital essence" of life in human beings, in land, and in things. When an object
embedded with the hau is given to others, the "spirit" of the thing
given seeks to find its place of origin, thereby creating a return. This
example provides Mauss with the "key to the whole problem," enabling
him to demonstrate more explicitly Durkheim's earlier point, that the
intimate relation between persons and things is the energizing force
making obligatory the acts of giving, receiving, and returning.

　　In *Crime and Custom in Savage Society*, in part a response to *Essai
sur le don*, Malinowski rejects Mauss's conclusions that objects such as

kula shells are associated with symbolic power. He argues instead that the dictates of custom are the motivating force behind reciprocal returns. Since then many other critics have joined the controversy.[9] Some claim Mauss overintellectualized the Maori text, mystifying the economic reality of reciprocity. Marshall Sahlins shows that the Maori hau, like all gifts, represents nothing other than the material "yield" of the gift, that is, the gain received through the transaction of gift and countergift.[10] Lévi-Strauss goes even further, insisting that Mauss's phenomenological approach kept him from recognizing that the hau is merely the Maori point of view and could never illuminate the universal structure underlying the acts of giving and receiving.

Throughout these debates, no one observed that in a few instances Mauss used the word *immeuble,* pointing out that not only Maori valuables and Trobriand kula shells, but Samoan fine mats and Northwest Coast coppers remained attached to their original owners even when they circulated among other people.[11] In the opening pages of *Essai sur le don,* Mauss begins with an example of Samoan fine mats (*ie toga*). He labels them "maternal goods" because they are given in marriage by the women's side, and, like the Maori *taonga* (valuables), they are "more closely linked to the soil, the clan, the family, and the person," in opposition to things *meuble,* such as food and crafted goods that lack these kinship connections.[12]

Here Mauss briefly suggests that an inequality exists between exchanges of Samoan fine mats and food. His intuition is unerring for in these exchanges, *oloa* is given for service and help whereas fine mats are always exchanged for each other. Since the name, rank, and historical trajectory of each fine mat has its own singular and absolute value, each exchange can only be understood in terms of the *difference* between one fine mat and another. The fine mat exchanges involve intricate strategies in which each one given elicits a return that either matches, exceeds, or is less than the original's value. Since all fine mats are ranked against each other and the most highly valued rarely circulate, the exchanges are as much about the identities of the particular fine mats that are hidden away as they are about the transactions of the moment. Politically, the challenge to exchange is a challenge to what is being kept out of the exchange. Although wide variation in local practices make the Samoan and the Maori examples each culturally distinct, the elementary principle of keeping-while-giving rather than the norm of reciprocity takes us to the heart of the problem Mauss evoked in his discussion of the Maori hau.

Difference and Hierarchy

In surveying other parts of Polynesia, Mauss found that the Maori taonga provided the most important parallel with the meanings embedded in Samoan fine mats.

In Maori, Tahitian, Tongan and Mangarevan (Gambier), it [taonga] connotes everything that may properly be termed possessions, everything that makes one rich, powerful, and influential, and everything that can be exchanged, and used as an object for compensating others. . . . [They are] strongly linked to the person, the clan, and the earth. . . . They are the vehicle for its mana, its magical, religious, and spiritual force.[13]

In Polynesia, cognates of taonga most often refer to fine mats, barkcloth, and cloaks, which, in most cases, are produced by women and exchanged by women and men as wealth at all major social and political events (see fig. 4).[14] Women are by no means universally the producers of cloth, but their important roles in these activities are found worldwide as is the symbolism of human and cultural reproduction that is associated with cloth and its production.[15] Yet theorists on Polynesian political hierarchy rarely consider cloth possessions as essential forms of material wealth.[16] Are these objects ignored by anthropologists because women produce them or is there simply a disinterest in fibers as opposed to food? Like Malinowski, has our involvement in a world of commodities closed our minds to the symbolic power embedded in cloth? Have we neglected the complex relationships that link women's roles in human reproduction with cloth production because Western cultures traditionally invest such roles with negative values?

In Polynesia, many forms of cloth made by women are highly prized and often guarded as inalienable possessions so that each one takes on its own subjective identity. But keeping these possessions inalienable while giving others away in exchange develops into a demanding economic and political commitment. Yet if a person or a group is successful, the benefits outweigh the challenges. The enhancement of a person's or a group's social identity is dependent upon strategies of conserving such possessions, be they names, myths, sacred cloaks, or bones, that distinguish the difference between one person or group and another. Grand displays and expenditures give the illusion that everyone shares in a ruler's largess, as any medieval nobleman or a Trobriand chief knows full well, but the political impact of these events resides in what has been kept. Political hierarchy arises out of the successful dual endeavors to preserve and expand one's social identity, not only through marriage and alliance, but by being bold and wealthy enough to capture someone else's inalienable possessions, embrace someone else's ancestors, magic, and power, and then, transfer some parts of these identities to the next generation. The processes of cultural reproduction involve the heroic ability to reproduce more of one's self or one's group through time by asserting difference while defining an historical past that looks unchanging. In varying degrees, we are all engaged in these heroic ventures.

The dimensions of this complexity are revealed by how politically compelling inalienable possessions are. The authenticity lodged in these possessions denies intergenerational difference whereas their ownership continually justifies difference in the present. Therefore, inalienable possessions are the material confirmations of these endeavors, controlled through the productive and reproductive exchange relations between women and men. Whatever the local cultural circumstances, constructing, guarding, altering, and expanding social identities into forms of rank and hierarchy are dependent upon the success of institutionalizing difference through exchanges that demonstrate one's ability to keep-while-giving. The ahistoric essentialism behind the traditional concept of the norm of reciprocity conceals the particular cultural configurations in and through which inalienable possessions are empowered to act as the source of difference and hierarchy.

With these principles in mind, I now turn to the Maori texts. There are three main threads that I follow. First, by pursuing Mauss's interest in the hau, I trace the way the hau is embedded in a special class of valuables called *taonga* that are ranked according to their historical and cosmological antecedents. Second, by reinterpreting classic Maori ethnographic texts on the semantic meanings and spatial and historical movements of taonga, I expose the economic and political significance of flax and feather cloaks that, historically, are the oldest kinds of taonga (see fig. 5). Third, since women are the producers of these cloaks, my ethnographic analysis of the hau and taonga brings women's production as well as human and cultural reproduction into prominence. The presence of cloaks corresponds to the universal unrivaled magnitude of cloth as a signifying medium for the strengths and limitations of social life. From swaddling an infant to wrapping a ruler, cloth delineates all levels of social relations, all supports for political alliances. Further, because of its variation in style and technical production, cloth has an almost unlimited potential as an emblematic marker of age, sex, status, rank, and group affiliation.[17] As a repository of human labor, cloth can convey complex meanings that symbolize the tying together of kin and political connections, humans to gods, the power of cosmology and history and, in the Maori case, the complex spiritual world of the hau. In this way, these three ethnographic threads converge to reveal the historical development of taonga and the need to reconfigure what we mean by reciprocity to account for inalienable possessions as the source of difference and hierarchy.

The Original Maori Text Reexamined

Among Robert Hertz's papers, Mauss found a reference to a Maori text that he felt illuminated the relationship between Samoan fine mats and the Maori taonga and was "the key to the problem."[18]

I will speak to you about the *hau*. . . . The *hau* is not the wind that blows—not at all. Let us suppose that you possess a certain article (*taonga*) and that you give me this article. You give it to me without setting a price on it. We strike no bargain about it. Now, I give this article to a third person who, after a certain lapse of time, decides to give me something as repayment in return (*utu*). He makes a present to me of something (*taonga*). Now, this *taonga* that he gives me is the spirit (*hau*) of the *taonga* that I had received from you and that I had given to *him*. The *taonga* that I received for these *taonga* (which came from you) must be returned to you. It would not be fair (*tika*) on my part to keep these *taonga* for myself, whether they were desirable (*rawe*) or undesirable (*kino*). I must give them to you because they are a *hau* of the *taonga* that you gave me. If I kept this other *taonga* for myself, serious harm might befall me, even death. This is the nature of the *hau*, the *hau* of the personal property, the *hau* of the *taonga*, the *hau* of the forest. *Kati ena* (But enough on this subject).[19]

Tamati Ranapiri's Maori text is very clear: the hau was not to be found in all gifts, only in those classified as taonga.[20] In all the later scholarly readings of the text, however, the enigmatic hau dominates attention, totally eclipsing the significance of taonga, the cloaks that women weave.[21]

Women, Reproduction, and Mana

The oldest and most cherished taonga are cloaks that still today are regarded by the Maori as the "greatest treasures of the land."[22] Woven with complex techniques to produce spectacular patterns from dyed flax or bundles of birds's feathers, these cloaks, as figure 6 shows, easily match the sophistication of other elaborate weaving technologies found worldwide. The complex symbolism associated with these cloaks refers specifically to women and human and cultural reproduction. Traditional Maori cloaks made from flax fibers are called *kahu* and the same term is used as a prefix for special cloaks, such as those made from birds' feathers and dogs' skins.[23] But *kahu* also designates the membrane surrounding the fetus.[24] The term *wharekahu* is the name for the special house in which Maori women give birth. *Whakakahu* refers to the person who cuts the umbilical cord.[25] Another set of meanings refers to death and ancestors. *Kahukahu* is the germ of a human being, the spirit of the deceased ancestor, a stillborn infant,[26] and the cloth used by women during menstruation.[27] In traditional Maori thought, lesser gods and ancestors were believed to come from miscarriages and abortions.[28] This latter belief, also found elsewhere in Polynesia, has puzzled scholars in large part because of the common analytical practice that assumes women and their activities are "profane" and "polluting" in opposition to the "sacred" domain of men who have access to mana.[29]

These symbolic meanings embedded in cloth that are associated with women and reproduction, however, cast light not only on the relationship between the hau and taonga but also on anthropology's long-debated controversy over the meaning of mana. In the last century, the missionary R. H. Codrington first described mana as a pan-Pacific magical force, bestowed by powerful ancestors and gods on certain people and their possessions.[30] Since Codrington's account, controversies over how to define mana continue into the present.[31] In relation to Maori cloaks mana draws our attention to how the authority with which taonga are imbued is authenticated through access to cosmological phenomena. Here is where we locate women's exclusive role: it is in the rituals surrounding human reproduction and cloth production where women gain control over mana which, in turn, gives them a domain of authority and power in their own right. And here also, we locate the source of "the spirit of the gift."

In the last century, Codrington collected extensive ethnographic information from Solomon Islanders who told him that mana is the source of a chief's spiritual power. Because mana originates with the "ghosts" of ancestors, a chief is able to bring this power to bear on contemporary actions, thereby enhancing his own chiefly authority.[32] Mana can be inherited but it also can be lost or used in antisocial ways to

bring sickness and death. Further, mana permeates a chief's possessions; its presence in things attracts others to him.[33] For Codrington,
mana represents power outside ordinary human agency and nature—a
substance transmitted from the dead to the living that continues to
pass from one generation to the next.

Mauss, intrigued with Codrington's descriptions, wrote an essay
with his colleague, Henri Hubert, to uncover mana's universal meaning
and structure.[34] This attempt was largely unsuccessful and Raymond
Firth, among others, faults them for grammatically confusing the issue
by describing mana as a noun, an adjective, and a verb. In fact, Firth
earlier dismisses Mauss's example of the hau as too metaphysical to have
any ethnographic reality.[35] But Hubert and Mauss conclude that because things, actions, and people are organized hierarchically, thereby
controlling one another, mana embodies "the idea of these differences
in potential."[36] Unfortunately, they take this thought no further and
resolve the issue by making mana a fact of collective life.

Recently, Roger Keesing argues against Codrington's description of
mana showing that such force is not metaphysical because Melanesians
and even some Polynesians define mana as luck or efficacy, referring to
mana as power only in a "quasi-physical" sense.[37] Yet Keesing also ad-
mits, following Codrington, that in certain Polynesian societies, such
as those in New Zealand, Hawaii, the Marquesas, and Tahiti, mana
became more "substantivized" with the emergence of a priestly class
that elaborated its cosmological implications as "metaphoric 'power.'"[38]
It is, however, precisely this metaphysical power of mana that provides
the underlying authentication of inalienable possessions—through
women and without the need of a priestly class.

A possession like a feathered cloak or a jeweled crown can affirm
rank, authority, power, and even divine rule because it stands symbolically as the representative of a group's historical or mythical origins.
The classicist Louis Gernet suggests this point when he notes that,
among the ancient Greeks, it is in the association of certain objects with
magical powers that we find "the earliest social understandings of the
different aspects of authority."[39] The absolute value of an inalienable
possession is this authenticity, its foundation in its sacred origins which
pervades its unique existence in the present.

In Polynesia, the highest cosmological authentication attributed to
inalienable possessions occurs through the authority of famous ancestors or gods and their mana. Like the authentication of inalienable ancient Greek libation cups and woven garments whose sacred source of

power came directly from gods and goddesses, to own these possessions is to participate directly in this power. In this way, one's claim to authority affirms one's genealogical or mythical history and therefore supports the ranking of one's social identity in the present. The Greek example shows that cosmological power resides in both women's and men's possessions, but in anthropological discussions about mana, most often men are the ones cited as having cosmological or divine powers. Yet women's activities involve them in the transmission of mana, giving them considerable authority in economic and political affairs.[40]

Throughout Polynesia, to become infused with mana a person must enter a state of *tapu,* where special taboos and ritual prerogatives are in effect. Anthropological accounts of this tapu call attention to chiefs or priests who occupy the only positions of authority. Even the translation by some writers of mana as "procreative power"[41] is discussed in terms of male rulers. Valerio Valeri, in defining the meaning of mana for ancient Hawaiians writes that "the real locus of mana is in the reciprocal but hierarchical relationship between the gods whose actions demonstrate efficacy and the men who, by recognizing that efficacy, increase and fully actualize it." It is this relationship that "truly causes their [i.e., men's] ownership of mana."[42] Although Valeri includes references to the mana of goddesses, to the power of barkcloth to invoke or curb mana, and to images and metaphors of giving birth,[43] these instances never temper his total emphasis on the authority and power that men claim through their relationship with male gods. Yet in ancient Hawaii, some women achieved great fame as powerful rulers exercising authority over their subjects including, of course, men. But for Valeri, the only cosmological pantheon that counts is that of male gods; biological reproduction merely reduces women to a profane life where they are excluded from all important rituals. Sahlins, too, ignores the power and authority that women gain from mana by analyzing Polynesian women's sexuality and reproduction as the cause of their negative, profane placement in the structural and behavioral scheme of things.[44] In fact, this ethnographic muddle of the data has a long history in Polynesian studies, not only in discounting women's power and their attainment of mana, but it also allows for a misreading of the fact that it is the procreative power of *women* that lies at the root of mana's metaphysical efficacy.

When early Polynesian accounts are read with care, we find that in all the ranking societies mentioned by Keesing elite women are imbued with mana directly through their own birthright as well as through

their tapu state during pregnancy and giving birth. Through human reproduction, mana is not only transmitted to an infant but through the
attendant rituals it confirms high-ranking titles and genealogies. In a
similar way with the Maori, mana is transferred through rituals to a
woman's flax threads that she uses in weaving cloaks. Not only the
weaver but the weaving poles are tapu and while working both the
poles and the threads have to be attended to appropriately or, like Codrington's examples, sickness or even death is thought to occur.[45]

These examples show how highly valued women's cosmological potency is and how its transformation into material possessions has the
highest value. The relation among women, reproduction, and mana is
as central to high-ranking women's access to power and authority as it
is to high-ranking men's political achievements. With high-ranking
women, all things associated with pregnancy and birth are infused with
mana and, in this state, women are tapu. Furthermore, women's sacred
rituals and tapu states surrounding weaving are as essential as are similar rituals and taboos for men in warfare. In fact, the Maori belief that
miscarriages become gods demonstrates that women provide direct
connections to deities and ancestors. The traditional opposition between male sacredness and female pollution is largely based on readings
of Maori myths that have been interpreted using simplistic male/female
symbolic oppositions to show that Maori female genitalia are polluting to gods and men. Yet as the Hansons point out, in these myths
women's genitals can also be interpreted as divine "portals" through
which sacred connections between gods and humans are established.[46]

Thus, like men in warfare, women exercise their own powers over
mana and tapu that can be both violent and sacred. Like men they are
both feared and acclaimed, as much agents of political success as harbin-
gers of political failures. Despite the anthropological record, which so
often ignores the political presence of women, high-ranking Maori
women achieved political prominence in their own right and some of
them became great chiefs.[47] As sisters, these elite women, as shown in
figure 7, are revered by their own natal community and become the
"pivot upon which the mana of the tribe rested."[48] Today, the presence
of a woman elder at political meetings with the high-ranking tattoo on
her lips gives her group an authority that cannot be surpassed by the
presence of any man.[49]

Once women's associations with mana and tapu are acknowledged,
we then can see the source of mana in women's cloth production. So
powerful do these fibers become that gods are thought to enter into

the threads themselves. For example, religious experts carried wooden staffs with carved heads which they used for calling upon the help of gods; these "god-sticks" were similar in form to weaving poles.[50] But only when the staff was placed in the ground and a piece of flax was tied around the neck of the figure could the god be induced. As the expert tugged on the flax while chanting a spell, the god was attracted to the thread. Without the precious cloth tied around it, the figure had no power at all.[51] The assumption is that such experts were always men, but women, too, had powers that made them able to induce tapu states and to dispel tapu.[52] This example returns us to the original problem of what Mauss meant by the hau as "the spirit of the gift." Only by understanding the intricate relationship between cloaks and human and cultural reproduction can we discern what Ranapiri meant by the hau.

The Hau and Cloth Taonga

According to Elsdon Best, the principal tutelary being of Maori women, Hine-te-iwaiwa, presided over both childbirth and the art of weaving.[53] The poles used by women to support themselves during delivery were similar to those used for weaving and as god-sticks.[54] Following a birth, a dedicatory formula was recited during which time a small hank of dressed flax fiber was placed in the infant's hands. When the umbilical cord was to be cut, it was tied with a piece of prepared flax, and in the case of infants of high rank, the cord was cut with a valued nephrite taonga;[55] these stones had special names that referred to famous cloaks.[56] In the naming ceremony following each birth, we find the associations between cloth taonga and hau even more specifically expressed.

After the removal of the umbilical cord, the child and mother left the birth house (wharekahu) to return to the village. Before returning, however, a special ritual, *tohi*, was performed in which the child received its name.[57] The parents, infant, and relatives went with a religious expert to a stream in a secluded place. Here at the bank of the stream a variety of the finest woven cloaks was spread out and arranged in a specific way so that the hems of the collars were at the edge of the water. Collars were the most sacred parts of the cloaks and the word for collar is the same as that for the early practice of plaiting mats that the Maori first brought with them to New Zealand.[58] The parents then seated themselves on the cloaks, now called *paparoa,* the place of honor, and if sacred possessions were available they also were placed on the cloaks.[59]

The expert recited a chant describing the strength and beauty of the child in which he invoked various gods. Calling upon the child to hear him and open his or her mind to his words, the expert proclaims the expected strength of the child for warfare if a boy or the ability to learn to weave if a girl.[60] Thus at this early age, both genders had specific domains that were comparable. The group then returned to the village and the cloaks were "lifted by the collars and carried away" by the father's parents or grandparents.[61] Back in the village the cloaks were again spread out in the same formal way at the sacred place, the window space on the porch of the principal house. The infant was placed on the cloaks, and gifts were placed around the child.

I described the tohi at some length because it is in this ritual that the hau is transmitted to the child and cloaks act as the agent of transmission.[62] An account by W. E. Gudgeon specifically explains the way the hau is conferred during the naming ceremony.[63]

We are told that the *hau* is conferred upon the child by its elder relatives when they perform the ceremony of tohi, hence if there has been no tohi there can be no *hau*. . . . It is a perfectly logical conclusion so far as the Maori is concerned to say that the tohi produces the hau; because according to their own traditions the first man was merely clay until life and intellect [were] conferred upon him by the breath of the god . . . and therefore the Maori is justified in assuming that the child is mere clay until the tohi has invested him with the divine spark.[64]

Thus the hau of each person was activated in the tohi ritual as a sign of each person's vitality, knowledge, and ability. Although neither Gudgeon nor others mention specifically whether flax threads or cloaks were the agents for transmission of the hau, numerous circumstances are cited elsewhere in which the Maori believe that threads and cloaks act as conduits to a person's hau. For example, when someone dies, a ritual is performed in which the tags from the dead person's cloak are pulled by her or his kin, thus sending the person's hau on its way.[65] At any time, the hau, once vested in a person, can be lost. A person's hau could be attacked by others, causing death, and the medium of such an attack was flax thread that belonged to the subject. An expert first had to obtain the thread and then it was inserted into a hole in a mound of earth made to resemble a human form. Spells were recited causing the

hau of the subject to descend the cord into the hole where it was confined and destroyed.[66] From these examples, we see that the hau can
be separated from the person. The hau brings to the person the potential for strength and knowledge, but the person always is in danger of
its loss. The association between persons and things, however, draws
on more than the hau. For threads and cloaks act as media, extending
the presence of a person into situations where the material object, the
cloak, or even its threads, stands for the person. In the semantic connections, rituals, and beliefs surrounding birth and death, flax threads and
cloaks figure significantly in the transmission of mana from gods to
high-ranking people. But these fibers and fabrics also transmit or interfere with each individual's personal life force, the hau. Because of these
connections, each cloak had its own identity, initially established by its
aesthetic beauty and the expertise of the woman who wove it. But its
mana is what imbues the cloak with a cosmological authentication, giving it more than a personal history. Here we begin to see how these
possessions reveal not only clan and individual histories but Maori history itself.

Taonga as Cultural History

Maori cloaks circulated as taonga from a very early time.
The ancestors of the Maori who first came to New Zealand brought
with them the techniques for barkcloth and mat production used widely
throughout Polynesia.[67] But the climate prohibited the extensive culti-
vation of the imported paper mulberry tree from which barkcloth is
most often made; this kind of cloth was inadequate against the colder
New Zealand weather. The subsequent use of flax, with the introduction of a more complex finger-weaving technique, ultimately created a
technology unique to the Maori while sustaining the wider Polynesian
tradition of cloth wealth and its sacred associations that gave such possessions absolute value.[68] Because of the traditional lack of interest in
cloth as wealth on the part of archaeologists and the fact that barkcloth
and cloaks disintegrate in a tropical climate, it is difficult to pinpoint
the prevalence of cloaks archaeologically. The earliest cloak found in a
burial site dates to the seventeenth century, but burials from the much
earlier Archaic period beginning around A.D. 800 include many cloak
pins and needles.[69]

Maori cloaks are not the only taonga. In ancient times, human bones were also considered taonga and like cloaks, the bones of high-ranking people were revered because they remained infused with a person's mana. Burials from the Archaic phase disclose that skulls and other bones were often missing.[70] Bellwood suggests that such bones "were very probably removed for ancestor rituals and to make ornaments for relatives."[71] In the late nineteenth century, Best reported that ancestors' bones were deeply cherished, and at a death they were placed around the corpse along with valued cloaks and other sacred possessions.[72] In the early nineteenth century, Joel S. Polack reported similar observances, especially for chiefs.[73] During parturition, a flute made from the bones of a woman's ancestors would be played by her father or grandfather proclaiming the infant's genealogical connections.[74] The bones of an important woman would be revered as a source of mana and her kin would use her bones to draw on their ancestors' accessibility to the gods.[75] Although a person's ancestral bones were guarded and protected in these ways, the bones of enemies taken in battle were made into fishhooks and spearpoints.[76] The most explicit reference for the use of bones directly as wealth comes from Firth who reports that when a person refused to sell his land for "garments and weapons" (the usual exchange medium), he would be tempted to give it over only if the potential buyer had obtained the skull of his ancestor, taken in warfare or gotten in an exchange, and offered it to him as payment.[77]

The Maori practiced secondary burial, and each time bones were exhumed, they were carefully wrapped in cloaks before they were reburied or finally deposited in a cave.[78] Best describes the ritual associated with the reburial of bones and it is exactly like the display of a child after the naming ceremony discussed above: "On reaching the village the bones would be deposited in the porch of the principal house, below the [sacred] window space, and on mats [cloaks] spread for the purpose."[79] At the completion of this final stage, if the deceased were a chief, the bones would be carefully wrapped in cloaks and deposited in some part of the ancestral land. Sidney Mead wrote that through these secondary burials the deceased becomes an ancestor whose spiritual presence is realized through bones and cloaks.[80]

Nephrite objects suddenly appear in the archaeological record in the Classic Maori Phase from about A.D. 1300 to A.D. 1500, at which time palisaded villages were in evidence and significant population expansion had occurred. Therefore, their use coincides with a major development in political hierarchy. Numerous writers report that the most valued nephrite taonga were fashioned into adzes, ornaments or weapons (see figs. 7 and 8). Each handle, buried with a chief, was refashioned at the installation of a successor whereas the stone, endowed with mana and representing the origins of clan identities, continued to pass from one chief to the next.[81] The adzes were used to make the first chips of a canoe or a new house, thereby invoking the authority of gods, goddesses, and ancestors. The sculptured *hei-tiki* (that is, nephrite neck pendants, such as those worn by the women in figure 7) that resemble a cross-legged human being carved with its head tilted to one side and in most cases, with female genitals, also received individual names and were inherited by relatives after an owner died. Like cloaks, all nephrite taonga were presented at naming ceremonies, ear-piercing rituals, marriages, and deaths, and when these possessions were on view, the histories of battles and ownership would be recounted.[82] Thus in the course of Maori history, with increasing social stratification and political control, sacred nephrite weapons and ornaments replaced bones as taonga, although the "economic" significance and sacredness of bones never completely disappeared.[83] Early Maori sources suggest that the hei-tiki represented the immortalization of an individual in the way that nephrite weapons represented the chief and the tribe.[84] At times, a nephrite taonga could be converted into a tiki as a way of honoring a special relationship. The mana in a taonga could be shared with someone by changing the object into a different form.[85] Altering objects in this way also suggests that the drawing of female genitals on the nephrite neck pendants was perhaps an inventive attempt to recreate in nephrite the reproductive symbolism conveyed by cloth.

Despite the increasing use of nephrite, cloaks continued to occupy the high status of taonga, even though nephrite was imbued with similar sacred connections to hau, mana, and the history of gods and humans. For example, cloaks, like nephrite adzes, were used as payment for ceding land titles to others,[86] as compensation payment for crimes, and for the performances of rituals.[87] Cloaks and nephrite possessions both moved in the same direction when they were distributed at births, marriages, and, most importantly, at deaths. They were displayed and handled with great emotion and elicited historical recountings.[88] Many early writers describe the large quantity of cloaks that, following a death, are brought by relatives and spread over the deceased as "coverings."[89]

In a general ethnological sense, cloth differs from bones because cloth is not an actual human physical substance, but rather a kind of symbolic skin, technically complex, that is most often used as a wrapping or covering. Like skin that reveals age and health, beauty and ugliness, cloth adorns and conceals, heightens and disguises these natural characteristics. It is not accidental that the very physicality of cloth, its woven-ness, and its potential for fraying and unraveling denote the vulnerability in acts of connectedness and tying, in human and cultural reproduction, and in decay and death. Contrastingly, hard possessions such as jade, precious metal, or bones are much more durable than cloth, making them better physical objects for symbolizing permanence and historical accountings. Cloth, unlike hard materials, is able to represent the more realistic paradox of how permanence in social, political, and ancestral relationships is sought after despite the precariousness of these relationships always subject to loss, decay, and death.

From Europe to the Pacific, bones (or other hard substances) and cloth, complementing each other, are still revered as sacred possessions and are vied over as significant economic resources. As early as the sixth century, saintly pieces of bone and cloth were prized and fought over by groups within the Catholic church as rights to such possessions were necessary to establish a new religious community.[90] Consider that it has taken over nine hundred years to disprove the authenticity of the famous shroud of Turin and even when recent carbon-14 dates showed that the flax was from medieval rather than Roman times, many Catholics still believe the shroud is inspirational.[91] In many other places, such as among the Indonesian Batak where gold and silver ornaments and fabrics are major marriage exchanges,[92] or the Northwest Coast Kwakiutl who say "this prized copper is our bones" but give it up in a potlatch, it is always hoped that the most ancient textiles imbued with special names and mythical histories preserved as inalienable treasures will not be forced to enter these exchanges. When a famous Maori nephrite adze that had been lost for seven generations was discovered in 1877, the Maori people still remembered the histories associated with the adze. But upon its recognition, it was wrapped in sixteen of the most valued and finest cloaks and more than three hundred villagers cried over these objects as they assembled to view them.[93] More recently, when the Maori exhibition, *Te Maori: Maori Art from New Zealand Collections,* toured the United States, no cloaks were displayed. The Maori elders in charge of organizing the loans decided that the cloaks were too valuable and precious to travel abroad.[94]

In general, cloth occupies a special place in human history, an analog to bones and shells that aesthetically and technologically transforms a natural substance into one that is culturally and symbolically complex. For example, before flax can be twisted into threads, the plant leaves must be cut, stripped, soaked, and then beat, dried and bleached. Dyeing, weaving, and further ornamentation require additional knowledge and skills. Within an entire spectrum of cloth production, such labor intensity and manifold technical practices can signify historical change through differences in style and fashion just as treasured cloths with their ancient patterns emphasize stability for those who are able to control their circulation.

The many examples of wrapping cloth around people, statues of gods or even human bones illuminate the way cloth represents all manner of human and cosmological connections. The photograph of an Ojibwa Indian woman, as shown in figure 9, illustrates how widespread are the connections between humans and cloth. Here, instead of wrapping bones in cloth as the Maori did, a widow (or widower) made a great bundle out of her dead spouse's clothes and carried it wherever she went. Similarly in the Trobriand Islands, a dead woman's skirt or a man's basket, each adorned with the dead person's personal possessions is carried everywhere by a mourning relative throughout the major mourning period.

The most dramatic political difference between cloth and bones, however, is the replicability of cloth. Whereas a famous cloak is protected from loss, other less valuable cloaks are produced and exchanged. Because cloth is like the body yet, unlike bones, not the body, increasing production leads to the stockpiling of cloaks—the development of a currency that, although still expressive of social factors, enables those in power to trade and exchange more widely. In the same way, shells, minerals, and metals, symbolic of bones, fill treasuries and enable a person to withstand competing forces by being able, with sartorial brilliance, to keep-while-giving. In this way, we see how certain possessions attain absolute value and how this value makes inalienability a major goal that is always being contested. At the same time, we also see the inventive responses to change, directing us to consider that when ranking and hierarchy are at stake inalienable possessions are the key to institutionalizing these political claims.

Inalienable Possessions and Hierarchy

Although all Maori cloaks are believed to take on a person's semblance (*aahua*), chiefs' cloaks are so heavily tapu that no lower-ranking person would dare to touch one. In this way, famous cloaks develop their own unique identities.[95] So great is the mana of high-ranking cloaks that if a woman throws a cloak over a man, he becomes her husband. In other circumstances, throwing such a valued cloak over a condemned person spares his life because the cloak serves as ransom.[96] To part with this cloak is a tragic loss because its mana enhances that of its new owner. In the last century, wars were fought just so a famous nephrite adze or a cloak could be captured.[97] If a chief knew that another group planned to attack his village and he thought that his own group could not defend itself, instead of fighting he would give up his most valued taonga. The chief knew that the real objective of the attack was to gain "tribal treasures." Therefore, he and his relatives would pay a ceremonial visit to those whom they feared and, before the fighting could begin, they relinquished their prized possessions.[98] As Sidney Mead notes, when a challenging party accepts cloaks instead of fighting, they have attained the *"aahua*—the semblance of victory." Each victory, however, is short-lived, because the loss of taonga triggers later attacks to return the valuables to their *"foyer d'origine."*[99]

Even after a person dies, these possessions remain active. Depending on the rank of the person, some taonga are buried with the deceased; others, with the tapu removed, are stored in large, carved wooden boxes to be brought out later and cried over (like kula shells) but ultimately, to be guarded as valued inalienable taonga.[100] An account of an incident in 1856 involving the sale of land to Europeans depicts Maori attitudes toward taonga and expresses how precisely they understood the absolute value of inalienable possessions in relation to the Europeans' use of money.

[A] chief . . . struck into the ground at the feet of the Land Purchase Commissioner a greenstone axe, saying, "Now that we have forever launched this land into the sea, we hereby make over to you this axe, named Paewhenua, which we have always highly prized from the fact of our having regained it in battle after it was used by our enemies to kill two of our most celebrated chiefs. . . . Money vanishes and disappears, but this greenstone will endure as a lasting witness of our act, as the land itself, which we have now . . . transferred to you for ever."[101]

Although both cloaks and nephrite objects circulated widely as payments for services and in other economic exchanges,[102] a contemporary account reveals the social and political significance of taonga as inalienable possessions. At funeral practices and all other major exchange events greenstone weapons and ornaments with names and histories . . . feather cloaks, and fine flax mats . . . [are presented]. Such gifts may be kept for years, but most are ultimately returned to the donors on a comparable occasion. *The recipients hold them in trust: they do not "own" them and should not dispose of them to anyone except a member of the donor group. Pakehas* [Europeans] *who are given such gifts as recognition of their social or political standing often offend in this respect out of ignorance* [emphasis mine].[103]

These most highly prized taonga, owned by individuals of distinguished rank, remain inalienable, transmitted only to those reckoning the same ancestors and, through time, all efforts are made to keep them within the "tribal boundaries." In 1888, John White recounted:

In the old custom it was proper for such men [chiefs] to exchange such weapons, because they represented the descent lines which held them in keeping. A prized greenstone weapon was kept for a time by the descendants in one line of descent, and then they carried it and presented it to those in another line of descent from the tribal ancestor who first made it.[104]

A few brief notes about Maori social organization show the way ownership of taonga affected kinship alignments. The Maori reckon descent cognatically; socially they are organized into territorially located tribes, subtribes, and extended families. Although genealogical links through agnatic lines are important, links through uterine lines are also consequential. In the last century, chiefs and elders forged alliances through marriages, large-scale distributions of food and other possessions, grand oratorical competitions, and warfare.[105] Except for warfare, these gatherings at the *marae,* a territorial space where a descent group's rituals and political meetings take place, continue to play a leading role in contemporary Maori life.[106]

In this complex kinship milieu, every major event in a person's life becomes an occasion for exchange that takes on political consequences. Junior lines compete with senior lines whereas the authority invested in a chiefly title can be diminished or expanded depending upon the titleholder's leadership skills. Having possessions to give away to others is essential but the guardianship and appropriate inheritance of those inalienable possessions that carry the mana of famous ancestors are strategic. Such possessions could be placed in the care of someone else, but could never be given away; "to do so would be to give away the chieftainship of the tribe."[107] To keep such possessions that authenticate one's genealogical and cosmological depth confirms one's right to a title. Keeping also attracts both allies and rivals who, through friendship or deception, want to share in this power. All sorts of political strategies are enacted to gain well-known taonga treasures; keeping heightens the political stakes while it also increases the taonga's value. To give away much that one owns at an important commemorative occasion is a worthy political victory, only if a chief is able to keep the group's most precious taonga intact. The ownership of inalienable possessions proves one's difference, making all other exchanges resonate this difference.

The Hau and Taonga: Keeping-While-Giving

Finally to return to the hau, we see that Ranapiri's text is not enigmatic, nor is Mauss's interpretation of the hau mystical. The hau as a life force embedded in the person is transmitted to the person's possessions. The ethnography shows that the hau must be given following birth and is lost through antisocial means or at death. The hau is permeable in that it must be replaced in people and things, instilling people with a creative force that creates a bond between them. However, the taonga and the hau are not identical because a taonga, as an inalienable possession, carries the force of history and tradition. The hau of each owner enters the taonga, but the taonga's value is based much less on personal identity than on the cumulative social and cosmological identities of past owners. Therefore, although the taonga is the vehicle of both the hau and history, these meanings are separable. In fact, Mauss sensed some kind of confusion in his own explanation when he wrote in a footnote, "Indeed the taonga seem to be endowed with individuality, even beyond the hau that is conferred upon them through their relationship with their owner." [108] The taonga given to someone should return because it is inalienable, but the hau can be detached from an object so that another taonga may carry the original "semblance" of the person. When Ranapiri explains that when a taonga is given to another person, it will be repaid with another taonga, this is a replacement for the original. But when an exceptionally fine taonga is given, there is no replacement possible. Each high-ranking cloak or nephrite possession subjectively defines an exclusive set of social and cosmological relationships. To give away a taonga to someone else is to make that person an intimate part of these relationships. To claim another person's taonga is more than a personal victory; it is to assume another's rank, name, and history.

The mana present in a taonga authenticates the differential ranking of chiefs and their tribes. Although the hau is a personal life force that is thought to imbue all persons and things with this vitality, mana is a cosmological power that can only be the prerogative of high-ranking people. Men's and women's status, rank, and access to mana originate in women's reproductive potency, which connects human beings to the feared yet ultimate resources of ancestors and deities. Not only in human reproduction but in the cultural activities of birth and cloth production, women bring these powerful sources of authority to bear on the negotiation of political relations. Mana infuses possessions with a power that, although feared, is coveted. So sanctified do the taonga of high-ranking people become that the possessions associated with them take on the same symbolic powers. When taonga were brought onto the marae, they were often greeted as persons (see fig. 9), as though the ancestors they represented were actually present.[109]

An individual's role in social life is fragmentary unless attached to something of permanence. The history of the past, equally fragmentary, is concentrated in an object that, with age, becomes increasingly valuable. In the Maori case, a person's life force, the hau, also penetrates these possessions. And among high-ranking people, mana, the source of reproductive potency and cosmological power contributes its sacred efficacy. The dynamics surrounding keeping-while-giving are attempts, paradoxical though they may be, to give the fragmentary nature of social life a wholeness, thereby strengthening each new generation with the fame of past generations. But these possessions do more than replicate the past. Their fame and power pervade all exchange events for giving and the status that ensues is measured by what has been kept.

Reciprocity only provides the outer manifestation of social interaction. Such acts appear to disguise difference, but in reality they proclaim the variation between participants in status or rank authenticated by the inalienable possessions a person is able to retain. The fact of ownership, be it an ancestral name, knowledge of a myth or ritual, or a magnificent flax cloak, enters into all other exchange events defending, usurping and in some situations, defeating political hierarchy. In order to play these games for high political stakes, participants require replacements, such as hundreds of other cloaks or fine mats, to keep their most prized possessions out of circulation, even as they must continue to keep these possessions prominent in people's minds. The ultimate solution which divine rulers attempted to attain is to establish difference without the need to defend it—the Andaman Islanders' myth of a world without exchange.

CHAPTER 3

The Sibling Incest Taboo: Polynesian Cloth and Reproduction

---

*. . . anyone brought up among Puritans knew that sex was
sin. In any previous age, sex was strength. . . . Everyone,
even among Puritans, knew that neither Diana of the
Ephesians nor any of the Oriental goddesses was worshipped
for her beauty. She was goddess because of her force; she was
the animated dynamo; she was reproduction—the greatest
and most mysterious of all energies.*

Henry Adams, *The Education of Henry Adams*

*This cruel death in exile, far from home,
Far from your sister. And I [your sister] could not be there
To wash and dress your body for the fire
Or dutifully lift the sad remains
In loving hands.*

Sophocles, *Electra*

In traditional theories of kinship, the accepted priority of
the norm of reciprocity focuses kinship studies on marital exchange and
human reproduction. The consequence is that reciprocity becomes the
pivot around which other important kin relationships—between men—
are established. Reciprocity, as traditionally defined, is not the mechanism that produces homogeneity between participants in exchange. It
is the many paradoxical solutions to keeping-while-giving that result in
the establishment of difference between participants and which make

the processes of cultural reproduction central to the development of hierarchy.

A child is both like and unlike its parents but, in genetic terms, it is sexual difference that makes human reproduction possible. The work of cultural reproduction also produces difference through the exchanges that begin from a person's birth and continue even after a person dies. To draw on other social identities, to enhance one's history, and to secure the appropriate transmission of inalienable possessions for the next generation involve voluminous exchanges, elaborate strategies, and productive efforts. The initial exchanges of social identities that begin at birth fall not only onto the child's parents, but involve a brother and sister whose exchange efforts with each other and with each other's children provide the kinship counterpart of keeping-while-giving.

For over a century, the sibling incest taboo has been at the core of kinship studies because this restriction, which prohibits sexual intercourse between brother and sister, is often conflated with the rules of exogamy, prohibiting marriage between cross-sex siblings and other close kin. Therefore, the inherent motivation that has been thought to underlie reciprocal gift exchange is extended to reciprocal marriage exchange. In these exchanges as traditionally defined, a woman's role in social life is limited to her sexual and reproductive role as wife, and in this role she is merely the sign of the exchanges between her husband and her brother. What is missing from these long-held views is that both before and after she marries, a woman is prominent as a sister. In this latter role, she is dynamically involved in a multiplicity of social and political actions that accord her a position of authority—as sister—in her own right.

As an anthropological concept, the incest taboo is encumbered with such heavily pejorative sanctions that the restriction on sexual relations is thought to extend to all other intimacies between a woman and her brother. How then do we account for the extensive data that show what a strategic role sibling intimacy has played in human history?[1] Although actual sexuality between brothers and sisters is prohibited in most societies, the cultural recognition of a brother's and sister's socially and economically charged intimacy creates a unique bond that unites them for life. Like inalienable possessions, this ritualized sibling bond remains immovable because in each generation politically salient social identities and possessions are guarded and enhanced through it. Therefore, the incest taboo and sibling ties must be reconceptualized as part of reconfiguring exchange theory.

Although in most cases, social and economic intimacy between brother and sister is surrounded with ritual avoidance and sexual separation, these prohibitions only heighten and culturally acknowledge the essential human and cultural reproductive potentialities in sibling intimacy. In fact, the stronger the sibling incest taboo the more it reveals this reproductive power and, instead of being suppressed, it is thrown into the political domain. Sibling sexuality appears in myths, genealogies, and among gods but its constituted power emerges from the intricacies of kinship organization, from contests over political legitimation, and from the economic and political actions of women as sisters. Although actual sibling sexuality may be culturally disavowed, it is at the same time, inexorable. My use of *sibling intimacy* encompasses this broad range of culturally reproductive actions, from siblings' social and economic closeness and dependency to latent, disguised, or overt incest.

The Maori example demonstrates how inalienable social identities and possessions are infused with potent cosmological forces and ancestral connections such as the hau and mana. What the Maori material only hints at, however, is that, like the symbol of a Maori woman's tattooed lips, the reproductive potency of mana, rank, and titles is sanctioned by and through women as sisters. This authority gives sisters an autonomous source of power that men cannot match or attain, making women feared and venerated whereas men are dependent on them for their own political endeavors. More important, such power, linked as it is to a multiplicity of sexual, reproductive, and productive domains, accords to high-ranking women as sisters political authority in their own right. Although the historical past of Polynesian societies cannot always be reconstructed with complete confidence from the many mixed messages in explorers' journals and other early archival materials, when sifted through judiciously, these firsthand documents show that sisters played important political roles in Polynesian history and that sibling intimacy was always politically vital. Although many contemporary ethnographers have called attention to the sacred power of Polynesian women as sisters,[2] formal analysis of brother-sister intimacy has not followed, in large part because of traditional beliefs in the inherent nature of the norm of reciprocity.

It is therefore important to examine how incest has been viewed historically to show the way a reciprocity model makes claims about a woman's sexuality that eliminates the power and autonomy of her reproductive actions. To show the economic and political significance of sibling intimacy even in societies where the incest taboo is rigorously upheld, I compare three societies, each of which is progressively more socially and politically complex. Although I am not necessarily proposing an evolutionary scale, there are important points of comparison, such as sibling intimacy, the reproductive prominence of sacred sisters, and cloth as an inalienable possession that have not been thought about in this way.

First I discuss the long-standing debates surrounding the incest taboo from the perspective of sibling intimacy. I then analyze the reproductively essential activities in which brothers and sisters are prominent in the Trobriand Islands, in part because of my research there, but also because Malinowski's ethnography sustained so many debates on the meaning of incest taboos.[3] I then focus on the same themes in Western Samoa because I also have done fieldwork there and I draw on this material as well as the work of others. Ancient Hawaii provides another appropriate case because sister-brother sexual relations and marriage were the rule for the highest-ranking nobles. Although the Hawaiian data are meager and difficult to assess and I am by no means a Hawaiian scholar, there are certain aspects of the Hawaiian material that are essential to my argument.[4] By including the Trobriands in this comparison, where elite chiefly matrilineages are set apart to some degree from commoner lineages,[5] I emphasize an analytical gradient rather than the traditional distinct separation between Polynesia and Melanesia.[6]

After comparing the processes of cultural reproduction in these three cases and showing the kinship centrality of sibling intimacy in relation to the development of rank and hierarchy, I then compare women's cloth production in the three societies. This comparative analysis of cloth reveals the political limitations in the scope of rank and hierarchy but also shows how, in each society, power and authority are tied to gender and, despite political limitations, give women, especially in their roles as sisters, political power and authority. In terms of political hierarchy the three societies may be ranked with Hawaii as the most complex and the Trobriands the least. I use this tripartite scale in both directions to avoid claims that the Trobrianders' social structure is the precursor to Samoan chieftaincy or that that chieftaincy is the forerunner of Hawaiian hierarchy. The examples I discuss are meant to promote a different mode of ethnographic description and explanation that reverses traditional priorities and assumptions about kinship, exchange, and gender and exposes the source of difference and hierarchy in a wide range of relatively unrelated societies.

The Sibling Incest Taboo and Reciprocity

Since the time of the ancient Greek philosophers, the act of incest has served as a parable to show the uniqueness of humans in opposition to animals and nature. Thus the universality of the incest taboo is thought to reveal that society is created in recognition of the limits to sexuality (even though the biblical account of Adam and Eve depended on sexual relations between their children for the creation of society). For the nineteenth-century social evolutionists, incest was cast as the representation of sexual anarchy (nature) that, with the imposition of its taboo (culture), established formal social regulations for men over women. Yet in eighteenth-century France, sibling incest was often portrayed as a political act, a revolutionary force that through universal endogamy would create a world of "brothers" and "sisters." This "natural law" of absolute equality prompted the Marquis de Sade to exclaim that "incest must be the law of any government of which fraternity is the base."[7] In Victorian England, a more traditional nature–culture view of the incest taboo prevailed in which social origins remained the main anthropological concern. Although Edward B. Tylor never explicitly tied the origin of the incest taboo to his theory of marriage alliance, his belief that people once had to choose between "marrying out" or being "killed out" firmly linked reciprocity to the origin of exogamy. Malinowski and Freud transmitted to modern anthropology these nineteenth-century debates, shifting the parameters of discourse from the evolution of social order to how the incest taboo specifically regulates sexuality, marriage, and the family. Freud located the universal origin of the incest taboo in the Oedipus complex in which a boy's sexual desire for his mother comes into conflict with his father's tie to his mother who he then sees as his rival. Later, fearing castration, the boy identifies with his father, "takes over the severity of the father and perpetuates his prohibition against incest."[8] Malinowski rejected the universality of Freud's theory by showing that a different configuration existed among the matrilineal Trobrianders. For Malinowski, the incest taboo functioned as a sociological regulator that divides "persons of the opposite sex into lawful and unlawful" relationships, which restrains "intercourse in virtue of the legal act of marriage and which discrimi-nate[s] between certain unions in respect of their desirability."[9]

In the kinship controversies that followed, the dual terms, sexuality and marriage, incest and exogamy, were continually conflated. Whether perceived as physical kinship or social kinship, a strong male-oriented biogenetic stance kept kinship studies narrowly focused on the repro-duction of social organization or the reproduction of a life cycle.[10] From either a societal or an ego-centered perspective, marriage exchange was cast as the point of fission and fusion, the event that regulates hu-man reproduction for the next generation. In a sense, these ideas simply continue the same nature–culture opposition in which the women's position is erroneously constructed. Quite ignored are the multiple transformations of women's sexuality and human reproduction into forms of cultural reproduction that entail production and politically vital cosmological domains and that give autonomy and a political presence to women.

Nowhere is this traditional view more substantively wedded to the incest taboo and reciprocity than in Lévi-Strauss's theory of marriage exchange. The incest taboo marks the "fundamental step" whereby the "transition from nature to culture is accomplished. . . . Before it [i.e., the incest taboo], culture is still non-existent, with it, nature's sover-eignty over man is ended."[11] The incest taboo not only marks out where "nature transcends itself" but by nature imposes alliance so that culture need only define the rules. In this way, Lévi-Strauss moves from incest to the rules of exogamy, defining society as relations among men over women. His approach was revolutionary in its theoretical sophistica-tion but his synthesis never departs from the traditional biogenetic assumption that defines kinship and society as the exchange of women's biologically ordained procreative roles.

Although Malinowski's functional analysis of the incest taboo as the basis for familial social cohesion is fraught with problems discussed by others,[12] his inability to understand why Trobrianders expressed such strong interest in brother–sister incest, despite the strictest pro-hibitions, offers an important clue into the kinship–incest problem. Malinowski argues that Freud's account of the Oedipus complex is Eurocentrically based on a model of the patrilineal Aryan family be-cause the presumed universality of the Oedipus complex cannot ac-count for the Trobriand "matrilineal nuclear complex" in which a boy's mother's brother—not his father—is the authority figure. The Tro-briand father, lacking jural authority over his children, remains loving

and affectionate and never becomes the hated rival for his mother's sexual love. So within the Trobrianders, the Oedipus complex becomes
the "repressed desire to kill the maternal uncle and marry the sister."[13]
Ernest Jones refutes Malinowski's position on the basis that a Trobriand son does not come under his mother's brother's authority until
adolescence whereas the resolution of the Oedipus complex occurs by
the age of six.[14] In all the decades of subsequent debates, however, only
Anne Parsons touches on the key element in the argument: the critical
relationship between a Trobriand sister and brother. In psychoanalytic
terms, Parsons shows how a son develops the Oedipal desire for his
mother as he is aware of the important presence of her brother in her
life. Therefore, the boy's ego censures this incestuous undercurrent and
his libidinal desires are transformed from this woman as his mother to
his mother as his mother's brother's sister.[15]

This interpretation calls attention to the psychological proximity of
a sister and brother in each other's life. Indeed, the ethnographic record
is filled with examples of women's close social and economic intimacy
with their brothers or their brothers' children long after they marry.
Thomas Beidelman is one of the few anthropologists who has pondered
extensively over this problem, exploring why the matrilineal Kaguru
give such prominence to brother–sister incest in folktales, jokes, and
gossip.[16] Not only in matrilineal societies but in societies with other
kinds of descent systems, sister–brother incest is a recurring theme in
genealogies, myths, or rituals and in some cases, such as ancient Egypt
or Hawaii, sibling sexual relations became a political fact.[17] These latter
cases are usually thought of as aberrant circumstances, but examples of
both the acceptance and taboo of sibling sexuality attest to the fact that
women are not merely a counter exchanged between brothers-in-law.
When a woman marries, the full range of her reproductive powers is
far too essential to be lost to her brother and the other members of her
natal group. Whereas in most cases, a woman's biological procreative
role is established within her marriage, thereby sexually upholding the
sibling sexual relations taboo, her other productive and reproductive
roles—those usually omitted in kinship theory—remain clearly tied to
the relation between herself and her brother. Even when the sibling
taboo is rigorously upheld, the desire for and possibilities of sibling intimacy are present, giving women as sisters a unique kind of power.[18]

Some societies make greater claims than others on maintaining close
relationships between women and their brothers. Lévi-Strauss acknowledges such differences by stressing that in cases where the

brother–sister tie is strong, the husband–wife tie is weak, as does David Schneider in his classic essay on the characteristics of matrilineal societies.[19] This opposition, however, skims over the important shading of these differences, the problems that matrilineal, patrilineal, or cognatically defined societies face when people marry out, and the solutions that emerge. Giving a sibling to a spouse is like giving an inalienable possession to an outsider. Some way must remain open to reclaim the sibling. In a Motu myth, a man poignantly says, "You can have our sister's body but you cannot have her bones."[20] But the reclaiming actions for keeping siblings when they marry do not wait for death; they are ongoing and remain a formidable part of kinship and political processes. The controls and avenues open for sustaining the stability of siblings' culturally reproductive roles play directly into the level of rank and hierarchy that some societies attain. Therefore, the intimacy of sister and brother directly affects a woman's presence in economic, cosmological, and political affairs.

Sibling Intimacy and Kinship

THE TROBRIAND CASE

The main kinship theme in the Trobriands is of a society divided between commoner and ranked matrilineages where, in the latter, chiefs have rights to specific prerogatives and authority. But a chief's power is limited by the number of wives he is able to take,[21] and neither chiefly titles nor rank can be transmitted to members of other matrilineages. Therefore, being born into one of these ranked matrilineages provides the only access to chieftaincy, making women the primary means to one's birthright. So unifying is this claim that women are thought to conceive through the impregnation of an ancestral spirit child maintaining the Trobriand belief that those who are members of the same matrilineage have the "same blood." This spirit child is believed to be regenerated from a deceased matrilineal kin. Most often, a woman is impregnated with the spirit child by another deceased kinsman who transports the spirit child from the distant island of Tuma where, after death, all Trobrianders continue their existence.[22] Although a woman's husband is not thought to play a part in conception, he contributes to the external growth and well-being of the fetus through the contribution of his semen in repeated sexual intercourse. But even this part of a husband's supposed biological role in reproduction is often suppressed: when a child is born it is not thought to have any internal substance from its father. Yet it is always thought to resemble him because now the infant's sociological affiliation with its father is of public concern; a father provides for his child's well-being by giving possessions, such as names and chiefly decorations, from his own matrilineage, as mapula, what Malinowski originally described as "pure gifts." [23] Publicly, a child is adorned with its father's matrilineal resources, showing its father's support, but since these possessions remain inalienable to the members of the father's matrilineage, they must be reclaimed by the father's sisters at a later time.

Although much effort is made to objectify the social presence of a man as father, the prominence of the brother–sister relationship diminishes its centrality because of the need to ensure the enduring strength of the matrilineage. Sexual intercourse or marriage with a member of one's own matrilineage is considered an inviolate transgression of the sister–brother incest taboo. Yet Trobriand belief demands that conception occur within the confines of the matrilineage. The "cosmological" intimacy between a woman and her deceased kinsman—the purveyor of her child—provides for the tightly controlled reproduction of matrilineal identity. The many anthropological debates that arose over Malinowski's description of Trobriand beliefs in reproduction were subsequently glossed "virgin birth." [24] Yet the enormous ritual attention that Trobrianders give to premarital sexuality ensures that no Trobriander is a virgin at marriage so that the opposition between sexuality and virginity as it has been defined in Western mores and religion is no more the issue than is the argument over whether or not Trobrianders are ignorant of biological parentage. Sibling sexuality, although overtly prohibited, is fundamental to the "pure" reproduction of matrilineal identity.

Women's sexuality has been cast in a sexually inflammatory way by anthropologists and Malinowski was no exception. He is quite emphatic about the sexual separation between a sister and her brother and constructs a picture of their life together which has become a classic rendition of brother–sister avoidance with the drama of women as seductive sexual symbols.

They must not even look at each other, they must never exchange any light remarks, never share their feelings and ideas. And as age advances and the other sex becomes more and more associated with love-making, the brother and sister taboo becomes increasingly stringent. *Thus, to repeat, the sister remains for her brother the centre of all that is sexually forbidden—its very symbol; the prototype of all unlawful sexual tendencies within the same generation and the foundation of prohibited degrees of kinship and relationship* [emphasis mine].[25]

Lévi-Strauss simply shows us these same views of a sister as an allurer when he defines a woman as the sign of marriage exchange because she is "the object of personal desire, thus exciting sexual and proprietorial instincts" and, "as the subject of desire" as well, she binds others through alliance.[26]

How then do we reconcile that when a woman marries, she assists her brother whenever she can, convincing her husband to help her as well. Since most marriages take place among young people living within the same or nearby villages, a woman's brother is geographically close to her; she sees him often and gives him cooked food whenever she can. Her brother is her protector and his major obligation is to make a large yam garden each year in her name, as figure 10 shows. The harvest is presented to her and her husband; these yams form the economic and political core of all marriages and all brother–sister relationships[27] because the yams obligate husbands to work for their wives, ultimately strengthening the brother–sister tie.

Sibling intimacy has other far-reaching implications because the relationship between a brother and his sister to each other's children secures possessions, relationships, and knowledge for the next generation. It is a sister who reclaims the inalienable possessions, such as personal names and lineage decorations, that her brother gives to his children. Not only is a man responsible for giving his sister's son the knowledge and information necessary for his eventual succession to a leadership position but his sister encourages and heightens the adolescent sexual life of her brother's children, transposing into the next generation the vitality of sibling intimacy. Technically, her own daughter is the preferred marriage partner for her brother's son.[28] The time for the most important sexual liaisons that eventually lead to marriage occurs during the yam harvest season when it is a woman's responsibility to perform beauty magic for her brother's children and even assist them with finding lovers. Sexuality is hardly suppressed since in all these incidents a sister is directly involved in sexual matters with her brother even though it is through his children.

In several instances, Malinowski alludes to the ambivalence that Trobrianders feel about sister–brother sexuality, pointing out the few actual cases he was told about. Clan endogamy is also considered incestuous. Still, it occurs with some regularity and such marriages are usually attributed to love magic that is so potent it overcomes the force of the incest taboo.[29] This belief is at the heart of a famous myth, Kumilabwaga, recorded by Malinowski about sibling sexual relations and the origin of love magic. By accident, a young girl brushes her brother's coconut oil (a powerful love potion) over herself and is overcome with passionate desire for him. After the two make love, they neither eat nor drink, then die. Subsequently, a flower emerges from their bodies whose fragrance is the foundation of love magic. Malinowski not only gives the transcription of the myth, but also gives an informant's commentary. In the latter, a change is made in the text, indicating that the sibling's shame prevented them from eating and drinking and therefore, their remorse was the cause of their deaths.[30] This shame is what Malinowski defines as "The Supreme Taboo."

As a general rule, when love magic is strong, the desire it instills is so intense that the person can neither eat nor drink.[31] For example, if a young person truly desires someone as a spouse but their relatives object, the person refuses food and water. The relatives then recognize that someone has used strong love magic and they accept the marriage. It follows then that the siblings in the Kumilabwaga myth died, as the original text stated, not because of shame but because of their passion for each other. In this sense, the myth is a celebration of sibling sexuality—the origin of love magic and the more hidden origin of matrilineal reproduction.

In everyday life, the social and economic intimacy of siblings in each other's lives and to each other's children is pervasive. At the cosmological level, sister–brother sexuality itself is not totally subverted; a woman conceives through the agency of ancestral spirits who are members of her matrilineage who are like brothers. In this way, Trobriand beliefs in conception sanction the "supreme" purity of matrilineal identity, thereby keeping rank and chiefly status uncontested. If ancestral sibling sexual relations act as a guard against losing or diluting matrilineal autonomy, the down side to this solution is that matrilineages cannot incorporate outsiders as permanent members, and even chiefly matrilineages sometimes die out. Spouses and fathers, whose resources are essential for political power, must be repaid for their care and efforts when a husband, wife, or child dies. In actuality, the exchanges spread much wider than these central participants, to relationships between each member of the dead person's matrilineage to members of other lineages connected to them affinally, patrilaterally, or as friends and allies. In this way, each death puts a drain on accumulating resources and the constitution of chiefly authority never builds beyond dependency on localized, ego-centered siblings and affinal relations. Although a chief's potential for expanding his authority occurs through the success of his marriages, his authority still must be authenticated in these exchanges by his sisters.

When a man is told of his sister's marriage, he stays in his house or lives alone at the beach for several days. Is it only from shame that he hides away or is this also a response to loss? One of the most devastating insults that any Trobriander can make is to tell a man, "Fuck your wife!" The lack of acknowledgment to the most obvious sexuality between a husband and wife speaks directly to the political potency of sibling sexuality.[32] Trobrianders acknowledge a strong sibling incest taboo, yet their beliefs in incestuous matrilineal reproduction as well as the basic organization of descent and kin relations are dependent on the intimacy—at once social, economic, cosmological, and sexual—of a sister and brother relationship.

THE SAMOAN CASE

Whereas in the Trobriands the beliefs and practices associated with matrilineality are centered in the attempts to keep lineage identity and political authority free from the claims of others while incorporating the work and resources of those from other lineages, Samoan descent is more complex but reveals the same prominence of sisters. In Samoa, the basic unit of descent is not a lineage but a multibranching group (*'àiga*) with genealogies traced back for ten or fifteen generations.[33] Given the enormous complexity in genealogical reckoning and the many ways that people can attach themselves to other kin groups, the core kinship relationship, like the Trobriands, still is a sister and brother.[34]

The founding ancestors of a descent group most usually are a woman and her brother, and in each generation they remain the foci for the two descent categories, *tamatane* and *tamafafine,* through which all major titles are traced. Titles are most often reckoned through women who stand in the tamafafine category to men in the tamatane category. In most cases, men compete to gain the highest-ranking tamatane titles because such a title gives rights to chiefly authority over people, land,

and other descent group resources. Tamafafine titles also are sought in this competitive way, as prior to changes wrought by missionaries the highest titles were associated with mana and bestowed upon the eldest sister, called by Samoans the *feagaiga* or "sacred" sister.[35] Because the original sacred sister had access to mana, subsequently all firstborn women in each generation through these titles are believed to possess this ancestral power, which gives them a domain of authority and political power with which men must reckon.

Shore sums up the authority of Samoan chiefs (*matai*) when he writes, "If asked to suggest the single most important pillar upon which their culture rested, most Samoans would probably respond without hesitation that it was their system of chiefs."[36] Access to chiefly titles and authority for women and men is further complicated by the fact that the many branches within each descent group own rights to specific titles and all titles vary in rank, status, and historical depth.[37] A person may simultaneously obtain titles from several branches; residence, adoption, and even marriage allow individuals to align themselves, work for, and even gain chiefly titles from different descent groups at the same time. With many possibilities to hold titles, competition is endemic.[38] Unlike Trobriand chiefs, who are for the most part *primus inter pares* and politically control villagers within a relatively small geographical area, a Samoan titleholder wields authority over widely dispersed members of the descent group as well as members of other descent groups who have attached themselves or over those in other descent groups who have given him (or her) a title. Since all titles are ranked, chiefly authority is also ranked, from titles that bestow nobility to those that bring minimal prestige.

Samoan women, much like the Maori examples, use mana autonomously in both subversive and regenerative ways.[39] On one hand, a sacred sister has the power to cause illness or even death; on the other hand, through her own mana, she insures that chiefly titles carry the potency and force of her mana.[40] Further, in political meetings, a sacred sister has the autonomous right to veto any decision concerning the conferring of a title on someone within the descent group. She also can arbitrate disagreements within the descent group to the point where she defies her brother. A sacred sister can "throw her weight around the 'àiga and tell off her brother even if he has a high title," a Samoan elder emphatically told me.[41] Even from an early age, relationships between a woman and her brother remain socially close. A young man is the protector of his sister; he should always treat her with respect. As Shore points out, a man is extremely shy and deferential to his sister, even though men are assertive and domineering in other relationships.[42] Although women should act with dignity in public, they can openly chastise their brothers for being lazy because men are expected to channel their energies productively for their sisters.[43] And, as in the Trobriands, it is exceptionally traumatic for a man to be told that his sister is married. But in contrast to the Trobriands, it is the sister–brother incest taboo that is extended as a standard for all young people to show, in general, the wrongness of premarital sexual relations.[44]

Thus the sibling incest taboo appears to be rigidly upheld and most writers emphasize the prominence of premarital virginity for women, in light of Samoa's traditional marriage ritual that proves a woman is a virgin.[45] But there is another side to the emphasis on virginity that involves the political power lodged in sibling intimacy. The virginity of a sacred sister until her marriage to a person of high rank ensures that her firstborn son and daughter have access to titles of high rank through their father.[46] The issue of virginity, however, involves the special relationship of a woman's oldest son and daughter to her brother. By adopting his sister's first son, historically a common practice, a brother retains claims to the important titles to which the sister's son has full rights through his father.[47] In the same way, a woman's firstborn daughter, who will become the sacred sister in the next generation, is also adopted to strengthen claims for her mother's descent group to the most sacred titles to which she may gain rights through her father and his sister. By marrying out, a sister reproduces children who, in becoming her brother's children, augment the resources to high titles for her and her brother.

Here at the core of the intricate complexity of Samoan chieftaincy we see that, although sibling marriage is taboo, its precepts are cultural practice as sisters reproduce children for their brothers. On another level, actual sibling sexual relations are neither denied nor subverted. Some of the most powerful spirits (aitu) who still return to the living even today are thought to have come into being through the circumstances of brother–sister sexual relations.[48] Historically, sibling marriage between a sacred sister and her brother was the ultimate way to achieve a titled chiefly line that had the greatest power. The genealogies of famous women and men chiefs reveal many cases of these brother–sister marriages because sibling sexuality was thought to produce the most intense mana.[49] Still today, these genealogies that trace ancestral cases of brother–sister sexual relations demonstrate one's authority and power. When recited in the midst of a political debate over a title, the power of this knowledge when publicly revealed conclusively proves one's legitimate right to the title.

In Samoan kinship, the sister–brother relationship is the controlling force in the midst of long, complicated, and often contested genealogies and political strategies that allow for the incorporation into the descent group of many outsiders and the ranking and proliferation of titles that intricately cross and recross descent-group boundaries. The social and political closeness between sister and brother and even the public dominance of a sacred sister over the chief are evidence of the essentialness of this core relationship. The importance of keeping a sister reproductively united with her brother is enacted through cosmological connections to ancestors and the highest mana, through the cultural reproduction of each other's children, through access to titles through her children's father's descent group, all of which increase the ranking and the prerogatives of power and authority from which both she and her brother benefit.

The components that constitute principles of Samoan descent differ significantly from Trobriand descent, yet in both cases, sibling sexuality, mythologized or historicized, and its transformations into other essential sister–brother culturally reproductive areas create the elementary locus and force for the cultural reproduction of kinship and the political order. In both cases, sibling sexuality guards the unity of cosmological forces as these forces are reproduced for the next generation by women as sisters. And in both cases, sisters reproduce children for their own natal group. The Samoan solutions keep these sibling connections politically intact in the face of kinship diversity and genealogical ambiguity in all other kinship relations, generating far greater political authority and control than in the Trobriands. Hawaii provides a different example. In Samoa, because of the competition to maximize claims to titles within and across descent groups, a strong commoner–chiefly opposition occurs within each descent group. But the embeddedness of titles within descent groups to which anyone outside the group potentially can gain legitimate access, prohibits the full emergence of a chiefly class, organizationally segmented from commoners with chiefly authority that, following Dumont, encompasses the group. This is the level of hierarchy that developed in Hawaii.

THE HAWAIIAN CASE

In ancient Hawaii the island populations were sharply segmented into chiefly and commoner divisions, with a noble class distinguished by eleven grades of sanctity involving rigidly held privileges and taboos.[50] Unlike those of the Trobriands and Samoa, Hawaiian descent groups were not the basis for kinship alignments. According to Valeri, kinship for commoners was ego centered without reference to ancestral connections, whereas kinship among the nobles was ancestor centered as individuals publicly had to verify their connections to specific ancestors to legitimate their rights to the prerogatives of noble rank.[51] Sahlins points out that in these latter cases, it is ascent rather than descent that matters as individuals chose "their way upward, by a path that notably includes female ancestors, to a connection with some ancient ruling line."[52]

Vast diversity surrounds tracing up, as affinal ties and genealogically related connections through myriad branchings and multiple genealogical interpretations allow for and prevent the attainment of ancestral legitimation. Within this genealogical maze of actual and fabricated ancestral ties, brothers and sisters form the predominant focus for reckoning ascent through sisters. According to Jocelyn Linnekin, "lines of women descended from a sister in a [brother–sister] sibling set— occur in the Hawaiian chiefly genealogies" revealing the importance of women's transmission of mana as well as the political strategies and negotiations over genealogies in which women must have been engaged.[53] Although there is only minimal information about social organization among commoners, there was great fluidity in terms of multiple liaisons, residences, and group affiliations after marriage. Here, too, even among commoner groups, the elementary kinship principle for residence and land rights is the sister–brother sibling set.[54] Brother and sister often lived together after marriage and older sisters served as the heads of households with considerable authority.[55]

Among the elite, great care was taken to ensure the highest and purest genealogical connections, at least for the first child, whether a boy or a girl, and the mother's rank always counted above the father's.[56] High-ranking women were surrounded by rituals indicating the sacredness with which all high-ranking births were held. Within the complexity of genealogical ascendancy, the pool for marriage partners that would produce the highest-ranking royal heirs was so rigidly segregated that sibling marriage was recognized as the most appropriate act for procreation. Although both women and men were polygamous, birthright and primogeniture for women and men provided the predominant claims to chiefly successions, with a child born to a very high-ranking brother and sister accorded the highest sanctity.

Sibling intimacy among Hawaiian Islanders was not disguised; it was an overt fact of the political order at the highest level of society. Samuel Elbert reported that seventeen marriages of blood relatives of high rank were noted in the tales and chants he examined, of which "ten were between brother and sister."[57] Keōpūolani, the first and most sacred wife of Kamehameha I, was born with divine rank because her parents were sister and half-brother to each other and their mother was of the highest rank. In fact, the sanctity and mana that surrounded Keōpūolani were so powerful that if a man inadvertently came into contact with her or her possessions, he would be killed.[58] Valeri, however, believes that Hawaiian women were denied access to gods and mana. Therefore, he describes the Hawaiian system of nobility as one in which the hierarchy of high-ranking men was encompassed by the gods within one single order because only men had access to the mana that came directly from the gods.[59]

As the example of Keōpūolani's powerful mana makes clear, high-ranking women were the agents who conveyed the most potent mana from the gods. This potency surrounded all rituals associated with giving birth as well as women's own temples and gods. Although Valeri denies that women had access to gods, female chiefs worshipped their own gods and certain women had so much mana that they could enter men's temple precincts.[60] Furthermore, because Keōpūolani was of the highest rank and accorded all taboos associated with extreme nobility, her husband Kamehameha I worshipped her goddess who was descended from Maui nobility.[61] And politically, a ruler's sisters were persons of great authority who held important offices in government, even after European contact, including the position of prime minister or queen, as in figure 11.[62]

Although the Samoans and Hawaiian Islanders differ in the organization and structure of their descent and kinship systems, in all instances, sibling intimacy is fundamental to the authentication of the highest mana and rank. Sisters act as a powerful stabilizing force, standing out as a link and autonomous executor in the great labyrinths of genealogical and affinal reckoning that occur in the pursuit of political power. In Hawaii, sibling marriage segments the highest ranks of society, affirming the uncompromised connections that sisters have to divine gods and the most efficacious mana. In Samoa, the sacred sister's mana similarly conferred ancestral sanctity and power on the highest titles with the public recognition that ancestral sibling marriage had unparalleled political advantage. Although contemporary sibling marriage is openly abhorred, exogamous marriage in which children were adopted by their mother's brother enables siblings to reproduce their own children with access to titles that potentially establishes political control in the next generation.

Setting the Trobriand example beside the Polynesian cases reveals similar political potential in sibling intimacy and the prominence of women in cultural reproduction. But Trobriand sisters' involvement is to reproduce matrilineal identity by conserving the separation between ranking and nonranking lineages. This reproductive work not only is invested in women reproducing their own children but extends to their culturally reproductive activities with their brothers' children. Further, sibling intimacy depends on gaining resources from fathers and then marrying out to gain additional resources from spouses, but all these exchanges keep the boundaries contained between one matrilineage and another. In both Samoa and the Trobriands, women's marriages are the means to reproduce resources for themselves and their brothers: cloth, titles, and children. In Hawaii everything of political significance is controlled through those who claim the highest mana; in Samoa this control can only be effected by claiming the highest titles; in the Trobriands only the claim of an ancestral conception belief allows such control. In each case, however, economic resources are essential and it is in these actions as they authenticate cosmological controls that the political authority of women as sisters is realized.

Cloth and Inalienable Possessions

THE HAWAIIAN CASE

In ancient Hawaii, brother and sister sexual relations and marriage create a political situation of autonomous endogamy in the marked division between nobles and commoners. We also find that cloth production was organized by class. Commoner women and men produced barkcloth fabrics, expressly as "tribute" for nobles and island rulers as well as for their own household use and exchange, although there is very little information about the ritual and economic circulation of cloth as wealth.[63] Noble women produced only special kinds of cloth but the highest veneration surrounded these fabrics. For example, sacred skirts constructed of ten thick layers of finely made barkcloth were worn only by high-ranking women. Such skirts were replicas of those worn by goddesses which were thought to have magical properties and the ritual restrictions and tapu states of women during cloth production indicated that the presence and powers of gods or goddesses entered into the cloth itself.[64] Women remained in a tapu state while producing this cloth, as did their implements and even the area where the cloth was prepared.[65]

Although Hawaiian barkcloth reached an unprecedented aesthetic zenith for the Pacific, Hawaii clothmaking is best represented today by the beautiful feather cloaks collected by early explorers and displayed in museums around the world. These cloaks, along with precious ornaments decorated with feathers, such as leis, feathered hair combs, helmets, and *kahili,* sacred insignia of rank (often called "fly flaps" by early writers) were the exclusive inalienable property of the highest-ranking men and women rulers.[66] Chiefs wore feather cloaks in battle and, like the Maori, capturing such a cloak gave the victor claims to a more prestigious genealogy, for these validated the connections to particular high-ranking genealogies. Kamehameha I, in his rise to power, captured the prized feather cloak from his higher-ranking rival, Kalani'ōp'u, and by this ownership, validated his right to rule.

Who made and owned these high-ranking inalienable possessions is a subject of debate. As Linnekin points out, the most often-cited references to the manufacture of feather cloaks are by Peter Buck who writes that because the cloaks were imbued with mana, they had to be the property of men and as such, they only could be made by men.[67] Later writers have simply accepted Buck's biased assumptions. However, feather garments and valuable feather ornaments were owned by high-ranking women and women did play a role in their production.[68] Figure 12 is an engraving made from an oil painting done in 1825 of Princess Nahi'ena'ena who married her brother, Kamehameha III. She is wearing a beautiful feather cloak. Louis Freycinet in 1819 describes women producing feather cloaks and Samuel Kamakau comments on a great feast for Ka'ahumanu, a politically powerful woman who was "borne by the chiefs upon a litter . . . spread with feather cloaks and cushions." In preparation for the feast, impressive feather fly flaps and a great feathered lei were prepared. In correspondence between Charles Reed Bishop and William Brigham concerning the collection of Hawaiian featherwork for the Bishop Museum, Bishop discusses that Liliuokalani loaned her few feather cloaks for photographs in Brigham's memoir on featherwork but Kapiʻolani, "who owned some of the finest capes known," declined permission to have them photographed (see the cloaks draped over her casket in figure 11).[69] Although these references pertain to nineteenth-century elite women, there are other indications that women's ownership of featherwork had a long history, as two of the earliest descriptions of women rulers recorded during Captain Cook's voyage to Hawaii indicate. David Samwell describes the visit of a woman "chief" who came on board his ship wearing great quantities of new barkcloth, boars' tusks on her arms, the prized whale-tooth ornament around her neck, and carrying the great chiefly fly flap—each a symbol of the highest-ranking chiefs.[70] After Cook's death, when his ships were anchored off Kauai Island, Captain Charles Clerke was visited by a "Queen" and her daughter. Dressed in chiefly regalia, both women carried the treasured fly flap made with sacred feathers attached to human bone handles as in figure 13.[71]

Unfortunately, data are unavailable on the actual circulation of cloaks among Hawaiians, but many were exchanged for Western goods brought by European voyagers.[72] This suggests, as we find with the Maori, that trade and payments were made in cloaks, keeping other cloaks and chiefly insignia inalienable. Just as the styles of Maori cloaks varied through time, so too did the Hawaiian styles change dramatically following the visit of Captain Cook. As Adrienne Kaeppler shows, the feather cloaks came to be more and more associated with warfare and conquest whereas the sashes were fabricated while genealogical chants were recited over them.[73] Kaeppler, following the traditional assumptions that because only men had mana only they owned these possessions, notes that the sashes would protect "the chief's vital parts for the perpetuation of the societal ruling lines."[74] When we recognize that women not only had access to mana but were the reproducers of the highest mana, then these sashes may have symbolized women's "vital parts" acting as ancestral conduits through which procreative power was transmitted. Given high-ranking women's strategic management of genealogical verifications, the accepted association of men, mana, and feather cloaks is another ethnographic muddle in which women are simply ignored.

A further source, and perhaps the most important one, leaves no doubt that women did fabricate and control cloth that was imbued with the highest mana. This cloth brought the presence of gods directly into human affairs, making these women, rather than men alone, the agents of transfer between humans and gods.[75] In Hawaii one of the most vivid recorded examples comes from the Luakina ceremony in which the consecration of a new ruler's temple took place. In Valeri's account, the Luakina ceremony is the precise ritual moment when chiefs become divine, but we never learn that during the major part of the ritual the prohibition about the segregation between the sexes did not apply.[76] As the moment of consecration approached, high-ranking chiefly women entered the temple precinct carrying huge pieces of specially fabricated white barkcloth. These cloths were exactly the same kind of fabric necessary for presentations at the birth of a high-ranking child.[77] This "life-giving" cloth sanctified the temple when the women wrapped it around the god figures. Only then did the presence of the god enter the figure. Without the cloth, the image alone had no power, and the ruler could not be sanctified.[78]

In Hawaii, however, women did not just serve male rulers, they themselves took on full political office, ruling over districts and entire islands.[79] Their daughters and sons inherited these positions of autonomous authority from them. A woman's high rank gave her equal rights with men of similar rank and many prerogatives over men of lesser rank, including her husband if she overranked him.[80] Although women as sisters were politically vital to their brothers, women as mothers and wives also had access to political office. Even though most cloth production was done by commoners, women and men rulers guarded their most prized cloaks as inalienable possessions that were to be inherited only within the appropriate genealogical lines. Elite women not only had access to feather objects that were the highest insignia of rank, such as fly flaps and cloaks, but they themselves controlled the most prized cloth of all—the sacred barkcloth described above used at high-ranking births and chiefly inaugurations to bring forth the divine presence of gods. As ancient Hawaii reached the highest level of political stratification found in Oceania, so too, elite women achieved full political and sacred status.

Although historically this sacred barkcloth expresses the power and status of Hawaiian women, the fabric also conveys the instability of power. The ancient Hawaiian political system gave women and men at the top vast latitude in autonomy and authority. But by excluding so many below who were less socially well-connected and less endowed

with ancestral and godly mana, the way was left open for rival successors who attempted to alter genealogical connections or marry their
way into higher ranks. This Hawaiian political drama intensified during
the century prior to Western contact leaving us with evidence of increasing warfare, the rising power of priests, and the elaboration of inalienable feather cloaks more as a symbol of men's victorious battles
than of a long-reigning nobility. Prohibitions leveled at women by male
priests impinged on women's autonomous hold over the highest sanctity and mana. Women's strong political hegemony over royal birth,
cosmological authentication, and sacred cloth had to be contested if
those without aristocratic privileges from birth were to gain ascendancy. To usurp women's containment of mana was, at the same time,
to erode the aristocratic powers of men born into the highest noble
classes. With the rise of Kamehameha I, these dynamics were already
set in motion shortly before Captain Cook anchored in Kealakekua Bay.

The many references to Hawaiian women rulers in ancient genealogies, even though fragmentary, attest to the long history of women
chiefs. Despite the erosion of the hegemony of the noble class and the
effects of colonial governments and missionaries throughout the eighteenth and nineteenth centuries, women continued to exercise power
and political autonomy to an unprecedented degree, another indication
of their ancient ruling presence. In the nineteenth century, the changes
that elite women initiated or carried out were strikingly radical, a sign
of their vital political dominance, support and power. For example, in
1823, the chieftainess Kapi'olani defied the ancient gods and the priests
by breaking with sacrificial rituals. Four years previously, the high
chieftainess Keōpūolani dissolved the traditional eating taboos, thereby
firmly establishing Christianity against rival factions. In another later
revolutionary and decidedly feminist venture, Liliuokalani opened a
bank for women, the first of its kind. Recognizing that the bulk of
Hawaiian money acquired through the inheritance of land was owned
and controlled by Hawaiian women, she established the bank to allow
women, especially those married to non-Hawaiians, to manage their
own affairs making it less likely that their Western husbands would take
these monies from them. These changes, including women's claims to
leadership roles, often were contested by strong rival political factions
but women managed to hold on to a large measure of their authority
and power. Such resistance also can be seen in cloth production that
similarly underwent drastic changes. The missionaries who arrived in
the 1820s taught a few elite women to sew patchwork. The skills of

these women quickly evolved into the fabrication of beautifully designed quilts that are still made today. These quilts, presented at births, marriages, deaths, and to visiting royalty, continue to accumulate histories that symbolize Hawaiians' indigenous, sacred origins, that include the political presence of women.[81]

THE SAMOAN CASE

The power of Samoan sibling intimacy is lodged in reproduction, mana, and the relation between a chief and his sacred sister. But political potentiality is also acclaimed in the keeping and giving of fine mats, the wealth of women and men. These are the plaited pandanus fine mats that Mauss alluded to in the first pages of *The Gift*: "feminine property . . . more closely bound up with the land, the clan, the family, and the person" than things called *'oloa*, manufactured objects and food.[82] Even though Samoans today have a cash economy, they still exchange hundreds of fine mats each time someone is born, at a marriage, a death, and the inauguration of a new titleholder.[83] For each event, fine mats are given and received in over twenty named categories that define specific kin and affinal relationships. Before being given, each one is ranked in terms of age, quality, name, and history; there are as many strategies in giving and keeping as there are fine mats.[84] The splendor of these presentations, especially when someone of high rank dies, is politically essential.[85] Samoan informants say that the sacred sister "sits opposite the chief" in her responsibility for the well-being of the descent group and it is she who officiates at the distribution of fine mats, as in figure 14, when a death occurs or when a title from her descent group is conferred.[86]

Samoan fine mats are the wealth of both women and men, with the highest titleholder able to draw substantially on the wealth of others. But even with the huge distributions of fine mats, chiefs have great difficulty in accumulating fine-mat treasuries. First, chiefs eventually must replace all fine mats they have taken from their supporters. Second, their sisters, especially the sacred sister, accumulate and guard the most valued fine mats. At the commencement of any fine-mat distribution, the sacred sister is presented with a special fine mat to honor her dignity.[87] Even more important, after the event is over, the sacred sister must be given the best one the chief (her brother) has gained. A chief's sons, continuing this practice, give the highest-ranking fine mats to their father's sister or to her daughter.[88] These are the exchanges between brothers and sisters and their respective children that mark vital connections to expand control over titles. These possessions are the indices of how the political process works.

Sibling sexual relations are alluded to in the circulation of fine mats as stories of incest figure centrally in origin stories associated with the ancient names of the most revered fine mats, giving these mats, when presented or kept, enormous political advantage. Most notably, the names given to high-ranking fine mats often refer to what are thought to be actual ancestral accounts of sibling sexual relations that were prominent because they involved the powerful mana of high rank. On the occasion of a woman's marriage and again at the birth of her first daughter, her brother brings her an extremely important fine mat. When she dies, her brother brings to her funeral another high-ranking fine mat, which he calls *ie o le measā* (*measā* means sacred genitals of either sex). This presentation symbolizes sibling sexual relations and reveals the sacred sister and her brother as the conserving and reproductive forces in the complex political and economic affairs of the descent group.[89]

Fine mats given at these presentations are among the most precious that people have. Usually they are kept for decades or generations, only to be presented when the politics of a marriage or, as in figure 15, when a death demands it. Such revered fine mats are carefully stored, guarded as inalienable possessions because, like Maori cloaks, they authenticate claims to titles and mana.[90] Traditionally, the production of fine mats was under the authority of the highest-ranking women; the work itself was considered sacred. In production, women's own mana was infused into the fine mat bringing women's access to the highest mana into economic circulation.[91]

Because of the inviolate power of a fine mat, its circulation was limited, as demonstrated by an ancient story.[92] A woman was to be married and the members of her descent group stood before her prospective husband's relatives with only one fine mat, whereas the latter had assembled a thousand of them. But when this simple fine mat was finally presented by the bride, thunder and lightning rent the skies, proclaiming the mana that made this fine mat prized far above any others. Since even a thousand fine mats could not match its honor and power, it was returned to the bride's kin. Even today, when a person brings a highly valued fine mat to a distribution and the receivers do not have an equivalent one to exchange, it must be returned to the givers. This is how fine mats become inalienable. They are not reciprocally exchanged for 'oloa, the category of manufactured things, food, or money, as most writers assume.[93] Fine mats always are exchanged for fine mats, but underlying this overt reciprocity are two endeavors: first, to keep the best ones inalienable, and second, with each exchange to show one's rank. This latter strategy takes great finesse because, in matching the values of fine mats, the game plan, unless one decides to comment unfavorably by returning a lesser fine mat, is to select one that is only a fraction more valued than the fine mat given. This is the way one asserts difference and conserves.

When a crisis erupts, however, the only strategy is to give up the most precious fine mat to which one has access. If a murder or rape is committed, the highest titleholder in the culprit's descent group immediately sits in front of the offended chief's house covered completely with a treasured fine mat.[94] If the offended chief accepts the fine mat, then further retaliation for the crime is brought to a halt. A Samoan friend asked me why I thought Samoans attributed such significance to pandanus strips that have no practical use at all. Answering his own question he replied that "fine mats are more important than your gold. They are protection for life." Much like the Maori example of giving up a treasured taonga to an enemy to thwart an attack, the strong possibility of defeat leaves no alternative but to give over one's most cherished inalienable possession.

Although Samoan women do not completely control the distribution of fine mats, in their roles as sacred sisters they have the opportunity to obtain those of the highest rank from their brother or his sons and even to keep them inalienable. In the past, a sacred sister's mana made her brother's title strong, just as women's production and control of fine mats strengthened the economic and political foundation of the title. In these ways, women as sisters assumed a base for political authority that, although less hierarchical than in Hawaii, still accorded them extensive political power as women could, and still can, hold the highest titles. In fact, the four highest titles in all of Samoa, traced through female ancestral connections, once came under the rule and authority of one person who was a woman. In 1500 A.D. Salamasina held these titles, an achievement that for the first recorded time united all major traditional political districts under one person's rule.[95] Schoeffel shows that most of the great titles of Samoa today are descendants of Salamasina; Neil Gunson traces the dates for many other famous Samoan female rulers.[96] Even in the early 1900s, Krämer wrote:

girls and women of rank enjoyed an almost godlike veneration. It is not only through their prestige that they have great influence over their husbands and relatives and through them, over affairs of state, but titles and offices, even the throne are open to them.[97]

What makes Samoa an important example is its illumination of how difference institutionalized into ranking through sibling intimacy and cultural reproduction supersedes gender distinctions.[98] Because women are accorded chiefly authority and power as sacred sisters, on occasion they gain the same access to chiefly authority and power as men. To be sure, today there are many more male Samoan chiefs than women chiefs, but my point is that because women play a reproductive role of fundamental importance, they do become chiefs. Even today, some women claim the privileges and prerogatives of the highest political office.

Over the past hundred years, the effects of colonialism, especially missionization, deeply disrupted women's political power. Missionaries terminated women's endowment of mana and halted polygamy and a brother's adoption of his sister's children.[99] When women's access to mana was decried by church teachings, the dominant role that sisters held over chiefs was undermined. It is not coincidental that the Samoan word for sacred sister (feagaiga) is also the term for pastor. By weakening beliefs in the notions of mana, the church effectively undercut the once awesome sacred role of women as sisters; as the belief in mana was discredited, reckoning rank through women diminished in importance since titles were no longer thought to be imbued with mana.[100] Preachers and priests, even today, define marriage in terms of women's submission to their husbands' wills, undermining the freedom that women had in their roles as sisters. European administrators, too, interfered with women's roles as they systematically tried to ban fine-mat exchanges. In the early 1900s, German and New Zealand administrators were shocked that fine-mat exchanges produced disagreements and fighting over debts and repayments, as well as over chiefly ranking.[101] Arguing that these huge distributions of fine mats prevented Samoans from learning the work ethic of capitalism, administrators tried to outlaw all fine-mat distributions, especially the more competitive ones at the installations of chiefs and at deaths, thereby further eroding, but by no means destroying, the power of all women, especially in their roles as sisters.

Yet the cultural configurations surrounding fine mats and the role of the sacred sister are so deeply embedded in what it means to be Samoan that missionaries and administrators could not completely dismantle these traditions. In order for a titleholder to be politically influential today, he must keep the support of his sacred sister; her veto power within the descent group's affairs still makes her a political ally or foe.[102] Elite women today who hold high titles are accorded the utmost respect and maintain a degree of dominance despite the strong patriarchal position of men. Although fewer women plait fine mats than in the past (see fig. 16), the demand for mats has increased as they now circulate internationally—an intimate part of the lives of Samoans who now live in San Francisco, Auckland, or Honolulu and who still recognize the power in keeping-while-giving. Fine mats still are the most public forum in which Samoan women negotiate their political presence and are as prized and politically influential as ever.

THE TROBRIAND CASE

In contrast to the Polynesian examples, where cloth is essential at all births, marriages, deaths, and the taking of titles or rulership, Trobriand cloth wealth—bundles of dried banana leaves and banana fiber skirts—is necessary only when a death occurs in a matrilineage. Then a major distribution of women's cloth takes place in which women disperse thousands of bundles and hundreds of skirts. Today more than ever before, trade-store cloth and even cash are added.[103] Villagers, primarily related affinally or patrilaterally to the dead person, are the major recipients of these cloth possessions and the largest distributions go directly to the deceased's father and spouse as in figure 17. By repaying all "outsiders," women as sisters reclaim for their own matrilineage all the care that went into making the dead person more than she or he was at conception.[104]

Women are the sole producers, as well as the controllers of Trobriand cloth wealth, but the full circulation of skirts and bundles involves men. Although annual yams given by a man to his married sister (see fig. 10) provide the fulcrum around which marriages thrive, cloth wealth is attached to this pivot in the most basic way. Because a man receives these annual yams from his wife and her brother, he is obligated to provide his wife with his own wealth to help her buy more cloth whenever a death occurs in her matrilineage. In this way, a man reduces his own resources to support his wife and her brother. Since most deaths are assumed to be caused by sorcery, his help makes his wife and her brother economically and politically strong when their matrilineage is most under attack.

The use of cloth at each death demonstrates the political vitality of a matrilineage and shows the particular strengths of every marriage as well as each brother–sister relationship within the lineage. The control over cloth wealth also enables women as sisters to participate fully in the politics brought into play at a death as one woman emerges in each distribution as the wealthiest and most important woman of her matrilineage (see fig. 18). Overall, these distributions give women a domain of political and economic autonomy that exceeds such roles for women in other Melanesian societies. Still, ownership of cloth and control of its distribution does not allow women public participation in most other chiefly political affairs.

These limitations are revealed in the very form of the Trobriand cloth that represents these relationships. First, the most valued Trobriand cloths are new bundles and skirts that are made specifically for each distribution, not ancient ones that have been treasured for years. Skirts and bundles not only lack historical substance but neither are they associated with ancestral connections, mana, or chiefly powers. Unlike land, ancestral names, and decorations, cloth wealth is not inalienable so that women's control over these economic resources must be built up and reestablished at every death. Second, cloth wealth is necessary only following a death; it does not demonstrate political support and alignments at a birth, marriage, or the inauguration of a chief as we find in Samoa or among the Maori. There, the presentation of cloaks or fine mats shows political support (or its absence) from each of the multibranching descent groups. In the Trobriands, neither marriage nor chiefly succession establishes immediate wide-ranging political networks. Such influence and patronage accrue slowly after years of building up alliances. Only death triggers an immediate need for economic and political accounting, not just to show political stability but to free the dead person's lineage from debts to members of other matrilineages for the care of the dead person during life.

Skirts and bundles symbolize the "purity" of matrilineal identity, reproduced through the ancestral and political union of brother and sister. This is the unity that each death undermines. Like the Samoan example of giving up fine mats in seeking absolution, skirts and bundles are used to exonerate the matrilineage from any retribution that the father and spouse of the dead person and their extended kin may claim for the care and attention they gave while the deceased was alive. In this sense, like Samoan fine mats, skirts and bundles are "protection for life." Protecting the survival of the matrilineage in its "purest" form proceeds without problem through marriage and birth, but by the time of death, the investments made by members of other matrilineages must be reclaimed and replaced with cloth.

Reconciling these debts is accomplished at the cost of giving up matrilineage and marital wealth and thereby limiting women's political power. Men, too, are limited politically, because death and women's needs for cloth continually usurp their own accumulations of wealth. Whereas cloth distributions provide the economic base for a degree of ranking that gives some men more authority and power over others, it ultimately checks the level of ranking and the scope of men's political engagement. Even for the few chiefs who are polygynous, each wife that a chief takes obligates him to provide her with cloth wealth each time someone in her lineage dies. A husband's wealth is leveled to build up the political presence of his wife and her brother.

In the contemporary Trobriand situation, the value of bundles and skirts is continually being inflated as younger men now have more access to cash and women's demands for larger quantities of skirts and bundles are an increasing drain on men's resources.[105] Some men, wanting to conserve their cash for other Western benefits, tell women that bundles have no practical use, making women rethink these traditions. But such challenges have unanticipated repercussions. Women insist that if they stop making bundles, the distributions will continue with skirts and trade-store cloth, thereby placing even greater financial hardships on men.

Keeping-While-Giving: Sisters and Inalienable Possessions

The exchanges that take place throughout a person's life dramatize social difference but when difference is institutionalized into rank, the stakes of how much is exchanged and what possessions can be kept increase. To reveal difference and rank induces images of finite monopolies over things and people, but behind these appearances, the realities of competition, loss, and death never disappear. For this reason, the privileging of one inalienable possession over another limits power as much as it creates it. The possibility of loss, what Beidelman

calls "the pathos in things," is so paramount to an inalienable possession's uniqueness that the more the possession grows in importance,
the greater is the threat of its loss. To participate in exchange is to be
conscious of this possibility. The relations between persons and things
negotiated in each exchange bring together the force of these paradoxical conditions where difference is most sought after at the very moment it emerges and is held back. To transcend these opposing forces
requires the will to destroy, usurp, command, and possibly die. Therefore, protecting one's social identity, searching for fame, and striving
for immortality are always enacted against the threats of loss, expenditure, violence, and death.

In the Polynesian societies I discussed, inalienable possessions are
the markers of the difference between one ranking person or group in
the face of the flux of exchange that repays debts and obligations to all
those outside the group. What creates the highest-ranking inalienable
possession is its sacred authentication through mana that is thought to
infuse the object itself. Here mana is not only reproduced in things via
women and human reproduction but this procreative force is transmitted to the activities associated with women's cloth production, making the cloth the carrier of political legitimacy. The Maori, Samoan, and
Hawaiian examples reveal that rather than the elimination of women
from participation in political affairs, gender is not subsumed by the
political; elite women as sisters achieve authority and power in their
own right and outrank many men.

Although the societies of the Trobriands, Samoa, and Hawaii each
exemplify alternatives to the problems of keeping-while-giving, each attempted solution reveals the strengths and limitations of the political
system. The labor-intensive process of making Trobriand skirts and
bundles indicates how much production is necessary just to discharge
indebtedness. Samoan fine mats are technically more elaborate; the
greater intensive labor increases the economic value of each fine mat.
With a kinship system of greater intricacy, Samoan fine mats are used
not only to discharge obligations but to signify the direction of political
contests in the continuous rivalry over titles. The ranking of fine mats
enables some to be kept out of circulation. To obtain this goal, huge
quantities that can be exchanged must be produced. In this way, replacements for the best possessions heighten the possibilities to attain
an impressive level of hierarchy. And in Hawaii, the most sacred cloth
in which the power of gods was directly present had an ultimate authority that, from the beginning, never circulated.

In each of these cases, what gives women a political presence is the cosmological authentication that they reproduce in things and people. Cosmological authentication not only is fundamental for creating possessions that are more than bits of flax threads or dried pandanus strings but such authentication is vital to kinship relations. Sibling marriage keeps the cosmological authentication of rank, mana, and gods intact. Where sibling marriage is prohibited, cultural approximations and substitutions give rise to the cultural reproduction of alliances and identities in siblings' children constituting strong sibling connections one or several generations removed. All these solutions are in response to a basic question with profound kinship and political implications: how to keep brothers and sisters reproductively active even with exogamous marriage. Marrying out is accomplished at a cost that involves much more than a pattern of reciprocal exchanges. Even when sibling sexual relations are safely embedded in the historical or mythical past, the beliefs and the political advantages of sibling intimacy continue to affirm that, contra Tylor, the choice is not simply between marrying out or being killed out. When reproducing rank is at stake, marrying out results in dying out unless sibling intimacy recreates rank through the reproductive processes of keeping-while-giving.

Yet sibling intimacy can also be the source of conflict and division, as the next chapter shows. The validation of rank through cosmological authentication is embedded in women's connections to and control over human and cultural reproduction. But reproduction as the locus of power for women also becomes the site of their subordination as women's control remains vulnerable to other powers and political ideologies. The potential for growth, production, and hierarchy is, at the same time, the source for decay, death, and domination. Women's control over cloth production is no exception. It is not easy to create heirlooms, to keep possessions inalienable and to authenticate hierarchical relationships while still creating enough replacements for other exchanges. The power to do so heightens one's political presence. For this reason the work of sisters in terms of what they produce and reproduce becomes the primary target for those who seek to redefine cosmological beliefs for their own economic and political aims. Western history is full of such examples, and so is that of Oceania.

From the perspective of changing world systems, it is not simply Western colonialism and capitalism that destroys traditional modes of production nor is it only Christianity that subverts these islanders' cosmological beliefs. Internal changes brought about by competing groups, such as chiefly rivals and the growing power of a priestly hierarchy, can change the technology or alter the meanings of inalienable possessions so that women's presence in political events is decreased and comes under the control of men. Not only do we see these changes occurring in eighteenth-century Hawaii but they have also been documented for the Andean region showing how the growing power of the Inka subverted the economic and political authority that local Andean women once held.[106] Throughout human history, reproduction in its biological and cultural manifestations has always been the site of great political intensity. In the United States, the current political controversies over abortion and new reproductive strategies raging on all levels of government are witness to the ancient and historical unrivaled potency and power that resides in women's strategic roles in reproduction.

CHAPTER 4

The Defeat of Hierarchy: Cosmological Authentication in Australia and New Guinea Bones and Stones

*She was weaving and sewing and mending because he
carried in himself no thread of connection . . . of continuity
or repair. . . . He wasted, and threw away, and could
not . . . contain, or keep his treasures. Like his ever torn
pockets, everything slipped through and was lost, as he lost
gifts, mementos—all the objects from the past. She sewed his
pockets that he might keep some of their days together. . .*

Anaïs Nin, *Ladders to Fire*

In 1963, Marshall Sahlin's essay, "Poor Man, Rich Man,
Big Man, Chief: Political Types in Melanesia and Polynesia," marked
out major cultural differences within Oceania by looking at the social
and economic implications of reciprocal exchange in Melanesian as opposed to Polynesian chiefly redistributive systems.[1] The underlying
assumptions about exchange that Sahlins first outlined in his seminal
article persist today. The high islands of Polynesia summon forth images associated with great male chiefs overseeing the redistributions of
their food and wealth accumulations; New Guinea's wide mountain
valleys reveal big men's reciprocal cycles of pig and pearl-shell exchange; the vast Australian desert evokes portrayals of esoteric cosmologies supported by men sharing their knowledge and scarce food
resources among close kin. In Australia, the anthropologist questions
how such complex ideologies arose among hunting–gathering peoples.

In Polynesia, the anthropologist asks, how did political hierarchy evolve? From the New Guinea side, William E. Mitchell's question How is hierarchy defeated? is much more insightful.[2] To begin with Dumont's observation that "equality and hierarchy must combine in some manner in any social system"[3] and then ask, as Mitchell does, why a hierarchy that minimally constitutes differences in age or gender fails to develop into more stable political forms in some places, bridges the analytical problems that make the labeling of societies as "egalitarian" or "big man" systems unsatisfactory.

To juxtapose Aboriginal societies with Polynesian chiefs and Melanesian big men is to recognize that the defeat of hierarchy is traceable to the various cultural constructions that are created in attempts to overcome the exchange and gender paradoxes of keeping-while-giving. The same efforts to keep sibling intimacy strong and to maintain inalienable possessions, in the face of all the demands to give, carry across islands and seas into other ecologies and cultures. In this chapter, I compare data from two Australian Aboriginal societies and two Papua New Guinea societies to show how other kinds of solutions to the paradox of keeping-while-giving shape whether political hierarchy is sustained or defeated. As with the Polynesian material, I am not proposing a set of traits or characteristics that can be imposed analytically to show a specific developmental sequence. My interest is to take ethnographic data from egalitarian and big-man societies, including examples of hunting–gathering societies, to reveal the cultural breadth of common problems in keeping-while-giving and show how local solutions establish difference of a sort while defeating the formal institutionalization of hierarchy. Like Polynesia, gender is at the core of these problems because the most elementary loci of power are located in the particular local forms of kinship relations that support yet challenge the strengths and weaknesses of sibling intimacy.

These processes involve the central themes of this chapter: first, to locate the source of authentication for inalienable possessions, given that in Australia and New Guinea mana is not perceived as a procreative force; second, to evaluate the limitations and potentials for keeping inalienable possessions out of exchange, given the necessity to exchange; and third, to see how these problems and their solutions politically impinge on and are affected by the relationships of siblings and spouses. These are the elements that reveal under what circumstances hierarchy is established or defeated. Although gender and kinship are central to the dilemmas of keeping-while-giving, inalienable possessions are the hub around which social identities are displayed, fabricated, exaggerated, modified, or diminished. What is most essential about the trajectories of inalienable possessions, however, is not their individual ownerships but the source of their authentication. The Polynesian cases reveal that shifting the ownership of an inalienable possession from one person to another does not reduce the possession's power as long as beliefs in its sacred authentication continue. In these situations, while the site of the most important source of authentication is located in the mana of gods and ancestors, this source, even though outside contemporary social life, remains ambiguous. Since mana can be lost or limited, great effort and attention are necessary to keep mana an active part of a person's or a group's social identity. Further, the most critical aspect that reveals the unambiguous nature of mana is that this force embodies the differences reflected in the ever-present hierarchical relations between people and their possessions.

Inalienable Possessions and Cosmological Authentication

I first compare two Aboriginal societies in the Australian Western Desert: the Pintupi, based on the recent research of Fred Myers, and the Aranda, studied by Spencer and Gillen in the 1890s and by T. J. Strehlow forty years ago.[4] I chose Australia as an important focus for comparison in part because, although these societies are rarely related analytically to Melanesian or Polynesian societies, I believe that important comparative insights are to be gained by bridging these traditionally defined culture areas that remain part of anthropology's nineteenth-century legacy. The source of Aboriginal social identities and social relations revolves around cosmologies that, although different in scope and cultural meanings from the Melanesian examples I selected, still are similar enough to make comparison important. Further, interest in Australian cosmologies has a long anthropological history taking us back to Durkheim's more general theoretical concern with totemic structures. Although totemism was never an adequate way to describe Australian cosmologies, as we will see, the central themes in the anthropological debates over totemism are not without interest here.

Given the significant local and regional linguistic and cultural differences among Australian Aboriginal societies, beliefs in the complex cosmologies called The Dreaming—composites of myths, sacred sites, ancestors, ceremonies, names, sacred possessions, and songs created by the totemic ancestors—play a central role in all Aboriginal social life.[5] As Fred Myers points out, The Dreaming must be treated phenomenologically as a given condition of the relationship between the cultural construction and practical logic of time, space, and personhood as well as the social circumstances in which the Aborigines defer to and recreate The Dreaming. This massive cosmology, as Myers explains, is a creative theory of existence in which everything in the Aborigines' world, such as persons, customs, and geographical features, originates.[6] It is a cosmology both beyond time yet simultaneously located in the social actions of Aboriginal daily affairs so that The Dreaming also objectifies and authenticates ongoing social relations.

As an ideology, The Dreaming is immaterial but in another sense, The Dreaming flourishes because it consists of material and verbal possessions—myths, names, songs, ceremonies, and sacred objects inherited from one generation to the next. In this way, The Dreaming itself encompasses vast inalienable possessions that are authenticated by the very cosmology under which they are produced. These possessions created in and authenticated by The Dreaming circulate from one person or group to another in a limited way. The possibilities of transmission in the face of the canon for guardianship establish for ritual leaders a domain of authority that in certain situations leads to a formalized position of rank.

For Durkheim, the domain of the sacred was apolitical. His reading of Baldwin Spencer's and F. J. Gillen's ethnographic accounts led him to conclude that the animated and rapt emotional actions of participants in The Dreaming ceremonies created the spontaneous awareness of communal social identity. For Mauss, too, Zuni rituals and Eskimo summer festivities produced a societal intensity through which names and emblems infused the living with the identities of their ancestors, thus creating a fusing of clan identities. Both Mauss and Durkheim failed to read into these accounts that the ritual authentications of social identities defined, promoted, and even exacerbated difference even as these events linked people together under the rubric of "one group."

What Durkheim's emphasis on the sacred most brilliantly reveals is the importance of locating the site of authentication in a domain outside the present. For Durkheim, however, this domain is unambivalent, the source of societal communion. Without a church or a god, the "primitive" sacred domain comes into being through the transformation of natural resources, such as animals and birds, into symbols of totemic representations; this transformation brings individuals into a state of shared solidarity. Totems, however, assert difference and, in the process, create and sustain ambivalence.

Lévi-Strauss and Roland Barthe also saw in totemic systems the "primitives'" attempt to naturalize their social world by locating the totem's authenticity in a source beyond that world. They, too, viewed totemism as verbal discourse, taking their analyses further than Durkheim by seeing the origins of totemism embedded in the structure of language. But totemic representations are verbal *and* material inalienable possessions whose exclusive properties are authenticated in particular cosmologies and thus they validate difference and hierarchy. Totemism, like all inalienable possessions, creates difference because these social identities, expressed not just in nature's terminology, but in verbal and material possessions, represent the unresolvable conflict between autonomy and relatedness.[7] Totems are not merely, in Lévi-Strauss's parlance, "good to think," they are good to keep.

When inalienable possessions lose the site of their authentication, then the power of difference is subverted. Only by destroying a possession's sacred authentication will it lose its formidable power. Benjamin pointed out that "to pry an object from its shell, to destroy its aura, is the mark of a perception whose 'sense of the universal equality of things' has increased to such a degree that it extracts it even from a unique object" by mechanically reproducing copies.[8] The copy then is detached from its place within tradition, emancipated from its dependence on the past. As long as the object's authentication is recognized and accepted by others, its presence generates competition and fear of loss. To hold a rival's inalienable possession, even if only on loan, allows an outsider to incorporate the power and prestige of additional vital social, cosmological, and political antecedents. To force a Northwest Coast Kwakiutl chief's famed cloak into the exchange arena enables the victor of the encounter to assume the chief's name, his ancestors, and his rank.[9] The huge resources given away in potlatches or Samoan title-taking are not a political end in themselves, but are the effort it takes to guard and, if successful, elevate the value of a kin group's inalienable possessions.[10] Success bestows upon the chief increasing power while it also provides increasing stability to the ranking of one kin group over another.

The concern about loss is more profound than the problems entailed with specific ownership. As long as the authentication of a possession exists, its movement through time and space from one owner, ruler, or group to another only transfers, rather than destroys, its power. But when merchants, administrators, missionaries, or new local cults or gods interfere with the cosmological locus of an inalienable possession's authentication, the absolute value of the possession declines, sometimes rapidly. In these circumstances, possessions are discarded, forgotten, sold as commodities, and in some cases, revived as symbols of ethnicity or revolution in later decades or generations.[11] Inalienable possessions attain what Susanne Langer considers the highest achievement in art: the representation of "permanence in change," because these possessions signal the potentialities for loss as much as they sanction immutability.[12] This makes the dilemma over the paradox of keeping-while-giving fraught with emotion and political vitality. It is a political achievement "to show who we are and where we come from"[13] creating a semblance of unity within a family, clan or dynasty that, in fact, is rife with rivalry. This is the power that inalienable possessions establish as in authenticating permanence in change, they verify the difference between one group and another.

To reveal how local solutions to the paradox of keeping-while-giving create difference that establishes or defeats hierarchy, I now examine the Pintupi and Aranda ethnographic data in greater detail and I then analyze two comparative Papua New Guinea societies. For one example of an "egalitarian" society I turn to Fitz Poole's ethnographic studies of the Bimin-Kuskusmin, an Ok speaking group in the Sandaun Province of Papua New Guinea.[14] Among this small group of about a thousand people, the locus of Bimin-Kuskusmin political authority is established through long-term cycles of initiation rituals organized through patriclan participation in which much of the ritual work involves creating inalienable possessions from human bones. Within these ritual activities, potentially this authority is transferred from one generation to the next. The fourth comparative case is a classic big-man society in the Western Highlands of Papua New Guinea where the Melpa peoples, like the Bimin-Kuskusmin, practice horticulture and pig husbandry. Here the similarity ends, and in the detailed ethnographic work of Andrew Strathern and Marilyn Strathern, we see that almost all Melpa production is committed to competitive exchange events organized by big men outside sacred domains, without inalienable possessions, thereby defeating the institutionalization of hierarchy.[15] Only in one men's ritual are stones viewed as inalienable possessions. The ritual is controlled by a leader whose authority, during this event, supersedes that of all big men.

Given the vital role of Polynesian women in cloth production and in transmitting cosmological authentication, what of women in these societies? Two major disparities separate these four cases from those I discussed in the last chapter. First, bones and stones, rather than cloth, are the most dramatic and politically visible inalienable possessions and second, the Polynesian prominence of sacred sisters and women rulers is absent; instead, the ethnographic literature emphasizes strong male domination and female–male sexual antagonisms. Yet, when explored with an interest in women's roles, the ethnography also reveals that sibling intimacy even when descent is reckoned patrilineally, both in its sexual symbolic representations and social and economic divisions, is politically consequential. Like the Polynesian examples, the presence of sibling intimacy in these four societies reveals how political authority and power for women and men arises and, at the same time, is restricted.

Therefore, despite extensive cultural dissimilarities, each of the four societies from Australia and New Guinea evinces common problems around the creation and guardianship of inalienable possessions. The cosmologies that authenticate these possessions, although widely different from one another in scale and cultural meaning, provide the locus and rationale for public displays of authority and power. Yet the processes of cosmological authentication are themselves a source of tension and anxiety because they involve a statement about hierarchy. Whose genealogical history is more renowned? Whose magic is stronger? Someone must attest to the authentication of a possession and to the history that surrounds it. And even when there are few inalienable possessions, someone must decide about their transmission within or, when necessary, outside the group. Those whose knowledge is honored by others enhance or diminish what an inalienable possession represents, creating what Judith Irvine calls "chains of authenticity" that, through time, are dependent upon a person's memory and the knowledge and/or possession that she or he originally inherited.[16] Taking a possession that so completely represents a group's social identity as well as an individual owner's identity and giving it to someone outside the group is a powerful transfer of one's own and one's group's very substance. This transfer is the most serious step in the constitution of hierarchy.

The Pintupi and the Aranda

INALIENABLE POSSESSIONS
AND AUTHORITY

Myers, in a penetrating account of The Dreaming's "practical logic" of space and time, takes seriously how authority, even though limited, is sustained momentarily among the Pintupi of the Western Desert. The laws, rituals, myths, and landscape that constitute The Dreaming deny "the creative significance of history and human action" and "the erosions of time."[17] Since The Dreaming was created by the first ancestors, all further experience *appears* continuous and permanent and outside the manipulations of contemporary people and events.[18] Yet although The Dreaming transcends time, it is also an extension of space, as people perceive themselves to be linked to each other through The Dreaming's resources. Myers points out that this gives enormous autonomy to The Dreaming, situating it in a privileged position vis-à-vis all other events and experiences, enabling some few men to draw on that authority for their own use in the control of others.

In The Dreaming, ancestral myths, each linked to unique features in the landscape and personal forbears, cannot be easily substituted for alternate myths or rocks and trees, so that The Dreaming authenticates itself by identification with the geographical immobility of the desert. If we recognize that both permanence and circulation encompass the political dimensions of inalienable things then, in another respect, the necessary transmission of The Dreaming's associated names, myths, designs, laws, and ceremonies means that the possessions that are an inherent part of The Dreaming enter into exchange. As Myers explains, Pintupi men exchange their names or the esoteric knowledge of sacred sites and ceremonies with each other. In this way, they establish ego-centered links with Pintupi who live in distant places, creating shared social identities drawing dispersed people together as members of "one country."[19] Pintupi elders "look after" other men by gradually divesting themselves of this sacred, secret knowledge and in these practices, they control the circulating parts of The Dreaming, as they alone decide who receives the knowledge and what parts they will teach.[20] Through their prior access to The Dreaming, elders garner and invoke authority over others created not only because The Dreaming is inalienable, but because they control the succession of its circulating, but still inalienable parts.[21]

Created through The Dreaming, a fragile degree of authority is sustained without extensive material resources. First, the transmissions of inalienable possessions take place within a ritual sphere of activity.[22] Ritual provides an important way of restricting exchange, by conserving the field in which inalienable possessions move between people, giving greater security to their transmission. Second, secrecy also promotes authority. As Simmel points out, holding secret knowledge "gives one a position of exception" that increases when its "exclusive possession is outside public scrutiny" and therefore, authentication becomes more restricted.[23] With the Pintupi, although the circumscription of transmission generates authority, this authority is limited to those who define themselves as members of "one country." Pintupi live in campsites dispersed over a huge desert landscape and through such transmission they establish a regional system of social linkages. Therefore, giving possessions to others ultimately keeps the possessions within the kin group.

The Aranda of Central Australia, however, provide an important counterpoint to the Pintupi political situation because the sphere of The Dreaming's ritual action allows for the inheritance of political authority. Based on similar beliefs and concerns with The Dreaming, the Aranda, at least until the 1950s, had leadership positions that were usually inherited from fathers to sons.[24] Strehlow emphasizes that Aranda leadership in comparison with the Pintupi was more than a kind of religious guardianship of rites, myths, and songs: such a "chief" had "very real secular authority."[25] Yet the basis for this hereditary authority grows out of one of the most essential circulating parts of The Dreaming for *all* Aborigines: the sacred tjurunga. Like the Pintupi and other Aboriginal groups, the stone and wooden tjurunga are thought to be "the changed immortal bodies of ancestors" who underwent this transfiguration when they finished their travels and, exhausted, turned to stone as they sank into the ground.[26] A child's father finds his infant's tjurunga left behind at the spot marking where the infant was conceived by its ancestor.[27] When initiated men are first shown their tjurunga, they are told, "This is your own body from which you have been reborn."[28] Although the ontology of conception is similar to the Trobriand case, here we see how biology and cosmology are fused not only

Fig. 1. *Despite Malinowski's dire predictions that colonial governance would destroy kula activities, men still build kula canoes, such as this one that was pulled up on a beach after a kula voyage in 1976. (Photograph by Annette B. Weiner)*

Fig. 2. *Although these two kula armshells on decorated ropes are too big to be worn, Boiyagwa Mosilagi displays them to show her father's kula fame. (Photograph by Annette B. Weiner)*

Fig. 3. *In this late nineteenth-century photograph from Franz Boas's collection, L!āKwē't, a "chieftainess" is wearing a prized cloak as she holds a highly valued copper that has been broken and restored. (Photograph courtesy of the Smithsonian Institution. Neg. 42 975-B. Photograph by C. O. Hastings)*

Fig. 4. *Huge piles of barkcloth and mats assembled for distribution at a wedding that took place in the Tongan capital, Nuku'alofa, in 1915. (Photograph courtesy of the Bernice P. Bishop Museum, Honolulu. Neg. CPBM 86416)*

Fig. 5. *This portrait of Ruruhira Ngakuira painted by Godfrey Lindauer in the 1870s shows off her feather cloak worn over a traditional kaitaka flax garment with its decorative taanako border. (Photograph courtesy of Wanganui Regional Museum Collection, Wanganui, New Zealand)*

Fig. 6. *This Maori woman, photographed in 1910, is weaving a korowai cloak similar to the one she is wearing of fine-quality flax trimmed with black-cord fibers, a style that persisted from the eighteenth into the early twentieth century. (Photograph courtesy of the Dept. of Library Services, American Museum of Natural History. Neg. 33121. Photograph by J. Kirschner)*

Fig. 7. *The high rank of these Maori women is evident by their tiwi feather cloaks trimmed with taanako borders, their jade hei-tiki pendants, the sacred club (pounamu), and their elaborate lip tattooing. (Photograph courtesy of the Dept. of Library Services, American Museum of Natural History. Neg. 32775. Photograph by Thomas Lunt)*

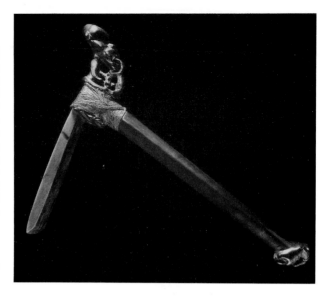

Fig. 8. *This sacred Toki Poutangata was once presented to a European who should have returned it prior to his death. Not understanding the honor and obligation bestowed upon him, he subsequently sold it as a curio. (Photograph courtesy of the National Museum of New Zealand, Wellington. Neg. B14272. W. O. Oldman collection. Photograph by Warwick Wilson)*

Fig. 9. *This lithograph made in 1838 shows an Ojibwa widow holding a bundle made from her dead spouse's clothes that she addresses as her husband until the mourning period is over. (Photograph from the Library of Congress. Gund Collection)*

Fig. 10. *Teyalaka Musumkunela views the yams, some decorated with lime, that shortly will be carried from the garden and presented to Chief Waibadi's wife. (Photograph by Annette B. Weiner, 1976)*

Fig. 11. *At Queen Kapiʻolani's funeral in 1899, some of her most famous feather cloaks adorned her casket and kahili feather standards lavishly decorated the aisle of Kawaihao Church. (Photograph courtesy of the Bernice P. Bishop Museum, Honolulu. Neg. CP 96201)*

Fig. 12. *In this engraving of the portrait of Princess Nahiʻenaʻena, she holds a sacred kahili staff and wears her own feather cloak, the insignia of high rank. (Photograph courtesy of Honolulu Academy of Arts)*

Fig. 13. *This kahili, collected during Captain Cook's voyage to Hawaii, is probably similar to the "fly-flap" carried by the elite women who visited Captain Clerke's ship. (Photograph courtesy of the National Museum, Wellington. Neg. 11135)*

Fig. 14. *Here a sacred sister directs the presentation of fine mats in Safoto Village, Savai'i Island, following the death of a young man in 1980. (Photograph by Annette B. Weiner)*

Fig. 15. *At this mortuary distribution of fine mats, women carry the highest-ranking ones to the house where the relatives of the dead person are assembled. (Photograph by Annette B. Weiner)*

Fig. 16. *Women from the small island of Manono still gather to work together on fine mats, each one taking up to a year to complete.* (*Photograph by Annette B. Weiner*)

Fig. 17. *Counting her newly made bundles, Boigipisi from Kwaibwaga Village readies this presentation for a forthcoming mortuary distribution where she will repay her deceased brother's spouse and father for their mourning. (Photograph by Annette B. Weiner)*

Fig. 18. *At a 1989 mortuary distribution of banana-leaf bundles held in Kwaibwaga Village, the deceased's oldest sister, Modubikina Tonuwabu, stands in the center as the big woman of the day and leads the bundle payments being made to those who have mourned. (Photograph by Annette B. Weiner)*

Fig. 19. *The photograph taken in 1984 shows an important Warlpiri woman, Judy Nampijinpa Granites, reenacting a sequence of the Emu Dreaming ceremony. (Photograph by Françoise Dussart)*

Fig. 20. *This is an example of a Pintupi hair-string wound on a spindle before it is used ceremonially. (Photograph by John Barrett)*

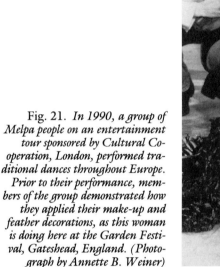

Fig. 21. *In 1990, a group of Melpa people on an entertainment tour sponsored by Cultural Co-operation, London, performed traditional dances throughout Europe. Prior to their performance, members of the group demonstrated how they applied their make-up and feather decorations, as this woman is doing here at the Garden Festival, Gateshead, England. (Photograph by Annette B. Weiner)*

Fig. 22. *This Mt. Hagen woman, photographed in 1936 shortly after European contact, is making a large net bag while sitting with another one draped on her head in the style women still use to carry their infants or their garden crops. (Photograph courtesy of the American Museum of Natural History. Neg. 285168. Photograph by M. H. Leahy)*

Fig. 23. *In 1980, the sisters of Tomuseu Toloyawa, who had died the year before, ended the major mourning period by presenting skirts to his spouse following the distribution of bundles in Kwaibwaga Village. (Photograph by Annette B. Weiner)*

Fig. 24. *In 1971, Chief Tokavataliya, a noted kula man from Sinaketa village, showed me two fine kula necklaces that he just received from his kula partner on his voyage to Dobu Island. (Photograph by Annette B. Weiner)*

to reproduce a child, but at the same time, to reproduce a possession that is believed to be the actual ancestral substance of the child.

Unlike the Maori taonga, the tjurunga needs neither the uniqueness of mana nor a group's cumulative history to be infused into it through production or ownership. Its discovery at a person's birth authenticates its uniqueness. As Myers points out, a person's identity is "not created but is already existing, already objectified through ancestral actions."[29] In this way, tjurunga are ranked according to the importance of each person's conception site but, through time, the age of a tjurunga adds to its power, establishing an overarching ranking whose authentication, even with the additional local history, still lies in The Dreaming, beyond contemporary claims.

To have a tjurunga at birth does not mean that ownership begins at birth. A man is not even shown his own tjurunga until he is at least twenty-five years old and has been initiated. Even then, the ancestral knowledge and myths associated with the tjurunga are not revealed for several decades more and only if the man is thought to be ritually responsible.[30] As with the Pintupi, Aranda elders guard the esoteric knowledge of the tjurunga myths and it is they who, in local affairs, control the processes of authentication and transmission. Unlike the Pintupi, however, the Aranda tjurunga possessions circulate as loans to other groups. Agreement to loan these ancestral objects outside the boundaries of a kin group acknowledges that the owning group has a large number of ranking tjurunga themselves to draw on. As with all vital inalienable possessions, even though these tjurunga are only on loan, the oldest and the most valued are never lent.[31]

Just as a Trobriand man gives his child use rights to his own ancestral name that will expand the social potential of the child linking him to the members of his matrilineage, the loans of tjurunga enable one group to enhance their own strength by drawing on the power of another group's ancestors.[32] Through the organization of these loans, individual men also enhance their authority and power. Although elders make many decisions about the circulation of tjurunga knowledge, according to Strehlow, only one man in each generation takes on the important role of deciding whether or not the tjurunga should be lent; he also makes decisions about the inheritance of the tjurunga within the kin group itself.[33] This leader benefits economically because, within his group, he is given meat from younger men before releasing any information about the tjurunga. Outside his group, he is given large quantities of other sacred objects made from opossum fur and especially highly valued human-hair strings from those to whom he lent the tjurunga (see fig. 20).[34]

Like the Pintupi, the transmission of secret knowledge makes the Aranda tjurunga highly political, but the Aranda loans of tjurunga make them an even greater political force. The Pintupi own tjurunga too, but instead of loaning them to others, these others become secondary members of the owning group when a Pintupi man teaches someone his tjurunga design who then fashions a new one for himself.[35] In this way, the Pintupi use inalienable possessions to create loci of ego-centered relationships among people scattered widely over the landscape, building up relationships in many sectors so that authority is diffused among many elders. But the original tjurunga remain carefully guarded and stored away so that copies rather than the originals are transmitted to others.[36] Only when Myers was ready to leave the field did his closest Pintupi colleague lead him to his isolated campsite where he kept the group's tjurunga—hidden from everyone. Turning to Myers, he told him that now he would show him who he really was. Even though his campsite was far away, isolated from other camps, it was his obligation to stay in this place, guarding the tjurunga. His knowledge would attract "millions, thousands of people" to him; they know him to be "the boss."[37]

Whether or not elite leadership roles traditionally existed in Aboriginal societies has long been a topic of debate. Strehlow has argued that Western intrusions into Aboriginal life diluted the power of these leaders whereas other anthropologists, such as Mervyn Meggitt and Ronald Berndt, present a strong picture of egalitarianism.[38] Recently, Erich Kolig, working in the Kimberly region, shows how vital are the prerogatives extended to elite leaders even today through their abilities to organize the transmission of sacred objects and designs from their own group to and from other groups.[39] Such exchanges have a long history in Aboriginal societies but, too often, they are either ignored or discussed as barter or trade.

In the comparisons between the Pintupi and the Aranda, we can see how different levels of authority evolve out of the control and transmission of inalienable possessions. In lending tjurunga to others outside the group, the Aranda formally expand their relationships through intergroup interests and alliances and in the process, one man is empowered with an authority that can be transmitted to his son. Through loans, inalienable possessions are kept while they circulate and a degree of hierarchy is instituted. In the Pintupi case, men of authority "look after" other men, "nurturing" them by giving them parts of The Dreaming and thereby creating nodes of ego-centered relationships where the source for autonomy and authority remains fixed in the protection of The Dreaming.[40] Although the boundedness of The Dreaming appears unbroken and, in a sense, nonarbitrary, the guardianship and transmission of inalienable possessions shows the ambivalence generated by The Dreaming in the emergence of political authority, minimally with the Pintupi, but in an incipient way, through right of birth with the Aranda.

In these Australian examples, unlike those from Polynesia, the ritual affairs of The Dreaming appear to be strictly men's concerns. Strehlow, however, reports that women, too, receive tjurunga when they are born; some even own exceptionally high-ranking ones. But he claims that even though a woman because of her conception site "may be entitled to a position of supreme authority in her own community" all tjurunga esoteric knowledge is hidden from her,[41] enabling Aboriginal men to dominate women's ritual life. Yet in a footnote, Strehlow comments that many of the most important stories and chant verses associated with tjurunga are the exclusive property of women.[42] Each tjurunga is wrapped with human-hair strings and when these are untied, the verses are chanted bringing the consecrating force of The Dreaming into the tjurunga. Although we know that this knowledge is the preserve of male leaders, enabling them to build economic support and wide reputations, Strehlow gives no other explanatory information about women's political authority or their ritual roles. The comparative question is whether or not the constitution of authority around inalienable possessions involves women, especially in their role as sisters.

COSMOLOGICAL AUTHENTICATION
AND SIBLING INTIMACY

A major problem in understanding how Aboriginal women enter into these affairs is that their rituals, as well as most other areas of social life, including living sites, are so sharply sex-segregated that it is difficult if not impossible for men to study women's rituals or for women to study men's. This research problem is further complicated by the neglect of women's ritual life by many early ethnographers and the long-term effects of Western values on women's roles. Only recently has there been a small but growing body of evidence that sub-stantively shows domains of women's ritual interdependence.[43] Diane Bell describes the ceremonies that women in the Central Desert per-form and demonstrates that women have direct access to knowledge of ancestral totemic myths and the ancestral designs for sacred tjurunga.[44] Bell further argues that prior to the Australian imposition of sedentary living among Aboriginal groups, women in this area were active leaders organizing separate and independent women's rituals that reinforced mutual values among women and men and gave women their own positions of authority and power. With the expansion of pastoral lands at the turn of the century, these economic and ritual roles were usurped as missionaries and administrators defined women as wives and mothers in a pattern consistent with Western traditions, relegating women to a domestic domain that depreciated women's cultural roles in reproduc-tion and elevated men's political roles in relation to Australian affairs.[45]

Bell, following Eleanor Leacock, firmly places the problems of gen-der around the historical circumstances that she posits undermined women's independence, especially in relation to the control over their own sexuality and their autonomous ceremonial life.[46] This view con-trasts with most male ethnographers who emphasize men's appropri-ation of women's sexuality in ceremonial events through actions, such as wife-lending, ceremonial sexual intercourse, and the exclusion of women from the most important men's rituals. Bell responds by argu-ing that men's and women's rituals are similar in context and content and that women's rituals confer power upon women through a focus on reproduction and women's sexuality, which traditionally gave them control over marriage and residence.[47]

Controversy has also been generated in Aboriginal studies over the question of who controls marriage bestowal and what effects polygyny has on women's roles, making the problems of equality and domination difficult to sort out.[48] Francesca Merlan points out, however, that sub-suming all the intricacies of power relations under the one rubric of male domination masks the particular domains in which women gain their own autonomy.[49] But a major problem is that the controversies over marriage practices and control over women's sexuality are de-scribed from the perspective of a traditional descent model—women as wives and men as husbands—but rarely from the way the intimacy be-tween sisters and brothers might be a major organizing principle in Aboriginal social life. Myers points out that while Pintupi women exer-cise power in autonomous ways, this power is not identical to men's power. He notes that women's ceremonies are concentrated around issues of "social dissonance, largely those within the residential group" whereas men's ceremonies, particularly those around male initiation, involve wider regional links through which men establish a sense of relatedness among widely dispersed Pintupi groups.[50] Myers, one of the few ethnographers who depart from the traditional descent model of women as wives and men as husbands, shows that sister and brother relationships in one generation join the children of sisters with the children of brothers as siblings rather than cousins in the next generation. In this way, the most important kinship relations—brothers and sisters—reproduce themselves in the next generation. Further, during a man's initiation ceremonies, his sister's dancing and other organizational work indebt him to her for the rest of his life.[51] These observations raise the question whether women as sisters in their own ritual practices are generating an aspect of social identity that strengthens the internal generational links between brother–sister sibling sets while men also work to develop regional relationships, all of which must be reproduced for each generation.

This question also calls attention to how little emphasis has been given to the way possessions, rather than women, circulate and who controls their circulation. Merlan documents how at birth, and at other times, a person may receive names that incorporate elements of another person's social identity.[52] The circulation of names validates connections to sacred sites and thereby broadens people's totemic-territorial associations. As previously shown for tjurunga, these names become heavily politicized because they give a person rights to social relationships, ceremonies, and territories that extend far beyond what a person had at birth. What is not clear from this example is how gender is organized through these exchanges.

Recently, however, Françoise Dussart gives extensive details of how contemporary Warlpiri women are socialized into gaining ceremonial knowledge and how they transmit this knowledge to other women. As with men, instructing others gives women the opportunity to gain economic resources and in the process, some women, as the one in figure 19, become well-known ritual experts who have economic independence in their own right. Dussart notes that in major ceremonies women have special sacred objects, called *makarra,* made from rope tied with thick cotton thread. The term *makarra* is also the word for "afterbirth," "womb," and "umbilicus" and its symbolic presence in ceremonies relates directly to ancestral events concerned with birth and rebirth.[53] The word *makarra* also refers to hair strings, shown in figure 20, a sacred ritual object that also signifies the above reproductive symbols. Among the Warlpiri, these hair strings are sometimes made by men but most often are produced by women from their own hair when someone dies. According to Barbara Glowczewski, these hair strings are exchanged from women to men and then among men for important uses in men's ceremonies, especially in initiation.[54] Women also participate in key exchanges of hair strings with their brothers through which ownership of a clan's sacred lands are validated.[55] Glowczewski argues that in Warlpiri myths, women's sexuality entices nonrelated men into the group where women remake them into Warlpiri men—an interesting mythic reversal of the incest taboo where women sexually create their own brothers.[56] But even more important, following the circulation of hair strings through kinship relations, the essential significance of this relationship is exposed and "affirms a certain dependence of men on women."[57] Today, cloth (usually store-bought blankets) is exchanged along with hair strings and often cloth alone is used for payments, for example to healers, where formerly hair strings were the medium of exchange.[58]

Hair strings are exchanged throughout the Central and Western Desert.[59] According to Myers, Pintupi men tighten their hair-string belts (also called girdles in the ethnographic literature) because they say this is the way they focus their power during special stages of rituals, and a boy's initiation cannot take place without these sacred, powerful objects. At times, the belt itself stands for the initiate as it may be sent for a ceremony to another group in place of the boy. Here hair strings are made by both women and men but following an initiation, women are allowed to take the boy's hair strings and keep them.[60]

With the Aranda, hair strings make up the major payments when the tjurunga on loan are returned. Most important, every Aranda tjurunga is wrapped with hair strings covered in red ochre and only as the hair strings are unwound can the verses of the ancestral names be chanted; at that moment the tjurunga are thought to obtain their magical force.[61] Like Polynesian cloth imbued with mana, they transmit a powerful force.[62] Since, according to Strehlow, Aranda women own rights to these chants like the Warlpiri, they also may be responsible for the hair strings themselves, further strengthening Aranda hierarchy.

Despite the lack of more complete information, these recent data on women's controlling interests in the circulation of hair strings, rope, threads, and cloth show how essential such possessions are to men as well as women and how these possessions constitute social identities as well as rights to territorial associations. Clearly, Aboriginal women had (and in some cases, still have) access to sacred objects that, infused with potency, have significant exchange value. Whether or not some of these possessions take on absolute value and become inalienable cannot be discerned from the available data. The close association of these objects with tjurunga indicates that women's presence in ritual life is connected to their control over some aspects of cosmological authentication and that women's roles as sisters may give them a domain of autonomy and authority even when their roles as wives are more problematic.

In the 1930s, Phyllis Kaberry noted that a woman's husband was under constant economic pressure to provide his wife's brothers with food and that the wife was not obligated in the same way.[63] The frequently reported cases of men's domination over their wives may result from the tensions created by the asymmetry between roles as siblings and roles as spouses. Although the Australian data strongly support these theoretical premises, the next example I draw on builds the case more completely.

The Bimin-Kuskusmin

INALIENABLE POSSESSIONS AND AUTHORITY

Among the Bimin-Kuskusmin, ritual events are also pervasive, demanding work and resources throughout a person's life, and within this ritual domain authority arises. Whereas tjurunga appear as the embodiment of a person's social and cosmological identity already created at conception, the ultimate result of Bimin-Kuskusmin rituals is the work of making human bones into inalienable possessions that over a lifetime become the embodiment of ancestors. These rituals involve long-term cycles of men's initiation, fertility rituals, and, traditionally, women's initiation rituals that, like the men's, last for twenty years or longer.[64]

The Bimin-Kuskusmin believe that male substances transmitted through human reproduction produce their children's bones but female substances, although representing fertility, decay within one generation.[65] To begin the long process of making bones into ancestral substance, men's initiation rituals involve the transmission of an ancestral spirit (*finik*) to initiates "through strictly patrilineal transmissions of semen."[66] However, children, including girls, obtain this finik spirit through fertility rituals in which a child's father's sister performs curing rituals that remove "antithetical female substances."[67] A man's sister takes his child from its mother as soon as it is weaned to perform these rituals and, to the child, she becomes "the most symbolically important female figure." So stunning is this detachment that the child's mother utters a violent curse at the moment that she loses her son or daughter to the ritual protection of her husband's sister.[68]

The authoritative presence of women as sisters also enters directly into men's initiation rituals where women are ritual leaders and assume political authority over men.[69] According to Poole, the most powerful sister is widowed, menopausal, and, although no longer marriageable, she must have had many children.[70] Like the male ritual leaders, she has the ability to incorporate both male and female substances within herself and embodies powers that differ dramatically from those held by ordinary women and men. She controls all rituals associated with childbirth, the male and female initiation, and other curing and divining activities.[71] Poole argues that these women attain equal authority with male leaders only because they are past childbearing age and are "androgynous," a kind of male-woman.[72]

Ultimately the political significance of women as sisters is generationally authenticated through bones. At death, only the bones of initiated men and those of their married sisters who have had at least one child are placed in sacred clan ossuaries,[73] later to be taken into the cult house to become part of the more formal ritual paraphernalia.[74] But when a female ritual leader dies, her skull is placed in the cult house with the skulls of other male ritual leaders. According to Poole, the Bimin-Kuskusmin believe that the skulls of these women represent a uterine line, created by sisters.[75] Thus, for men, agnatic identity is joined ritually with a uterine line of sisters who are the ancestral leaders in men's rituals.[76] Sibling intimacy, not only between brothers and sisters but between brothers, is essential for the ritual development of women and men in a patrilineage and, ultimately, to authenticate sibling bones that embody the shared sibling intimacy of a patrilineage. Women as wives and men as husbands together produce the beginning of a human being. But wives' contributions to human reproduction wane within a lifetime, whereas their ritual activities as sisters insure that bones become inalienable possessions for future generations.

COSMOLOGICAL AUTHENTICATION
AND SIBLING INTIMACY

Men's initiation rituals in which the cultural reproduction and guardianship of inalienable bones take place call attention to the multiple reproductive contexts in which sexual antagonisms are grounded. The sacred power of women among the members of their own patrilineage is perceived conversely as polluting powers among their affines. Unlike the Trobriand case, where the work and resources of affines are essential to political status and power, the polluting power of wives makes it dangerous to incorporate their work and resources.[77] As a wife, a woman has her own domain of power through association with birth, death, menstruation, and witchcraft that makes her perceived as a potentially highly polluting person, especially to her husband and his kin.[78] That these powers are sacred and dangerous, and that they are active and may even change in intensity throughout a woman's life, means that women occupy a position of being feared and dominated as wives, while being revered and dominant as sisters. A wife's curse at the loss of her child to the ritual protection of her husband's sister is an especially powerful reminder of where antagonism lies.

Although a woman changes her residence at marriage to live with her husband, "neither marriage nor motherhood alters the identity of a woman as an agnate of her natal group."[79] When a woman marries, she still remains ritually under the protection of her brothers.[80] When she is injured, or at her death, compensation must be given by her husband to the women and men who are members of her patrilineage. For any kind of pollution that occurs in the gardens where a married woman works, she directly compensates her husband's sisters, for these women "own" the gardens and make them fertile with the positive power of female substances.[81] Since these payments are considered significant, a sister's role economically in relation to the circulation of such wealth is important.[82]

Within men's initiation rituals, the cultural reproductive dominance of women as sisters is powerfully present. Even though Poole argues that the older female ritual leader gains her power because she is androgynous, he does not account for the fact that other younger women are also necessary participants in these men's rituals. In fact, among neighboring Ok groups, such as the Baktaman, Telefolmin, and Faiwol, younger women similarly play an active part in men's initiation.[83] First, a man's sister is chosen to participate in these rituals before the start of her menses. Second, a woman who is married and preferably has given birth also will return to her brothers' place to take part and these younger women will eventually replace their older sister as the most powerful leader.[84] Therefore, within a seemingly total male ritual domain, a full range of sisters' biological and cultural reproductive powers are necessary and provide for the reproduction of these relationships in the next generation.[85]

Women give birth but the substances they transmit to their children are those that wane rapidly. Women nurture their own infants but it is their husbands' sisters who, through extensive rituals, culturally reproduce in these children the essential elements of fertility for their own and their brother's lineage. The highest-ranking female ritual leader, containing and controlling all symbolic forms of male and female reproductive elements, is nevertheless no longer physically reproductive. The polluting danger in the exogamy of heterosexual relations between husband and wife can only be offset by a sister's ritual obligations in her brothers' ritual affairs as well as in her "brothers'" sexual relations. Authority and power for a few women and a few men as ritual leaders develop out of this ritual complex and are authenticated by the inalienable possessions produced through the ritual work of sacralizing bones.

Each of these features are covariants, mutually dependent but also undermining a broader development of hierarchy. On one side, the essential dependence on sisters enables the Bimin-Kuskusmin to maintain sacred bones as an inalienable possession, and in turn, these bones authenticate authority for those few women and men who, through cosmological knowledge and control, hold dominant positions over others. The sexual and material resources of the highest values are kept within the patriclan in the ritual domain in order to produce inalienable possessions that symbolize the success of patrilineal cosmological authentication. In order to concentrate these efforts, the boundedness of the ritual domain keeps resources and relationships focused internally on the cultural reproduction of the lineage and clan, thereby limiting authority and power in other political domains. To filter out the negative but necessary reproductive elements brought into the group by spouses demands intense ritual energy and work that keeps both male and female siblings' fertility within the clan. Success in these efforts results in culturally reproducing the patriclan through generations by keeping sisters socially and politically connected to their natal kin group. Simon Harrison describes the ritual life of the Avatip community in Papua New Guinea in a similar way when he writes that the clans maximize their "reproductive security: the clans have closed in upon themselves so as to reproduce and ritually 'nurture' one another."[86] The Avatip also keep their ritual resources, such as myths, names and the knowledge and symbols for fertility within the clan so that they do not become wealth to be used in exchange with outsiders.[87]

Like the Australian cases, the nature of Bimin-Kuskusmin inalienable possessions arises out of a complex cosmology. But the scope of Australian inalienable possessions that includes not only tjurunga but ceremonies, songs, ancestral designs, and mythic knowledge allows much broader transmission to many other individuals. This correlates with more complex kinship organization than we find among the Bimin-Kuskusmin and, in the Aranda case, allows for the development of a hierarchy that integrates a clan's internal political actions as well as external political events. Even in the Pintupi case, the ability to authenticate sacred knowledge, guard its secrets, and transmit it to others creates the locus for authority and control that Aboriginal elders exert over others outside of ritual activities. In the Bimin-Kuskusmin situation, the cultural reproductive efforts are so encapsulated by clan rituals that external affairs, such as political alliances and even marriages, are the source of danger and pollution, thereby necessitating the long years of ritual work by siblings to filter out these dangerous elements. The ritual use of bones also mirrors this internal confinement as, unlike Australian tjurunga, personal names, and hair strings, these bones do not become the kind of exchange medium that draws others into the group or defines differences between one group and another.[88] As I discussed in chapter 2, human bones are a limited exchange media when compared with cloth. They cannot be produced or replicated to provide replacements for exchange. Loss remains a critical problem. As Fredrik Barth insightfully states for the Baktaman, western neighbors of the Bimin-Kuskusmin, less commitment to ritual affairs by leaders sometimes results in the loss of highly valued human bones. This loss has the capacity to interfere not only with authority and a person's own leadership but with the ritual itself, as without the appropriate bone parts the ritual cannot be performed.[89] Among the Bimin-Kuskusmin, the commitment to the regeneration of clan social identities through intergenerational sibling sets is vital, creating a limited degree of hierarchy within ritual life. Although the constitution of authority within ritual actions provides a counter to the gender discontinuities between roles of spouses and siblings that, unlike those of the Trobrianders, are not bridged by complementary exchanges, these solutions undermine, and thereby restrict, the constitution of authority and power in domains external to the kin group. The Melpa example provides an opposite solution—reliance on extensive exchange media that are turned to political encounters much more frequently than to authenticating the reproduction of the kin group.

The Melpa

INALIENABLE POSSESSIONS AND AUTHORITY

Among the Melpa a big man competes to gain ascendency over the leaders of other clans by holding huge exchanges, *moka,* in which the winner gives away more than the others.[90] To compete, big men build up a productive support system from kin and affines, as well as lower-status men, but still these exchanges never provide big men with the means for direct political coercion nor do they establish ranking.[91] The control over possessions through which authority arises is ego-centered and the possessions themselves have no ancestral identity or cosmological authentication. Although their loss diminishes the political status of a leader, it does not destroy the ancestral authentication of the leader's clan or lineage in the way that the loss of a tjurunga or a Maori taonga does.

Without the presence of inalienable possessions, Melpa exchange is geared toward giving rather than keeping. But the history of moka exchange suggests this was not always the case and reveals similar problems in creating inalienable possessions that we have encountered in other Pacific cases. In the last century, pigs were the most important exchange objects in moka, and economically, women figured centrally in these events because they were, and still are, the producers of pigs.[92] A variety of shells, stone adze blades, and mats were also prominent in moka, but there is little specific information on the production and ownership of these items. Around the beginning of this century, pearl shells were traded in from the Papuan coast and when the shells reached the Hagen area via long and hazardous trade routes, they were already polished and refined.[93] Because the source of these finished shells was unknown, the Melpa thought of them "as wild things (*mel romi*) which men in a sense hunted by their magic" and only big men were thought to have the necessary magic that would enable them to obtain these shells.[94] This magical knowledge gave men who could control the shells' circulation greater power, as it also freed them from complete dependence on pigs and women.[95] Since durable pearl shells provided easier avenues for financial arrangements than did pigs, which had to be farmed out for raising and feeding, Melpa big men devalued the use of pigs in moka by making pearl shells the standard of value.[96]

Although these pearl shells were individually owned, they gradually began to be enhanced in ways that made them subjectively unique, taking on some of the attributes associated with inalienable possessions. First, each shell received a name and was wrapped with a knotted rope tally, woven by women, indicating the number of times it had changed hands.[97] A man's fame now could circulate widely because his possession of the shell gave it value and ranked the shell in relation to other shells.[98] The association of a shell with a particular history based on the names of men who owned the shell is a prominent criterion of kula shells, as I discuss in the next chapter. According to Andrew Strathern, at this time Melpa shells were also historicized in this way.[99] Although details of the shells' wrappings and how the tally weaving was organized among women are absent from the early literature, these were attempts to create ranking in the most famed shells.[100]

Second, a major criteria for a shell's initial value was its luster because brightness was associated with those magical powers that would attract other shells. As Andrew Strathern and Marilyn Strathern note:

In the past, when shells were scarcer, especially bright pearl shells were withdrawn from circulation and kept privately inside the owner's men's house. It was thought that their gleam would attract other pearl shells to them and the owner consequently [would] be successful in moka.[101]

This example illustrates how much people themselves perceive the advantages to be gained by keeping something valuable in the face of all the pressures to give it to someone else. As in the case of the most valued fine mats or taonga, holding fast to a possession attracts other allies and rivals because the ability to keep such possessions exemplified one's political expertise and power.

With these magical attributes and personal histories affixed to shells, moka exchange might have begun to institutionalize rank, but these magical properties and fame remained connected to individuals rather than to a cosmological domain of ancestors or gods. Although shells were becoming unique, historical possessions, other external events abruptly changed the situation when the first gold prospectors, the two Leahy brothers and J. L. Taylor, entered the region in 1933 and hired Melpa men to work for them or to sell them food, paying them in pearl shells. Five hundred pearl shells were flown in monthly by the Leahys[102] and in order to maximize their own profits, the Leahys continually inflated their value.[103] For the first time, any man willing to work or sell food had access to shells and men now found it more beneficial to sell food for shells than to raise food to feed pigs for future moka exchanges.[104]

The earlier control that big men had over pearl shells was disrupted as Melpa men competed in this European market to become wealthy.[105] Quickly, the pearl shells lost their historical markings as the tallies that signified the shell's circulation were abandoned and men simply attached rough handles of cloth or sacking.[106] Big men took up the ways of the colonialists and began to exploit less-advantaged men, gaining back through this labor their earlier positions as financiers.[107] What big men were discovering at their own peril was the freedom to be had when shells lost their absolute value and circulated widely in exchange. No longer were they dependent on the attainment of particular shells that had magical powers or were previously owned by particular men. No longer was there an urgent need to keep shells out of circulation to attract other important shells. It is not surprising that later the Melpa were quick to appreciate the sweeping power of money with its abstract economic value and as soon as they had the opportunity to obtain money, they used it in moka to replace shells.[108]

The history of pearl shells reveals how hierarchy can be defeated. Even when the best shells were wrapped with tallies and relatively rare, giving them absolute value, a shell ranked an individual's abilities and not the ancestral identity of a kin group. In time, the woven tallies that women made might have added ancestral authentication to each shell, but pacification halted any developing claims to clan differentiation and the establishment of hereditary chiefs.[109] Since the first pearl shells reached the Melpa area sometime around the turn of the century, the big men's monopoly in them could not have been much longer than one generation before the Leahy brothers altered the dimensions of exchange. This span of time probably is too brief for the development of the kinds of possessions that represent clan identity. The suddenness with which shells lost their individuality through colonial inflation could not have occurred if specific shells embodied clan and ancestral identities and therefore ranked both individual owners and their kin groups, like the ranking of taonga, tjurunga, or fine mats. What Melpa shells lack is this shared identity that is authenticated through cosmological connections, such as ancestors, mana, or The Dreaming. Yet a cosmological domain exists in Melpa social life that involves sibling intimacy—except in this ritual, women's roles are enacted by men symbolizing a deeply seated disjuncture in gender relations that interferes with the formalization of hierarchy.

COSMOLOGICAL AUTHENTICATION
AND SIBLING INTIMACY

Even with male dominance over women, Melpa men still literally dream about and ritually act out the advantages of sibling intimacy. Men tell a myth that accompanies their performance in the Female Spirit cult (*Amb Kor*) in which the spirit is thought to be a virgin because her vagina has never been cut open.[110] Yet as a young, beautiful woman, she appears before men in their dreams and promises to marry them and bring them fertility for gardens, pigs, and many children.

Although Andrew Strathern does not elaborate, he notes that the spirit "embodies the idea of sister as well as wife, the one to be given away as well as the one who comes to be married; she is a composite in this sense, and can stand for the overall flow of exchange."[111] In analyzing exchange from the perspective of inalienable possessions rather than a norm of reciprocity, we can see that the female spirit symbolizes the critical problem of keeping the intimacy of siblings when siblings must be married to outsiders.

Men find the reality of the Female Spirit's presence verified in special stones in the ground that are believed to be the embodiments of her powers of fertility.[112] The ritual drama of the cult focuses on these stones, which are celebrated and then secretly buried to bring continued fertility long after the ritual activities cease. Women are excluded from the major events and men enact the paired roles of husband and wife. Yet in the rituals a series of reversals occur.[113] First, the Female Spirit, jealous of the men's real wives, brings men the power of fertility but without physical sexuality. The reason her vagina is closed is because, as sister, she symbolically frees men from the incest taboo. Second, in Melpa ideology, sexual relations with women are polluting, thus the spirit woman dispels the fear of pollution. Third, the husband–wife roles are never paired in real life with the cooperative equality that is demonstrated in this cult. Fourth, although the moieties represented as men and women appear to be divided, the actors are dressed alike, combining in each person both female and male characteristics. Fifth, the spirit is polyandrous and dominant over men, whereas in social life, it is big men who are polygynous and men who dominate wives. Finally, in these affairs the ritual expert has absolute authority over the men, a role unprecedented in secular life even for big men.

For the Melpa, sibling intimacy is the dream of the best of all possible worlds: unlimited fertility without the need for exchange or polluting sexual relations. Since the spirit has no genitals, she is as safe as men can get with a woman. It seems no accident that during these events, the authority of a Melpa ritual expert far supersedes the power of any secular big man. The spirit woman is represented in stone and these are the inalienable possessions that, like early European Venus stones, remain buried in the ground following the ritual in which cosmological authentication is assured. Authority over the guardianship of these possessions is the ultimate Melpa authority.

The dependency that men have on sisters is not only expressed in buried stones. It forms the basis for male–female relationships and, like the Bimin-Kuskusmin, sharply divides the role of sister from that of wife. Since affines become so important both in assisting a man with his own moka exchanges and demanding his valuables to help them with non-moka events, to keep a woman as both wife and sister circumvents the problems that are basic to the inequalities in kin and political relations. This is the underlying theme of the Female Spirit cult. Because the issue of Melpa male dominance has been a subject of debate in gender studies since the 1970s, it is important to explore more fully the social and economic intimacies between sisters and brothers.

ANOTHER VIEW OF SIBLING INTIMACY

Marilyn Strathern has questioned many times why Melpa women accept their roles in raising pigs when their productive work is devalued by men, even though men themselves are dependent on these pigs for moka. She argues that the answer lies only in the husband–wife relationship: "It is the husband–wife relationship, and not other male–female pairing, that provides a particular combination of mutuality and separateness, in terms of the division of labor, for it is only over the labor of their own wives that men have a controlling voice."[114] Yet the social, economic, and even the more covert sexual intimacies that surround sibling relationships are crucial issues. Melpa women as wives accept their situation wherein they are denied transactional power by their husbands precisely because through their role as wives they have the power to negotiate economic benefits for their clan brothers, which eventually benefit women's own children. As wives, women present men with problems because they try to direct their husbands' resources to their own brothers in order, subsequently, to benefit their own children.

The title of Marilyn Strathern's book, *Women in Between*,[115] conveys a sense of the separation between Melpa women as the producers of pigs and garden foods and their husbands as the transactors of pigs and money in moka exchanges.[116] But the roles of women *between* their husbands and brothers are not given the same prominence. Unfortunately, we know little about women's productive roles in the last century when pigs were most important in moka exchanges nor do we know much about how women became more exploited by men when pearl shells displaced the prominence of pigs.[117] In contemporary times, however, women dance at the moka feast with elaborate decorations (see fig. 21), celebrating their own success in raising the pigs; they also beat the drums saying "it is they who enabled the moka to take place."[118] Still, in this century, it is men who negotiate, plan, and amass political power through their moka transactions.[119]

When we reexamine Melpa kinship from the perspective of sibling intimacy, we see where the problems of women's subordination lies. We also understand more substantively how Melpa kinship is organized. For two decades beginning in the 1960s, many debates took place over the "loosely structured" highlands' descent systems and specifically over whether the Melpa could be considered patrilineal when Andrew Strathern reported so many genealogical connections traced through women.[120] Georg Vicedom, a missionary who spent five years in the 1930s among the Melpa, points out that sisters provide important economic connections into patriclans other than those into which they marry. Because a woman has close affective ties with her sisters, even acting as a surrogate mother to their children, she has economic ties with members of the clans into which they have married. This strengthens a woman's tie to her brother because she herself can negotiate economic arrangements that help her brother in moka exchange.[121] In this way sibling social and economic intimacy is strongly united above the diversity of affinal and lineage affiliations. Further,

Andrew Strathern also emphasizes that Hagenders are classified into lineages that mark their "man-bearing" or "woman-bearing" identities through the brother–sister relationship.[122] Although Melpa reckon descent through men, a woman's child can become a member of her own patrilineage so that the Melpa "speak of interpersonal kin ties through women as 'blood' ties."[123]

These blood ties are not affirmed automatically. They occur only through the exchange efforts between women and their brothers. In the importance of this sibling relationship, we find the answer to Marilyn Strathern's question about why Melpa women accept their secondary role. The conflicts between affinal obligations and moka exchange are perennial and women as the producers of pigs, once the major element of moka exchange, are at the center of these stresses. But that is only a partial view. Although the role of Melpa women as wives is often onerous, their role as sisters gives them more equity in their economic relations with their brothers.

In her most recent work, Marilyn Strathern still considers the central issues of kinship and gender from the perspective of reciprocal marriage as a form of unmediated exchange by which one marriage metaphorically substitutes for another through time and space. She claims that bridewealth is "compensation" for the "detachment of the woman" and so the circulation of bridewealth merely cancels each marriage in succession, compensating for one "detached" woman after another. In her analysis, the role of women as sisters is essential only for their "transformations into wives."[124] In Marilyn Strathern's view, a fundamental separation exists between a woman as a member of her natal clan and her subsequent movement to a group of affines. Women appear of concern to the welfare of their natal clan only at the time of marriage ("detachment" and "transformation"). Their future role as sisters potentially benefiting their clan brothers and their own children through the provisioning and channeling of wealth are downplayed as critical features of the marriage process.[125]

Yet, when a Melpa woman marries, "she goes to 'help' her husband's group . . ." and her husband must continually repay her own group, remaining in their debt until he has finished all bridewealth payments, which takes many years.[126] Although a woman's husband has the advantage of establishing a moka partnership with her brother, he has other payments to her group at their child's first haircutting and at weaning for the breast milk a woman gave to her child.[127] These payments continue for a much longer time so, for example, if a woman has grown sons, larger payments are made to her natal kin which become part of protracted moka exchanges.[128] If a man refuses these affinal obligations his wife will leave him or her brother will stop moka transactions with him.[129] Although to some extent these internal exchanges may become part of moka transactions, they essentially support a woman's patrilineal kin providing wealth needed for other bridewealth payments, payments to sons' wives and their children, and for compensation and other kin obligations. They also secure a fundamental kin connection for a woman's child that strengthens sibling intimacy. Bridewealth alone cannot secure children's affiliations or their future exchange potentials with their maternal kin. This is the reason that so much pressure is put on a woman's husband's payments to her brother at each major stage of her child's life.[130] Big men have even larger debts to their affines in the name of their children. With several wives, these affinal obligations set limits on the range of their own economic and political power. Yet a big man's sister is his important supporter as she assures that her husband undertakes the long-term social and economic obligations that benefit her brother and also link her children to her natal kin into the next generation.

At marriage, a woman goes to her husband's group with many net bags, the largest of which symbolizes the "womb" and "fertility." In the 1970s, I noted that in many social contexts, objects, including Melpa net bags similar to those in figure 22, are exchanged by women and are imbued with social and economic significance that gives women some kind of power, although not necessarily political power. I argued even then that we must include "the cosmic order as an integral part of the social order" and not simply perceive of power only in relation to men's political domain.[131] Marilyn Strathern countered these assertions about Melpa women stating that women's production was devalued on all counts and that there "is no sense in which publicly yet exclusively female exchanges could have meaning in Hagen; and no sense in which women's part in reproduction could stand for social reproduction in general."[132]

Recently, Andrew Strathern notes that traditionally, barkcloth and net bag coverings wrapped around young people's long hair were thought to hold in "the life-force supplied by the spirits," marking the children's assumption of adult roles.[133] Although this example only suggests the cosmological implications of net bags and barkcloth, the use of these net bags at marriage shows how strong are the ties that still bind women to their natal group. As Nicholas Modjeska points out, the intensification of exchange that occurs with the Melpa in contrast to most other highlands groups is accompanied by a growing emphasis on affinal exchange relationships.[134] But these relationships both support and limit political authority because of the unresolvable intensity of women's economic relationships with their brothers in opposition to their husbands' control.

This is the conflict metaphorically expressed in the reproductive rituals and economic obligations that vex husbands and wives yet aid them in their roles as brothers and sisters. In the Female Spirit cult, a sister is available for many brothers to marry—the dream that brings ultimate control over fertility and one's destiny in exchange. During these rituals, the authority of a Melpa ritual expert far exceeds the power of any secular big man whereas the spirit woman is represented in stone. These are the Melpa possessions that are inalienable and they are literally buried within the ritual domain.

The Expansion and Defeat of Hierarchy

The cases from Australia and New Guinea demonstrate the narrowness imposed on kinship and gender analyses when the norm of reciprocity is considered the primary feature of exchange relations. Then, all objects, including women, remain signs of the transactional relations between men rather than signs of the reproductive imperatives surrounding keeping-while-giving that involve women as central actors in their own right. This traditional view not only affects our understanding of the fundamental role that inalienable possessions play in political events but emphasizes women as wives at the expense of the equally essential exchange roles of women as sisters.

In the comparative cases I presented in this chapter, sibling intimacy creates tensions in the roles that women and men play as spouses. These same tensions appear in the larger kinship and political domain where the need to regenerate the social identities of one's kin group stands in opposition to the competitive demands of others outside the group. The Bimin-Kuskusmin succeed in maintaining the former by directing enormous reproductive attention and resources into their ritual life. With strong sibling support, the degeneration and death represented most dangerously in relationships between spouses is combated. The demands made on producing inalienable possessions that affirm the

strength of patrilineal identity leave little room for shifting these resources and reproductive and productive efforts into large-scale external
exchanges. The necessity for sibling intimacy gives some women as sisters and some men as brothers the opportunity to assume positions of
leadership and authority that accord them economic and political autonomy and create a level of hierarchy within the kin group itself.
Bimin-Kuskusmin women also have their own subversive domain of
power as wives—the ability to cause pollution and death. Whereas with
mana Polynesian women as sisters control both positive and negative
forces, among the Bimin-Kuskusmin these powers are split between
women as wives who are dangerous to their husbands and their own
children whereas only as sisters can they contribute beneficial powers
to their brothers and their brothers' children.[135] The negative power
associated with wives is transferred to all outsiders who similarly are
dangerous, yet this danger dialectically enters into the natal group
through marriage. The ritual domain separates outsiders and spouses,
using their reproductive efforts and then reconstituting them through
siblings into the reproduction of the clan. Although ancestral authentication in bones provides the source of power and political authority
within the clan, these bones do not circulate as an individual's property
nor are substitutes or replacements made, so that keeping inalienable
possessions out of exchange fails to establish difference between one
group and another. The line of skulls authenticates the difference between ritual leaders and other members of the kin group but this internal hierarchy, visually represented in women's skulls, does not extend
beyond the clan.

In the Australian instances, women and men control separate ritual
domains with access to their own cosmological resources. Among the
Warlpiri, for example, senior women hold a hierarchical position over
other women, that accords them a measure of economic and political
autonomy within their group because they have the right to transmit
sacred knowledge. At the same time, their exchange roles with their
brothers secure rights to land and other important resources beyond
the kin group that accords them a wider context for the exercise of
power. The individual ranking of social identities is authenticated in
the ranking of tjurunga and other resources that themselves originate
in and are authenticated by The Dreaming. Because The Dreaming
creates this expansive authenticating force, sacred objects and knowledge are desired by other groups, enabling parts of The Dreaming to
become possessions that are transmitted to others. Here, then, is the

locus of authority enabling some few men to gain political autonomy that, in some cases, is inheritable. The level of ranking achieved is directly related to the circulation and guardianship of inalienable possessions. Similarly, the sacred possessions that women control are essential to men so that, in these cases, women do have a domain of political autonomy. Hair strings and other fibers traditionally have been ignored by ethnographers more taken with the elaboration of men's ceremonial paraphernalia. Yet when compared with Trobriand banana fiber bundles, Samoan pandanus leaves, or Maori flax threads, they appear to be an incipient form of cloth wealth.

In comparison, the Melpa are the antithesis to the above examples. For them, the locus of large-scale production is geared toward external exchange events set into motion by the desires of clan leaders. Melpa pigs, pearl shells, and money lack cosmological or ancestral authentication so that they never assume absolute value. Where at one time pearl shells began to be ranked in such a way that others were attracted to the power of big men, this shift toward the creation of absolute value was subverted by colonization. Without keeping some valuables out of circulation that give a leader the ability to attract others to him, each big man must work continually to develop allies for each large-scale moka transaction, as the film *Ongka's Big Moka* so sensitively portrays.[136] By increasing production through wives, sisters, and other men, a man builds up reciprocal networks, but these can never expand into the authority necessary to build personal reputation into lineage or clan chieftaincy. Lacking possessions that differentiate one kin group's ranking over another, the institutionalization of authority as a birthright does not develop. The bamboo tallies men wear today epitomize a striving after individual prestige; such fame is not regenerated through time in a way that ranks one lineage over another. The male and female cults are symbolic enactments of this dilemma. The cult of buried stones offers Melpa men an unfettered claim to fertility if only they could marry their sisters. Instead Melpa men and women are caught up in the complex social situations where their exchange roles as siblings take precedence over, and therefore, conflict with, their exchange roles as spouses.

Of all the societies I discussed, Melpa women are most constrained in their relationships with men. As married sisters they exert power but this power only fuels the tensions in moving resources from husbands to brothers. At least in this century, Melpa women, excluded as they are from powers attained through rights to authenticate cosmological

linkages, lack autonomous control over economically significant resources (except for net bags), that validate sacred, powerful forces.
Their efforts are segmented within the economic domain where they
are strictly confined to the difficult role of negotiating between husbands and brothers. Because Melpa women's production is critical to
men's external moka exchanges, husbands dominate wives in efforts to
lessen their brothers' control over them. But husbands are held in
check by these very circumstances; in the role of another man's sister,
a woman makes claims on her husband that he cannot ignore. The reliance that men have on sisters is expressed most clearly in the myths
and dreams associated with the female spirit where men envision the
advantages of marrying in. The net bags that women carry in marriage—a prominent cloth symbol of human reproduction—are a poi-
gnant example of Melpa women's lack of access to possessions that in
authenticating historical or mythical origins also become an economic
resource. Melpa women have neither their own extensive economic resources nor inalienable resources to draw on, and therefore their roles
in cultural reproduction and production severely limit the dimensions
and scope of their power. The extent of men's power also is confined
to their negotiating, noncoercive roles as big men rather than chiefs.
Only in the men's spirit cult where women, although absent, are associated with cosmological resources can a man as ritual expert coerce
and dominate other men. Yet this role, like the Bimin-Kuskusmin, remains in the ritual domain. Missing from the Melpa exchange system
is the culturally reproductive stability within the kin group provided
when inalienable possessions mark intergenerational social identities
authenticated in cosmological origins. What occurs is that the constant
flow of shells, pigs, and money exaggerates difference without locating
the source of such difference in genealogies or cosmologies. Only men's
individual fame expressed by their debts and gains in moka ranks one
man against another. Since this ranking rises and falls idiosyncratically
without a source of authentication that is outside contemporary social
life, external commitments continually diffuse resources and authority
into a kind of endless mobility with momentary fame, rather than intergenerational reproduction, the most sought after goal. Whereas the
Pintupi have resources that are cosmologically authenticated, the transmission of inalienable possessions bridges distance and makes people
fanned out over a wide region into one group. At the same time, this
diffusing authority among many elders constrains the institutionalization of hierarchy. The Bimin-Kuskusmin's most treasured resources are

cosmologically authenticated and since they strengthen and reproduce the internal relationships within a clan, they create a limited hierarchy, but only within the clan. In contrast, the Aranda, keeping inalienable possessions guarded but still using them to create exchange relationships across clans, institutionalize a leadership position that is ranked over others, and substantively differentiate one leader and clan from others.

There is a historical reason that inalienable possessions are the oldest economic classification. All societies attempt to make some things into inalienable possessions, to keep something out of the flux of events that demand giving. Bambi Schieffelin tells of how the egalitarian Kaluli deeply treasure bits of cloth or tiny pieces of shell that once belonged to a deceased kin, carrying it with them wherever they go.[137] The Trobrianders enlarge upon these feelings, ritually carrying a dead person's hair or fingernails that have been inserted into shell necklaces. But Trobrianders also produce vast quantities of bundles and skirts. Although they are not inalienable possessions, they have one of the most important distinguishing features of inalienable possessions. Skirts and bundles symbolically represent the authentication of matrilineal origins conceived and socially supported through sibling intimacy. Outside debts are repaid with cloth while the inalienability of matrilineal identities are secured. If skirts and bundles were transformed into the Samoan system, the most beautifully made skirt, as in figure 23, would begin to circulate among high-ranking people. As it got older, it would finally be kept out of circulation by a high-ranking chief and his sacred sister who, having enough other fine skirts to repay obligations, would endeavor to hide it and carefully control its future history. Had the skirt been produced by a high-ranking woman, it would have been imbued with mana that, from the beginning, would have set it in a special category only to be brought out on the most auspicious occasions. Possessions like these are what strong political hierarchy is made of.

CHAPTER 5

Kula: The Paradox of Keeping-While-Giving

Whose gifts are so readily recognized as some of those which the king gives, such as bracelets, necklaces and horses with gold-studded bridles? For, as everyone knows, no one there is ever allowed to have such things except those to whom the king has given them.

Xenophon, *Cyropaedia*

Such things Aeneas admires on the shield of Vulcan, The gift of his mother and, although ignorant of the deeds, he rejoices in the image, holding up on his shoulder the fame and fates of his descendants.

Virgil, *The Aeneid*

Malinowski's description of the reciprocal exchange cycle of ornately decorated white *conus* armshells and finely chiseled red *charma* necklaces made Trobrianders' kula exchange immediately famous.[1] But beyond its importance as a classic statement regarding the form and process of exchange in "savage" societies, it provides us today with a classic example of the cultural significance of keeping-while-giving and the inherent problems in sustaining this goal. The societies I discussed in the last chapter clarify how essential it is to the development of hierarchy that certain possessions authenticate a kin group's descendants and origins. Kula is the most dramatic case of these processes, as players attempt to recreate the processes of internal cultural reproduction in external kula exchanges.[2]

Malinowski had a novelist's flair for titling his Trobriand ethnographies. In the 1920s, few readers were well informed about "primitive" economics so that *Argonauts of the Western Pacific* imaginatively drew parallels between Trobriand kula players and ancient Greek heroes. Had Malinowski pursued these links beyond the title he might not have been so perplexed about why Trobrianders were dedicated to kula. Like the ancient Greeks, Trobrianders endure hardships of travel, disappointment, and even death in their search not just for immediate fame but to achieve the regeneration of their names. In the Homeric case, eminence depended upon one's social identity as an aristocrat and one's ability to compete successfully among equals in what Beidelman calls "agonistic exchange" that was the only means through which one could elevate one's authority over others.[3] Being equal demanded the appropriate background—a legacy of ancestors, correct marriages, and particular allies and only among aristocrats could the jockeying for a reputation that made the person appear totally autonomous take place. It was not an accident that Alexander the Great exploited a genealogy that supposedly stretched back to the *Iliad* and the *Odyssey*; Alexander used Achilles and Odysseus as his own ancestors, fabricating a genealogy that gave him the legitimacy to transcend his own blood descendants and even the social order.[4] Indeed, he repeatedly claimed divine antecedents, hence his being pictured with the horns of Zeus jutting out of his hair.

The examples in the last chapter from Australia Aboriginal and New Guinea societies show what a difficult accomplishment it is to transcend kinship in order to achieve political autonomy without the backing and ranking of a particular kin group or ancestors. Yet this is exactly the opportunity that kula offers. Kula players meet in an arena that is located outside village boundaries; here, like the ancient Greek aristocrats, some Massim Islanders compete for fame that will transcend the statuses of their own lineages or clans. Taking on enormous moral, financial, and even dangerous obligations, kula players engage in a kind of mental combat as they seek to outmaneuver all competitors in efforts to obtain the highest-ranking shells. Like Alexander the Great, kula players attempt to transcend their own genealogies, to validate their political authority with the possession of the most valued kula treasures. Only those players who have the knowledge and the ability to sustain this agonistic exchange have a chance to gain the most prized shells;

when successful, their names circulate throughout the islands for many years.[5]

Throughout the kula districts, those few players who become truly celebrated in kula are political leaders within their own villages.[6] Kula provides them with an arena to win over others who are not related by kinship, defining their authority through a wider network of political relationships that are all ranked. The possessions that circulate in the top ranks of kula transactions sustain a system in which definite criteria that not only define a shell's ranking but support one's political authority are continually authenticated.[7] Fundamentally, kula is not about reciprocating one shell for another because every player seeks to attain and then keep as many famous shells as possible. In essence, these prized shells are like the famous trophies for which ancient Greek aristocrats vied; one's esteem was measured by the number and fame of the chalices or suits of armor acquired through "ritualized friendship."[8] Each kula shell presented to another player is given up at a great loss because its history and reputation cannot be replicated. For this reason, a kula player who is able to obtain a famous shell tries to keep it out of circulation, guarding it for ten, fifteen, or even thirty years. By Melanesian standards, given the continual demands of local kin and affinal obligations, keeping a highly sought-after valuable out of circulation even for a short time is a major accomplishment. Twenty or thirty years is a generation and so from a player's perspective, to keep a shell as if it were inalienable is a possibility even though eventually the shell must reenter kula exchange.

This dilemma takes us to the heart of the keeping-while-giving paradox. Although kula is played for the highest political stakes, ultimately kula is as bounded as the ritual exchanges produced through The Dreaming. The most sought-after shells take on the kind of absolute value attributed to inalienable possessions although, unlike prized Aboriginal tjurunga or Maori taonga, the shells lack sacred powers. Their legitimation does not come from an authority located outside ordinary social life. Neither gods nor mana nor ancestral spirits sanction the historical force of kula possessions. Whereas these other inalienable possessions reaffirm a group's social identity and ranking through their attachment to particular clans or lineages, kula shells distinguish only the ranking and esteem of individual players. Authentication of difference occurs only within kula, dependent upon contemporary situations that limit the establishment and affirmation of political succession. This is the illusion in kula—the constitution of a pan-island political hierarchy without, except for the Trobriands, an institutionalized local base of ranked chieftaincies.

The Hierarchy of Shells

All kula shells are ranked according to explicit standards of weight, circumference, length, and age (see fig. 24). Only when certain armshells and necklaces meet the highest standards are they eligible for the top named category and only then is each shell given an individual name.[9] These are the shells that carry the history of their former owners' eminence creating their own specific identities through time.[10] Such high-ranking shells are the ones that move slowly from one high-ranking player to another. Unlike the Melpa example where the historicity and ranking of shells were dislodged almost overnight by the Leahy brothers' importation of shells, nineteenth-century colonial adventurers who similarly brought new shells into the kula areas never disrupted the main target of kula—to seek out and keep the highest-ranking shells. Although changes occurred in specific kula networks as well as in the kinds of kula valuables exchanged, some of the most famous kula armshells and necklaces that Malinowski described by name still circulate today.[11] A decade before Malinowski embarked on his field research when Seligman traveled through the Massim, he collected the histories of well-known shells and stone axe blades, some of which then were three generations old.[12] Beatrice Grimshaw in her visit to the Massim in 1909 remarked that just as some American women yearn for the most famous historical gems that have names such as "'The Koh-i-Noor,' 'The Sancy,' 'The Pitt,' 'The Cullinan,' so the Papuan shell armlets of unusual size and thickness have their native names, known to everyone, and bringing celebrity and distinction to the possessor of the jewel wherever he goes throughout the whole extent of Papua."[13]

To support the slow circulation of these large, well-known shells, many other less highly valued shells as replacements are necessary. What Malinowski never recognized was a category of shells called *kitomu* which are individually owned and therefore are alienable.[14] Such shells not only can be bought or sold but they can be put into kula play or taken out by their owners for other kinds of obligations. In a sense, kitomu shells are like having enough fine mats to enable one to deal in exchange strategically while safeguarding the high-ranking ones.

Kitomu shells are used effectively by a player to forestall a partner's expectations of an anticipated shell when in fact that shell has already been promised to someone else who, at the time, is more strategically valuable. In this way, individually owned shells are like wild cards in poker, enabling a player to multiply the possibilities for success by negotiating simultaneously with several partners on different paths over the same sought-after shell. Until the 1930s, villagers in the southern part of Kiriwina produced shells that, although not as finely made as the top-named shells, were used as kitomu and chiefs used these shells to enhance their kula strategies.

Once kitomu shells enter into kula they are evaluated and ranked following the criteria for other kula shells. In the same way that a new huge Samoan fine mat has much less value than an old, rare one, new shells, even if large and well decorated, do not take on the highest ranking until they have gained the appropriate histories and the shell, itself, takes on a smoothness and patina from having been handled many times.[15] If a kitomu shell is extremely fine and has circulated in kula among the highest-ranking players so that its reputation has usurped its individual ownership, then it is reclassified as a high-ranking shell.

This vertical movement from private ownership to an inalienable possession within kula to becoming an individual player's inalienable possession for many years is the trajectory that the highest-ranking shells follow. If a player owns a large kitomu shell and elects to give it to another kula player, the strategy behind this move is the expectation that eventually the kitomu owner will receive a shell that has greater renown. This return shell is actually the replacement for the original kitomu while the original one still circulates in kula.[16] Whoever gets the original kitomu shell has the right to keep it until that player decides to release it to someone else in pursuit of capturing another high-ranking shell. The dilemma is to find a shell that is highly prized and sought after by others and then to persuade that player to give up the shell. But no one gives up a high-ranking shell easily or quickly because, in all cases, the hope is to find a shell more famous than what one already holds. These shells, with names, histories, and individual rankings, comprise a hierarchical level of exchange that is missing from Melpa exchanges where shells are not individuated in this way.[17]

In kula, less valuable shells individually owned or already in kula for many years circulate most frequently and underwrite and stabilize the much slower passages of famous shells. Like the lesser-valued Samoan fine mats, these shells circulate between players providing the support necessary to sustain long-term relationships with partners residing throughout the kula areas. Sometimes these shells, even when not owned by a player, will be removed from kula activities because of a player's local kin obligations. But each time a player diverts a shell, if he lacks a kitomu shell as a replacement, his reputation diminishes. This disjuncture between internal kin obligations and external political commitments is a continual struggle for most kula players and undercuts their opportunity to make substantial gains within kula. This perpetual problem means that most players remain "small" whereas only a handful become famous.

Younger and less successful participants act too quickly with their shells, immediately giving a kitomu shell to another player, thinking that this one shell will solidify a kula relationship. But these novices lack the many other shells to back up this one play and so the recipients keep their shells giving them to other partners because they know that new players cannot bring any pressure to bear on them for a return. This is why novices and even older players often lose many shells in their unsuccessful attempts to gain eminence. In contrast, successful players manipulate transactions for ten years or longer, dealing in many shells of all categories, just to gain possession of one important shell.

Politically, authority in kula is dependent on controlling shells that promote and validate the right to be higher than others and the right to win when others lose. To be victorious is always a dangerous matter. With the Maori, gaining the possession of a famous taonga could trigger a war. In the Massim, a political triumph can lead to sorcery or loss of reliable partners. This puts all kula players at risk as they are locked in contention for the highest prize. Beidelman points out that among Homeric Greeks, a person of esteem gains nothing by competing with inferiors and he might actually risk being demeaned by deciding to do so. This same philosophy pervades kula playing as only the top-ranking kula men exchange the most valuable shells with each other.[18] Although every kula player dreams of gaining the highest-ranking shells, it is extremely dangerous (and unlikely) for a lesser-ranking player to excel over renowned players. This is what kula players refer to when they say that many men died because of kula shells.[19]

Like Polynesian inalienable possessions or even the Melpa shells that were once associated with magical properties, successful control over a few high-ranking shells draws other players to those at the top. In kula this creates a coterie of equals. Only by demonstrating that one has the ability to aim for and win the highest shells may a player compete in the top leagues; defeat to an equal rival over an acclaimed shell is far less shameful than a loss to a subordinate player. Other players find their own levels with partners who have the same experience and potentials.[20] Picture the conical pile of yams in figure 10 as a motif of kula activities. The most valued inalienable shells are at the top of the heap; few in number, they are supported by the many thousands of shells that circulate in kula as well as those that are individually owned and are used both in kula and in local kin affairs. In the same way, throughout the Massim, those few highest-ranking Kiriwina chiefs are at the top of the political elite, joined in kula by other men, leaders on other islands, who similarly gain distinction from their acumen in attaining the highest-ranking shells. On Gawa Island, known for its egalitarian political relationships, villagers told Nancy Munn that when they are able to obtain high-ranking shells, they become "chiefs."[21] In this way, the capture and possession of the highest-ranking valuables give a precise form to the goals of kula interaction just as the status of chief gives a political form to the whole enterprise.[22]

Chiefly Hierarchy in Kula

Throughout the Massim, the word *guyau* and its variants means "leader," but in the Trobriands, guyau refers to inherited chiefly positions and to all members of the ranking lineages into which they are born. The question of why certain Trobriand matrilineages are ranked with hereditary chiefs, when chieftaincy is absent among all other Massim island societies, has been the subject of long anthropological debate ever since Seligman, and later Malinowski wrote about Trobriand "paramount" chiefs.[23] But among other Massim Islanders, the presence of Trobriand chiefs is never in doubt as they often discuss the differences between themselves and "famous" Trobriand chiefs.[24]

The hamlets owned by the highest-ranking and most powerful chiefly matrilineages are found in the northern half of the main island of Kiriwina, the largest Trobriand Island.[25] Land mass and population density are the largest here and unlike the three other small Trobriand Islands (Kitava, Vakuta, and Kaleuna) where only one chief resides whose authority is limited, Kiriwina's important chiefs vie with each other for power. Basically, an individual chief has autonomous decision-making authority only over those particular villagers who are related to him through matrilineage, patrilateral, and affinal relationships. If, however, a chief makes strategic errors in political matters, his power is sharply curtailed. Yet the ancestral ranking of his lineage remains intact, so that his successor may be able to reconstitute a more stable position of power.[26]

Throughout the Massim, only in Kiriwina are skirts and bundles essential wealth for women and men.[27] Bundles represent a division of wealth into smaller tokens that can be distributed to hundreds of people, as figures 17 and 18 show. Although neither bundles nor skirts are inalienable, their symbolic representation of ancestral authentication makes them an effective symbol for validating matrilineal identity. Economically, when they are distributed following a death, the distribution attests to the strength of sibling intimacy and validates the relationships between one matrilineage and the members of other matrilineages linked through marriage and patrilateral relationships. Unlike Melpa women who face continual stress between their husbands' and their brothers' needs for the same wealth, Kiriwina women, with their own domain of bundles and skirts supported rather than drained by men, counter the threat to the stability of matrilineal identity by showing where each person belongs vis-à-vis her or his obligations to others. Like a Samoan chief covered up in a fine mat that must be given up for "protection," women's skirts and bundles protect the matrilineage by replacing affinal and patrilateral debts. And thus, cloth wealth, formalized to the degree that it acts as a kind of currency, provides the underpinnings for the authority of Kiriwina chiefs.

Consequently, kula is organized differently in northern Kiriwina from other kula communities. First, until early in this century, Kiriwina kula was restricted to chiefs, their brothers, sisters' sons, and their own sons. In the rest of the kula communities, including the villages on the other Trobriand Islands, almost all adult men (and today, a few women) are active in kula.[28] At present, only a small percentage of the Kiriwina population engages in kula and all the players of importance have kin or affinal associations with chiefs or are the sons of former chiefs.[29] Today, villagers often discuss how money is changing kula as more young men who work on the mainland buy large shells there and then enter kula. Although competition to enter kula is keener than in the past, the traditional leadership of chiefs still remains dominant as these younger men usually lose their shells to more experienced players.

Second, obtaining kitomu shells on Kiriwina differs from the other islands. On Kiriwina, kitomu are acquired through individually established networks in which a man gives yams or today more often money—to someone as payment for a shell.[30] Although yam production itself involves relationships between affines and patrilateral kin, at a harvest the recipient of yams has full control over their future use. So when a person acquires a kitomu, it truly belongs to him; other members of his matrilineage are not involved in decisions about its destiny. On Muyuw and Gawa Islands, however, where there are no chiefs, a person's access to kitomu shells depends upon the labor of his own kin and affines.[31] Kula canoes are produced for exchange and then sent overseas to other islands for a large return payment in kitomu shells. Because a man must draw on the productive work of his kin and affines throughout the making of a canoe, these people then have a claim to the shells and their future circulation.[32] As Munn recounts for Gawa, final decisions over whether or not to put a kitomu into kula are usually made by the shell's owner but in consultation with other members of his matrilineage.[33]

Third, on Kiriwina, armshells and necklaces are not the major source of wealth for internal exchanges. The most important items of men's wealth are stone axe blades (with clay pots and now money acting as secondary resources).[34] Unlike other Massim Islands, this diversification of resources frees men from a dependency on kula or kitomu shells for most local obligations.[35] Conversely, on Gawa or Vakuta Islands, when the need arises for shell exchanges at a death or a marriage, a villager may have no choice but to put his kitomu shells into these local exchanges rather than enter the shells into a kula transaction.[36] In other instances, a villager will be forced to take a shell that is promised to a kula partner and put it into a necessary village exchange. Overall, these ever-pressing kinship obligations keep most kula players much more dependent than Kiriwina men on the demands of their own kin and affinal relations, restricting their political autonomy and authority in kula.

Men from Vakuta Island to the south of Kiriwina and men from Sinaketa in the southern part of Kiriwina Island, the two other major Trobriand areas for kula, make the long voyages south to Iwa and Gawa Islands and west to Dobu in canoes similar to that in figure 1. The highest-ranking shells they obtain usually are destined for Kiriwina chiefs in the north, who only travel the comparatively short distances to the other islands in the Trobriand group. Throughout the Massim, the best kula players seek to have Trobriand chiefs as their partners because the fame and fear of these chiefs circulate independent of their kula exploits.[37] The ranking of shells and players is so pervasive that even the routes that shells follow around the Massim are ranked in this chiefly manner. Although chiefs are not the only distinguished kula players nor are they the only successful players, their presence and their ranking create the chiefly identity in which all top kula players participate. Kula provides the field of action and the symbolic edifice in which chieftaincy for all players becomes a political possibility.

Kula Partners and the Paths of Exchange

In Malinowski's ideal view of kula, players living on a continuum of islands who reciprocate serially with each other constitute the path along which particular shells are passed from one partner to another—the armshells moving in a counterclockwise direction, while the necklaces move in the opposite direction. When I first discussed kula with some village men, one man, exasperated at my ignorance about kula paths (*keda*), went to his house and returned with a piece of paper listing the names of his kula partners. He told me how he personally knew those who live on the closest islands where he himself travels to kula, but he had never seen his other partners from more distant places. Bweneyeya said proudly, "They never see my face, but they know my name." Malinowski never discussed kula paths, yet what is most strategic about kula action is the routes that shells follow. Special care and attention are given to the paths on which the highest-ranking shells circulate, and particular efforts are made to keep other shells on the path in a stable trajectory. Stability remains a problem, even for chiefs. If high-ranking shells are diverted from one path to another, the shells' names are changed and their former histories lost.[38] Since the top-ranking players are active in five to ten kula paths, diversion is always a part of their kula strategies and a danger to which they also are at risk from others.

In practice, although players know the names of their partners associated with specific paths, at any point in time, the only part of the network over which a player has any direct influence is to either side of him. Each player has a few partners situated geographically to the right and a few others to the left, giving each person access to necklaces coming in a clockwise direction and armshells coming from a counterclockwise direction.[39] Each small segment links into other segments further away, but a particular segment of the network becomes activated only when the owner of an important shell is located and the owner is willing to give it up. It takes years of work to convince the player to release the shell and this necessitates having many other shells to move along this particular path. Further, the point where each partner stands in relation to the large shell determines the kind of work the player must do for that particular sequence of exchanges. In this way, each player's role vis-à-vis the closest partners—those who he personally knows—differs with each stage of kula action.

Shells given from one partner to another in either direction convey specific meanings about the vitality or weakness of that segment of the path. Only when many shells are moving along a path's segment is it considered strong; if only a few shells circulate, partners become discouraged and turn their attention to other players associated with more active paths. Even an important chief who tries to gain complete autonomy by switching crucial shells too often will discover that his partners are withdrawing their support. Kula as a topic of conversation with nonpartners abounds with accounts about the lost chances, the broken promises, the things given to someone in an attempt to get a shell only to be faced with an empty return. Kula talk with partners, however, is full of bravado, expounding on the location of all one's promised and forthcoming shells and all the debts that one is owed. But as one kula player told me, all kula talk is dangerous because most of it is lies, specious rhetoric set forth to serve one's own ends.[40]

At all levels of kula playing, a player attempts to link up with partners who have access to better shells by soliciting them with kitomu shells, other kinds of wealth, and yams and pigs. Knowledge of what others plan is an obvious advantage and good players must learn to carry in their heads reckoning of all their debts and obligations and also the past histories of former paths and debts while conceptualizing all the future moves that they plan to make, much like the complex knowledge necessary for a chess champion.

Instead of perceiving kula transactions simply as gifts and countergifts, it is essential to visualize the maze of plays and strategies as *layers* of exchanges which one must constantly build up over time and then keep track of.[41] There can be no dependency on one gift for one return. Rather, a player must keep giving to convince partners that he is someone whom they should trust. This layering of giving begins when someone has an impressive shell, one that is in the upper ranking. Then many people want it and are willing to give many things in an effort to attach themselves to this path. Initiatory shells are called *vaga,* a term that indicates they are the opening shells that begin each new circulation. But these vaga are neither equivalent to nor exchangeable for the original sought after shell. They represent persuasive attempts in Western parlance "to sweeten the deal" and convince an owner to trust a player and have the shell travel along his particular path with his particular partners.[42]

When the owner receives vaga shells, he thinks carefully about each person who, having given him the shell, announces a desire to have the high-ranking shell.[43] As one Trobriand villager explained, "like a woman looking over the men who want to sleep with her," the owner decides which player he wants for his partner.[44] Once a partner is decided upon, he receives the sought after armshell because he has convinced the owner that eventually he can find a replacement for that item. The other players who vied for the chance to exchange receive only a return shell for the vaga each one gave the owner. In these latter cases, reciprocity is used to reject a person. Giving a vaga shell and quickly receiving a return denotes an end to further advances; no kula path for the large shell has been opened. The intricate plays and delays for making the final move in which a high-ranking shell is given to someone else are vast and complex.[45] Briefly, the partners on both sides of the original owner must find intermediate or what I call replacement shells that continue to move along this segment of the path. Diversions of shells are a constant threat so it is essential that replacement shells of the next lower ranks are exchanged along the path between the eventual recipient and the person still holding onto the sought after item. In the later stages of these transactions, three, four, or five shells at a time will be sent along the path to show the strength of the player's intentions. Yet even the destiny of these replacement shells is never secure. Each player will be enticed by others who have partners on other paths and need these replacement shells themselves. A player with many paths has more freedom to juggle shells and make diversions from one path to another. These ploys can be covered if the player has other kitomu at his disposal. If not, each time a diversion occurs partners are angered, but anger must be weighed against the breakdown of the entire path segment.[46] Taken to an extreme, however, a path may become so encumbered with even one player's switches and losses that the other partners decide to let the path "die."[47]

Kitomu are essential to the whole edifice as they play a key role not only in building up the strength of a path but in effecting the final exchange.[48] According to kula rules, once the high-ranking shell is released, that path segment is finished. But with the long-sought-after shell, another shell called *kunivilevila* meaning "to turn" in the sense of turning a corner is also given. This shell is considered a "profit" (*katumukolava*). According to Trobriand players, the marriage of two high-ranking shells "gives birth" to this additional shell, although the gestation period requires years of effort. The shell, although perceived as profit, is actually an investment in the future, much as children are perceived as eventually working hard for their parents. Like "giving birth," the shell allows the recipient to reopen the path's segment and not "let it die" by initiating another cycle of exchanges with the same partners.

From a more global perspective, the many less successful players who often lose shells are as essential to kula as are those who succeed. In order for increments and profits to occur, losses are necessary. Although kitomu shells enter kula as new shells, the continual loss of shells from one player to another allows other players to sustain paths, to make increments, and to provide profits and even more important, to make promises that may never be met. If at any one moment someone stopped all kula playing and demanded that all debts be covered immediately, the many losses would be apparent. Kula players say that kula is like having a passbook—they are banking their money. For a long time, this analogy left me perplexed until I read R. K. Narayan's novel, *The Financial Expert*.[49] In this tale set in India, villagers from miles away bring all their savings to a money lender renowned for the high interest rates he pays. When, however, someone spreads a rumor that the money is not safe with him, a sudden run on his self-styled "bank" occurs and he, of course, cannot return all the villagers' money.

Winning, so easy to aspire to but so difficult to achieve, illustrates that although the essence of kula strategy assumes winning, the essence of kula manipulation necessitates losing. In each kula area, only a few players can play at the top with all the capability necessary to control their kula destinies better than other players. The threat of loss of shells is matched by the danger that paths may die and sorcery may defeat those who go too far in their risk-taking. In kula, the intentions of overseas partners are not dictated by kinship ties so there is little in the way of close checks and balances on players' work and attention to one another.[50] When a player dies and a younger relative inherits his kula partners, these new players often lose their inheritance because of their inexperience. In some cases, if the former player's reputation for diversion and lying surpassed his or her successful deeds, then his successor may be ignored. Like any Melpa big man, each player, including a Kiriwina chief, must compete anew to reaffirm his succession to a deceased player's rank. Reciprocity in kula only establishes the beginning stages through which the first vaga shells are exchanged. These lead to the more important expectations that will enhance a person's reputation and create a profit. More frequently, these desires of victorious pursuits end in despair. The perceptions that surround kula combine fact and possibility, success and failure, with loss as much a part of the system as gain. In a general sense, these problems reflect the issues surrounding the constitution of ranking and hierarchy that I raised in the previous chapters. People's co-involvement with one another over time is critical to the process.

Kula and Inalienable Shells

Small wonder that the attainment of these most coveted shells, encrusted as they are with the histories of people's successes, fills a person with emotional feelings for the shell itself. When Malinowski wrote how kula shells are held in front of a dying man as if "to inspire with life; and at the same time to prepare for death," he could hardly have recognized how prophetic these words were. Although kula is about profit and loss in an economic sense, it can also signify other more existential concerns. Although the shells themselves are not infused with mana or powerful ancestral forces, kula actions are associated metaphorically with seeking lovers, being married, and giving birth; kula paths die and are reproduced.

The paradox that underwrites the entire project is apparent. Men engage in these events without the connections through women that exist in the Polynesian examples. The symbolism of kula resembles more closely Melpa cosmological concerns with the "female spirit," references to women's reproductive powers that are controlled and enacted primarily by men. Like Melpa inalienable sacred stones, on Gawa Island, kitomu are metaphorically referred to as "ancestral stones," because, as Munn points out, the ideal is to keep them in one's control over generations so that they continue to reproduce more shells for future generations.[51] Although the organization of kula is an attempt to frame the legitimacy of ranking for all participants, ultimately it cannot succeed in institutionalizing ranking at the local level. Like moka, these practices are associated with individual fame and reputations rather than the reproduction of previously objectified ancestral-lineage identities. Except for Trobriand chiefs, succession to ranking in kula is not inherited and ranking is validated by the reputations and abilities of individual kula players rather than the ancestors and sacred powers of lineages or clans. But given the dynamics of kula action, the disjuncture that this idea expresses between what is possible in kula and what is not shows what happens when the inalienability of kula shells is restricted entirely to a political domain, segmented from kinship. Unlike the most famous inalienable Maori taonga or Samoan fine mats, the inalienable kula shells do not move back and forth between local lineage and political affairs, bringing the ranking of lineages directly into political encounters. With the Maori, the Samoans, and the Kwaikiutl, clan and interclan obligations were met in the circulation of the same class of objects. Yet some individuals, members of particular groups, were able to keep the most prized and valuable possessions intact and free from circulation outside the kin group. Thus these possessions symbolize the inalienability of the group and, at the same time, a chief's growing reputation and potential immortality.

Kula players have the same intention with their high-ranking kitomu shells, for the competitive goal with each large shell is to seek another with a distinguished history.[52] Through these shells, a person transcends the history of lineage origins and becomes a part of kula history. What is of consequence is that this kula history is inscribed in the fame of particular shells. Therefore, in exchange, the difference between one player and another is inscribed in a meaningful framework recognized as "fame." The authentication of fame legitimates a person's right to win over others' losses and to be ranked as a winner in a coterie of equals—with the highest honor, ranking in the coterie of those who traffic with chiefs. Fame in kula also enables a player to demonstrate difference by holding valuables for a long time without having to give them up to relatives for use in internal exchanges. Keeping a kula shell out of exchange because it is promised in kula allows a person to store wealth in the face of other social and political obligations. On the one hand, the assignment of the shell to kula may protect it from loss in internal exchanges; on the other hand, unless the promised shell or another as famous finally enters a path, the owner's own eminence diminishes.[53] Each shell that is given up by one person is a defeat, a bereavement of sorts, because no high-ranking shell is the exact equivalent of another. To bestow a high-ranking shell on another player is an emotionally charged moment as the player releases a renowned shell that he had kept out of circulation for twenty years, he drops it with disdain, as if it had no value. At that moment it is without value for him; he finally has been coerced into giving it up; he has lost it and the power that its ownership has given him. Although he now has (or has been promised) another valued shell, it is not an exact equivalent. The shell may be of the same rank, but it has a different persona because it has had a different exchange trajectory. His work to hold this newly acquired shell begins again for only by keeping it will he reestablish his power. The talk of magic spells and sorcery indicates for us as onlookers the drama and even the possibility of violence that are part of the opposing forces present in each exchange.

This ritualized gesture of dropping the shell expresses the fundamental dilemma: the difficulty in establishing hierarchy. The shell profit, that I previously called a token, further illuminates the paradox. This profit that kula players seek is at the same time the reproductive token that reconstitutes a path too valuable to die—at one moment symbolizing the ultimate achievement of hierarchy as it encompasses the system while simultaneously symbolizing its defeat, in the need to begin again. Only by reentering the shell (i.e., one's profit) in kula, as a replacement shell for what has previously transpired, can the partners be held in place and the path segment be reproduced. Malinowski noted that once a player is in kula, he remains in kula for life, a seemingly strange observation when so much risk and danger are involved.[54] But risk itself, as Beidelman pointed out for the Homeric Greeks, can become a great feature of value.[55] Not to play the game at all leads to defeat without eminence and likely dishonor, just as withdrawing from kula diminishes a player's claims to authority and superiority. Ancient Greek competition outside the kin group was the only avenue for establishing the ranking of one above others within a coterie of equals, but even here, these claims had to be worked at again and again.[56] The alternative of hoarding one's shells in order to guard them from circulation so that they are truly inalienable defeats the very processes that constitute authority and renown.[57]

Cosmological Authentication and Hierarchy

Kula actions hold out the promise of attaining a hierarchical stance over others, but kula plays never succeed in structurally creating rank at the local level. Yet this promise is what motivates and underwrites the intense energy and work that makes kula possible. Only in kula do players act with some kind of autonomy and achieve a level of prestige that is not possible to obtain through politics at the local level. Even Trobriand chiefs, who enter kula as feared and significant men, still can be beaten and undercut by other players.

Ultimately, the comparisons developed reveal that kula playing does not institutionalize succession to positions of rank, either within the boundaries of kula or at the local level because kula shells lack cosmological authentication and women's participation is minor. Although a few individual women gain renown in kula, women rarely travel on overseas voyages and their long-distance efforts in kula are transacted by their male relatives. Further, women do not have their own domain, which brings the value and power that reside in cosmological authentication into kula action. The defeat of a broad-based hierarchy and the partial inalienability of shells are the results of what is most essential in the constitution of hierarchy: the authentication of the group one comes from.

Kiriwina chiefs own rights to specific shell body decorations that are ranked according to what a lineage's ancestors wore. These shells explicitly define each chiefly lineage; guardianship to prevent members of other lineages from imitating the shells is a constant preoccupation.[58] These are the shells that circumscribe ranking and remain inalienable within each lineage as they are held in trust for subsequent generations. Their uniqueness is authenticated by ancestors outside contemporary actions, and their display is a testimony to the establishment of difference that exists through time and is acknowledged by others. The only circulation of these shells outside the kin group is on loan to a man's children, later reclaimed by his sister. Therefore, the enduring identities that they symbolize do not enter into exchange competition with others. Rather, it is women's cloth wealth that in signifying ancestors and origins brings these authentications into social and political interactions. But when this wealth is compared with the Polynesian examples, its limitations are apparent. If cloth wealth is limited as an inalienable possession, so too are kula shells. Authenticated only through the histories of other players' exchanges, kula shells become inalienable for years rather than over generations. Although ranking is achieved, ultimately it is restricted by the shallow historical and ancestral authentications reproduced in women's and men's wealth. In the Polynesian examples, the most essential domain of women's cultural reproduction revolves around possessions that are cosmologically authenticated and more completely transform difference into rank and hierarchy.

Men's kula shells and women's cloth confirm the essential problem that arises in the dissolution of the political domain from kinship. Men go outside to kula, but the highest-ranking inalienable shells that circulate in kula are not inalienable outside kula—marking the identity of a local kin group. In Kiriwina, men rely on women's cloth, which affords them less dependency on their own wealth, such as stone axe blades and shells, but at the same time, the constant need for bundles usurps other wealth, such as cash, yams, and pigs that are necessary to procure more bundles.

Once again we see how authority is contained and limited by the very objects that validate it. In every aspect of kula, we observe how the potential for more shells, greater distinction, and even hierarchy is continually undercut by the limitations set by the paradoxical nature of inalienable possessions. Yet in Kiriwina the presence of women's cloth partially ameliorates complete dependency on men's wealth at each death, authenticating the ancestral renown of men, women, and their kin group and reenforcing the ranking of lineages. But neither chiefs nor women completely realize their destinies, especially when we compare the Trobriands with the institutionalization of ranking in Polynesia. A man's role in kula with its direct engagement in individual political action is ultimately as frustratingly bounded as is the role of women in their guardianship of matrilineal identity. The attainment of kula shells provides the means to realize fame, but such illustriousness still must be attached to the more elementary kind of inalienability—that of the lineage. Kula holds out the possibility that a person can build fame into a permanent hierarchy—one person encompassing the group—but like the token profit shell, it can never be fully attained.

In the Trobriands, much greater complementarity between women and men in their dual roles of siblings and spouses exists. Women are directly supported by their husbands and brothers through formal public exchanges of yams and cloth wealth. Although as sisters and as wives, Trobriand women (especially when compared with other Melanesian societies) attain a considerable degree of autonomy, their production and reproduction support rather than enable them directly to assume chiefly roles. Although the relation of difference to cosmological authentication gives women as sisters a considerable public presence in which they display autonomy and power, the political domain does not override gender as it does in Polynesia. However, in the Polynesian cases, the realization of chieftaincy and hierarchy although giving elite women a firm domain of power and authority results in the domination of men and women commoners in all arenas of social life. Hierarchy for a few comes at the expense of domination for many.

Afterword: The Challenge
of Inalienable Possessions

*And when the age of faith was over and the age of reason
had come, still the same flow of gold and silver went on;
fellowships were founded; lectureships endowed; only the gold
and silver flowed now, not from the coffers of the king, but
from the chests of merchants and manufacturers, from the
purses of men who had made, say, a fortune from industry,
and returned, in their wills, a bounteous share of it to endow
more chairs, more lectureships. . . . If only Mrs. Seton and
her mother and her mother before her had learnt the great
art of making money and left their money, like their father
and their grandfathers before them, to found fellowships and
lectureships . . . appropriated to the use of their own sex, . . .*
                                    Virginia Woolf, *A Room of One's Own*

Throughout the history of anthropology, one theory, the
norm of reciprocity, stands inviolate. The anthropological belief that it
is the expectation of a return gift that motivates exchange in "primitive"
society is, unfortunately, as strong as when Malinowski first postulated
it. Whereas earlier Marx revealed how belief in the "magic" hand of reciprocity fetishized the actual social relations between people as commodity producers and mystified the historical developments that led to
the commodity form itself, the norm of reciprocity in primitive society
remained unexamined, the gift perceived merely in relation to the return it would elicit. As this book reveals, it is the tenacious anthropo-

149

logical belief in the inherent nature of the norm of reciprocity that impedes the examination of the particular cultural conditions that empower the owners of inalienable possessions with hegemonic dominance over others. It is, then, not the hoary idea of a return gift that generates the thrust of exchange, but the radiating power of keeping inalienable possessions out of exchange. For even in the most mundane exchanges of greetings or Christmas cards, the social identities of the participants—what they have that makes them different from each other—color the styles, actions, and meanings that create the exchange.

Although the natural facts of sharing or giving and receiving are the observable data, anthropologists, by passing over the historically and culturally constructed ideologies that permeate economic and political pursuits, mystify what these facts stand for. Inalienable possessions are embedded with culturally authenticating ideologies associated with mana, ancestors and gods that give shape and drive to political processes. They are imbued with history composed of their own exceptional trajectories and the beliefs and stories that surround their existence. These encompassing ideologies are active forces that both validate the absolute value of inalienable possessions and verify the difference among individuals who own these coveted objects.

The inherent tension in keeping-while-giving follows from two fundamental contradictions: one, the challenge to give is at the same time a challenge to the ability to keep, and two, the challenge to surrender the documentation of difference between exchange participants is, at the same time, a challenge to the guardianship of autonomy. When the Pintupi man, as recounted earlier, shows the ethnologist his tjurunga hidden away and movingly says, "You might think your uncle is nothing. No! I am the boss of all this," we feel the power of inalienable possessions and sense the owner's proud possessiveness. We also feel the responsibility that guardianship entails. Yet to overcome these contradictions is to erase the difference between one inalienable possession and another, thereby nullifying the difference between oneself and another.

The work of keeping relationships, possessions, and cosmological authentications dynamic and vital, given the natural and cultural propensity for loss, entails the creation of difference that activated nodes of power and domains of authority while delimiting constraints against hierarchy. It is against these opposing forces that difference is established so that the power that difference generates is, simultaneously sought after, yet submerged; proclaimed, yet disguised; nurtured, yet defeated. Analytically, inalienable possessions provide us with these ambivalent texts and sibling intimacy is their kinship analog.

The established theories of descent rules and marriage exchange ignore the social prominence of sibling intimacy as a basic kinship principle, thereby reducing women's social roles to those of sexuality and human reproduction. Yet the multivariant references to sibling incest abounding in symbols, myths, genealogies, rituals and other social acts, signal the political vulnerability that results from the taboo itself. Although the brother–sister incest taboo may separate sisters and brothers sexually, a woman's or a man's sexuality as manifested in other culturally reproductive and productive domains, remains too important to the natal group to be completely transferred in marriage to those outside the group. What makes the equivalency rule of exchange misleading is that when siblings marry, they do not relinquish their sibling roles. On the contrary, with marriage these roles now assume weighty economic and political significance for all the participants. To overcome the problem of keeping siblings while giving and taking spouses, sexuality and human reproduction are replaced by a multiplicity of other vital reproductive roles between brothers and sisters as the examples from the Pacific elucidated in this book confirm. These examples show that the human and cultural reproductive work of spouses is enhanced, reenforced, or undermined by the exchange relations of brothers and sisters through the process of keeping-while-giving, a process that simultaneously affirms the historical strength of one's natal group as it authenticates its difference vis-à-vis others. These exchanges are vital for they protect what is not exchanged and, in so doing, provide women a domain of authority and power. Such exchanges are not only contingent upon brother and sister intimacy in one generation but extend to the generational linkages between siblings in their roles as mothers' brothers and fathers' sisters that nurture, command, and support the political potential of each other's children. The potency of sibling sets may even involve sibling ties genealogically removed by several generations as the kinship connections reproduced between the children of siblings anticipate the gender-based power relations in the next generation. By reducing these processes to simplistic acts of reciprocity, anthropologists negatively distort and malign the strategic role of women in human society.

Regardless of how descent is reckoned, the roles of spouses and siblings reveal the possibilities for, and the limitations in, the scale of authority that can be configured through keeping-while-giving. The exchange processes through which these social and political actions are set into motion skew gender relations in particular ways, in some cases bringing women into political prominence, in other situations securing only male hegemony. But the issues are more complex than the analytically prevalent simple symbolic oppositions that equate men with the political domain and women with the domestic, prosaic side of social life. It is the commingling of symbols, not their separation, that reveals the tensions, mystifications, and mediations around the problematics of sexuality and human and cultural reproduction through which political action occurs.

Power relations are not separate from gender relations but are inextricably lodged at the center of how women and men play out their dual roles as siblings and spouses. The processes of keeping-while-giving project political potential onto every essential exchange, making women's reproductive capabilities as siblings and spouses integral to how power is generated. The examples I discussed from Oceania show how women's control over cosmological phenomena is linked directly to human reproduction and provides the most powerful resources for their roles as siblings in cultural reproduction. Throughout the Pacific and other societies of similar political scale, women as sisters and spouses gain their own domains of power through controlling economic resources and protecting inalienable possessions and the various cosmological phenomena that provide authentication of historical, ancestral linkages. When the cosmological source of this authentication is transmitted to material possessions that women produce, the domain of women's power expands. And when women as sisters retain control over inalienable possessions that rank difference politically and therefore authenticate hierarchy, they achieve political authority and power in their own right. In these instances, it is women's control over human and cultural reproduction that is politically vital to the establishment of hierarchy.

The vexing question of how to reproduce the past in and through loss is answered politically by an individual's or a group's efforts to keep inalienable possessions while being challenged to surrender them. Although each local situation reveals an alternate solution to the problem of keeping-while-giving, comparison is possible, not via traditional typologies, but by evaluating ethnographically the intricate processes that both enhance and confine the sources of men's and women's power through their dual exchange roles as siblings and spouses. These are the paradoxical situations that provide comparisons across seemingly diverse culture areas to show how local solutions are disjunctive and partial in their promoting while restricting authority and power.

A further complicating factor is that in the light of human history, women's production, guardianship, and authentication of these unique possessions becomes a target to be undermined by men. Hawaiian priests, Inka rulers, Greek philosophers, Christian clergymen, and Western capitalists, to name only a few, systematically strip away women's control over cosmological resources, thereby denying women's roles in cultural reproduction and restricting their influence to reproducing the species. Today, when we remove the pomp and circumstance that mark a society's political domain, regardless of its economic or political scale we find that men appropriate, subvert, imitate, and generally try to control women's roles in human and cultural reproduction. And when we delve into the histories of Pacific cultures, we find the same historical problems—not because women are closer to nature but because these roles are the key to power for women and for men. In Oceania, the development of ranking and hierarchy depends upon the work of women in their economic roles as the producers of wealth and, most important, in the power of their sacredness in confirming historical and cosmological authentication. These examples also point out how men are constrained politically when women's access to these economic and sacred resources is blocked.

The dominance of elite women in the development of Polynesian hierarchy is not an arbitrary cultural instance. Nor is it merely a capricious act that women's cloth production provides economic and political stability for men and women. When elite women attain high-ranking status and chiefly authority they, like elite men, dominate both untitled women and men. As gender is subsumed by the political domain, dominance of high-ranking over low-ranking people becomes a general issue about the political dimensions of hierarchy that transcend a focus on gender alone. The many examples of gender complementarity between women and men in terms of hard and soft (cloth) possessions, weaving and warfare, and cosmological and political powers attest to the cultural differences surrounding gender that are not interchangeable. Yet to read these examples as oppositions between male and female is to miss entirely the commingling of symbols and actions that define the political domain for men and women in terms of reproducing relationships and possessions in the face of loss. Cloth may be the most apt metaphor to visualize the paradox of keeping-while-giving as societies in all parts of the world associate weaving with acts of tying and unraveling, sacred threads and dangerous dyes, woven warps and unworked woofs, expressions of longed for unity juxtaposed against the realities of death, destruction, and change.

Over the past century, anthropological theory has not accounted for keeping-while-giving or for sibling intimacy. Instead, anthropology remains an accepting partner to the prevailing assumptions about the norm of reciprocity and the singularity of women's sexual and reproductive roles in social life. Bringing these Western ideologies to bear on "primitive" societies, anthropology then became the paramount purveyor of exchange and kinship theories as discovered in other social systems and other cultures. In championing the domain of the Other, however, anthropology has not been notably sensitive to the way its own ideologies are deeply embedded in nineteenth-century Western social theories that were constructed on the basis of a vast intellectual separation between the then relatively unknown "primitive" world and the supposedly rational world of Western economics. My references throughout this book to examples from Western history are specifically directed to overcoming these divisions and to show how the sources of difference and hierarchy are profoundly similar because they arise out of the universal paradox of keeping-while-giving. The solutions to this paradox, in turn, shape other paradoxes that surround the organization of gender and power. Although local solutions are spectacularly diverse—a tribute to human imagination and ingenuity—they are also poignantly distressing. The creative human imagination has made things as diverse as myths, shrouds, crowns, cloaks, and bones into inalienable possessions—the coveted prizes around which wars are fought, leaders installed, and local groups assert their authority.

The mass re-production of capitalism, with its need to generate obsolescence, continually challenges the privileged position of inalienable possessions but the intense longing for possessions to mark who we are has not abated. Commercial traffic in inalienable possessions continues today as auction houses like Sotheby's and Christie's now act as the authenticating purveyor in the transfer of one family's documented heirlooms to another. From the growing commercial revival, as reported recently in *The New York Times,* of "heirloom-worthy jewelry for children" to the celebrated works of art that corporations display to authenticate their reputations, keeping-while-giving is still an extraordinarily active part of Western economics.

Reconfiguring exchange theory to accommodate the world's most ancient and profound economic classification represents only part of the problem. The global and historical presence of inalienable possessions calls our attention as anthropologists to the pressing need to extricate the prejudices in Western social theory from their embeddedness in old ethnographies. It is imperative that we sever what is left of the Enlightenment's partition of humanity into two camps—the "primitive" and the West. To achieve this goal we must recognize that creating inalienable possessions is a human endeavor, universally practiced, and that local manifestations, as diverse as they are, can be compared. But these universal processes are not reducible to orderly typologies or innate structural laws. They are the sources of a society's creative inspirations and they become the exacting paradoxes of social life—persistent dilemmas that can be ameliorated but never resolved. To analyze exchange practices as "wholes" as "systems in their entirety," as Mauss once directed, reduces the scope of our inquiry to an old-fashioned cultural relativism. Where we need to begin is with the gender-encoded spaces in which women and men struggle to manage and alter the ambivalence that surrounds their often visually unremarkable yet symbolically portentious possessions. It is these possessions, encrusted with meaning of identity and pride, that energize the processes of exchange and bear active witness to the paradox of keeping-while-giving.

Understanding the scope and limits of gender-based power in the ethnographic record demands giving serious attention to the essential domains in which women participate in economic and political actions in their own right with their own resources. Since the ethnographic examples from which traditional exchange theories are formulated rely almost exclusively on examples of men's production and men's exchanges, the reproductive energies in such things as women's bones, sacred cloth, hair strings, banana-leaf bundles, weaving poles, and birthing houses, are largely unrecognized or, when recorded, are reduced by anthropologists to prosaic categories lacking economic or political provenience. The increasing ethnographic recovery of what women do or did, previously left out of the ethnographer's published observations, still has not led to revisions in anthropology's most fundamental theoretical assumptions about the norm of reciprocity, gender, and the incest taboo. It is the intent of this book to begin that essential process.

Notes

Introduction

1. My usage of *cloth* is glossed to include all objects made from threads and fibers, such as Australian Aboriginal hairstrings and Maori flax cloaks, leaves such as Trobriand banana-leaf bundles, and bark, such as Polynesian barkcloth.

2. Arens and Karp point out that "power must be viewed as an artifact of the imagination and a facet of human creativity" (1989:xii) and that power must be understood in relation to "other aspects of the encompassing cosmological system" (p. xv).

3. Beidelman 1966:374.

4. Lévi-Strauss [1949]: 1969:497.

5. Bateson [1936] 1958.

6. Unamuno [1921] 1954:9.

7. Ibid.

8. Becker 1973:5.

9. See Wechsler 1985 for a sensitive analysis of the changes in and manipulations of ritual practices by T'ang emperors as they associated themselves with other dynastic emperors from earlier periods. Also see Tambiah 1982 who shows how the mobility of the Sinhala Buddha heightened and sustained the legitimacy of Thai kings; Cort (1989:383–386) shows how Japanese emperors from the Yamata clan gained ascendency over other powerful clans and then created ceremonies and the use of ancient cloths to assert their genealogical connections to powerful neolithic rulers.

10. Becker (1973:15) notes the importance of ancient Egyptian mummification techniques to the Russians as they embalmed "the leader of their Revolution" as a "permanent immortality-symbol." A further footnote is that as the statues of Lenin were being dismantled following the collapse of the Soviet

Union's communist party, some Russians called for the destruction of Lenin's tomb in Moscow and for burial of his body in the family plot in St. Petersburg (*New York Times,* September 7, 1991).

11. Dunlop 1972. During this stage of initiation, the boys in the film are also adorned with shells and net bags that their mothers or other female relatives have given them. Overall this part of the film sets a different tone on the role of Baruya women than is evident from Maurice Godelier's ethnographic study, *The Making of Great Men* (1986), in which Godelier writes that women are excluded from the material means of production and therefore are completely dominated by men.

12. Sahlins 1985:xii.

13. Marx [1867] 1976:711–724.

14. Tambiah 1982 and 1984.

15. Bean 1989:373; Cohn 1989.

16. Benjamin uses the word *aura* to signify the uniqueness of original works of art. This uniqueness is determined by "the history to which it was subject throughout the time of its existence" and in the age of mechanical reproduction, it is this aura that "withers" ([1955] 1969:220–221).

17. Myers 1986.

18. See Murra 1989 for a revised version of his earlier essay. Although in many other climates cloth disintegrates more rapidly than hard objects, archaeological remains of spinning and weaving implements can give some indication of cloth production.

19. See the essays in Weiner and Schneider 1989.

20. Pierre Bourdieu 1976:141.

21. Engels [1884] 1972. But also see Leacock 1972, 1981 who argued strongly against the oversimplification of analyzing women's roles only from narrow perceptions of the "family" unit. See Ginsburg and Rapp (in press) for a comprehensive review of recent research on the "politics of reproduction." See also Ginsburg's (1989) analysis of how the abortion debate in the United States has roots in the nineteenth-century history of women's social movements in which women's roles as mothers have been the source of their cultural authority while denying them authority in economic and political domains.

22. Atkinson 1982; MacCormack and Strathern 1980; O'Brien 1981; Rapp 1987; and Sacks 1979.

23. Ortner 1974.

24. G. Rubin 1975.

25. M. Strathern 1988.

26. Rousseau [1762] 1966.

27. See discussions of this problem from a Marxist perspective in Sacks (1979); also see, e.g., Bennett (1983) on Nepali high-caste women who as wives are given negative status whereas as sisters their ritual purity and association with cosmological forces give them high status. Anthropologists doing field research in Polynesia have long noted the importance of the "sacred sister" (see Goldman 1970; Gunson 1987; Huntsman and Hooper 1975; M. Mead 1930).

28. Marc Shell (1988) points out that some orders built monasteries and

nunneries together as "double cloisters" and a few cloisters even allowed for cohabiting Sisters and Brothers. Not only was "spiritual siblingship" fundamental but sibling incest was admitted as a "universal principle" (pp. 181–182). See also Shell pp. 49–75 and n. 44.

29. These particular examples have been selected only because of my own interests in applying these analytical criteria to a diverse range of societies.

Chapter 1: Inalienable Possessions

1. Malinowski 1922:95. Malinowski also writes, "every ceremony, every legal and customary act is done to the accompaniment of material gift and counter gift" (1922:167).

2. In Weiner 1980, I present a more detailed account of this problem in Trobriand ethnography as I initially resolved it by introducing the term *replacement* to show that when certain things were given to others, they had to be replaced with other kinds of wealth in order to have these possessions returned.

3. Malinowski 1922:178.

4. Ibid.:182.

5. Ibid.:179.

6. Ibid.:176–177.

7. Mauss [1925] 1954:71.

8. See also Firth 1951:123–131.

9. Malinowski 1926:40. Although Malinowski noted Mauss's objection, he wrote that he had already thought of it himself and so he had reached his conclusions independently (p. 41, n. 1). In fact, Raymond Firth had helped Malinowski with editorial work on this book and had raised some of these issues with him (Firth, personal communication).

10. Malinowski 1926:41.

11. Mauss [1925] 1954:24; see also Leach 1957:133–137.

12. Lévi-Strauss [1949] 1969:116.

13. Ibid.:496.

14. "These gifts are either exchanged immediately for equivalent gifts or are received by the beneficiaries on condition that at a later date they will give counter-gifts often exceeding the original goods in value, but which in their turn bring about a subsequent right to receive new gifts surpassing the original ones in sumptuousness" (Lévi-Strauss [1949] 1969:52).

15. Initially, Lévi-Strauss praised *Essai sur le don* as inaugurating a new era for the social sciences, much as phonology had done for linguistics ([1950] 1987:41). But Lévi-Strauss also concludes that it was Mauss's attempt to develop theory solely out of ethnographic facts that prevented him from fully recognizing the structural features of exchange.

16. Locke [1690] 1963.

17. Smith [1776] 1937.

18. Cited in Meek 1967:303, n. 36.

19. As Albert O. Hirschman (1977) so perceptively describes, during the eighteenth century the economic and philosophical problem was how to hold men's passions in check so they could pursue their own individual interests without the state's control.

20. In *The Wealth of Nations* ([1776] 1937), Smith reiterates his earlier claims that individuals must have the freedom to pursue their own economic interests which, even if this freedom were misappropriated by some, in the long run, still would create positive economic results. See also Hirschman 1977:70–80 on the Baron de Montesquieu's views about the advantages of commerce that would overcome any disproportionate riches.

21. But Hirschman (1977:4) argues that scholars have missed the importance of how much "the new arose out of the old."

22. Dumont writes that relations between "men" that traditionally formed the primary mode of interaction in holistic, hierarchical societies were supplanted by relations between "men and things that now predominate in modern, individualistic society" (1977:5–6).

23. See Baldwin's (1970:228–251; 261–295) excellent discussion of these economic issues.

24. Little 1978:213.

25. Ibid. The appearance of urban saints, notably St. Francis of Assisi, the patron saint of merchants, further stimulated wealthy merchants to give huge sums of money to religious services and institutions (ibid.: 216–217). See also Baldwin 1970; Kettering 1988; M. Rubin 1987; and White 1988.

26. Cited in Maine 1875:244.

27. Durkheim [1893] 1984:21–22.

28. Durkheim [1912] 1965.

29. Ibid.:495.

30. Malinowski 1922:89.

31. Ibid.:19.

32. Malinowski 1926:52.

33. Ibid.:52–54.

34. Maine 1875:264.

35. Maine wrote that "the history of Roman Property Law is the history of the assimilation of Res Mancipi to Res Nec Mancipi. The history of Property on the European Continent is the history of the subversion of the feudalistic law of land by the Romanised law of moveables; and though the history of ownership in England is not nearly completed, it is visibly the law of personality which threatens to absorb and annihilate the law of realty" (1875:264–265).

36. Benveniste [1969] 1973. I thank Beidelman for this reference. In a fascinating essay, Michael Herzfeld (1980) explores definitions of terms for property in a contemporary Greek village, pointing out his difficulty in understanding these terms when he initially assumed they were abstract, legal terms. In fact, these terms define inalienable and alienable property, especially in relation to marriage and dowry payments, and the context in which the terms are used (whether, for example, a man is talking about his wife's property or his own, or vice versa) is critical to their meanings.

37. Simmel ([1907] 1978:240–241) further notes that by the beginning of the fourteenth century, almost half the English soil and, at the time of Philip II, half the Spanish soil was owned by the clergy. Just as the Catholic church stood for the inalienable moral obligations of life, it also encompassed the foundation in the real as well as the symbolic sense. Beidelman (1989) shows in other ways how much anthropologists have neglected the importance of Simmel's work on exchange.

38. Marc Bloch (1961) and Georges Duby (1980) have written about these gifts to saints and there has been extended discussion without much consensus about the history of these practices as well as the kinship connections that lie behind these signatures. Only certain members of a family signed a petition and their kinship relations differed from one case to another. But see White's study (1988), which I draw on for my discussion, for excellent insights into these practices.

39. White (1988:109–114) also emphasizes that these material returns were flexible and variable, making the whole question of kinship in relation to the signing of the *laudatio* much more complex than earlier writers supposed.

40. White emphasizes how instrumental the practical role of medieval ritual was in reproducing medieval social structure. He also cautions that these bequests to saints were not conflict-free. These transactions (as with exchange events) could be undermined and negotiated for different ends (1988:162, 172–173).

41. White 1988:26–31, 158–169.

42. Cited in Laslett 1963:114. The law professor, Margaret Radin, points out that Locke's view of the body as personal property leads to "interesting paradoxes" as bodily parts, such as blood for transfusions, hair for wigs, and organs for transplantations, become fungible commodities (1982:966).

43. According to Locke, only in this way could men proceed "from the abstract world of liberty and equality based on their relationship with God and natural law, to the concrete world of political liberty guaranteed by political arrangements" (Laslett 1963:115).

44. I thank Beidelman for pointing out to me that the interplay between wealthy merchants and poor nobility was part of a much older pattern. The Samurai married Osaka merchants' daughters, and the grandfather of Elizabeth I was merely a merchant, although a very wealthy one. Similar connections were established across the Atlantic as noble families such as the Marlbouroughs took rich American wives.

45. In *The Return of Cultural Treasures* (1989), Jeanette Greenfield documents the legal cases concerning the return not only of the renown Icelandic manuscripts and the Elgin marbles, but also pre-Columbian art, Maori carvings, and Benin bronzes.

46. See Hirschman (1977:109–113) for an extended discussion of this contradiction.

47. Quoted in ibid.:101.

48. Ibid.:121.

49. Hirschman (ibid.:95, n.g) comments that the hopes and fears concern-

ing the eighteenth-century growth of alienable wealth is paralleled in the late twentieth century by contradictory attitudes regarding the growth of multinational corporations.

50. Simmel [1907] 1978:102, 174–176, 240–241.

51. Grahame Clark (1986:100–101) discusses how the named gems embedded in Western dynastic and Papal crowns often were picked out and sold in emergencies or usurped by other rulers. The jewels remained irreplaceable, not merely because they were precious stones but because of the history they represented. Clark also notes that even when European monarchs lost gems to others through warfare or because of financial circumstances, the gold crown frames rarely were taken; these remained inalienable.

52. Hayden 1987:150.

53. Ibid.:151.

54. In chapter 4, I discuss these views more fully. The extensive and complex myths of the origins of ancestors and social groups that comprise the Australian Aboriginal Dreaming are connected to actual geographical locations, such as caves, stones, and streams, so that the inalienability of the landscape gives material form to the myths. See Munn 1973:23–24; Myers 1986:57–58; also see Basso 1984 on similar relationships among the Apache Indians.

55. See Carruthers 1990 on the numerous devices that people used during medieval times to memorize extraordinarily lengthy texts.

56. Frederick Soddy, a Nobel-prize winning chemist, subsequently published a book on economics, *Wealth, Virtual Wealth and Debt,* in which for the most part he holds to all sorts of out-of-date nineteenth-century evolutionary notions. But his insightful observation on how food and fuel differ from all other commodities has relevance to my discussion (1933:116–118).

57. Kahn 1986.

58. Young 1971:195–196.

59. Simmel ([1907] 1978:240) considered that landed property was valued above any utility it might have because men had "a relation of sovereign power over the soil."

60. Veblen 1899:38.

61. Before the United States Constitution was amended in the nineteenth century, only men who owned land had the right to vote and in many contemporary rural U.S. communities today, local taxes are calculated on the acreage of land owned rather than on earned income.

62. Out of a total of 56,000,000 acres, the British Crown, for example, owns 274,000 acres and the Duke of Buccleuch, 300,000 acres (Hayden 1987:113–115).

63. Similar beliefs occur among the Wape of Papua New Guinea whose ancestors' ghosts reside within their lineage lands to ensure the fertility of its resources (Mitchell 1987).

64. Strehlow 1947:117. Strehlow notes elsewhere that stealing a tjurunga was also avenged by death (p. 19).

65. Henry 1928:189.

66. Of course, Durkheim never lived to see how fascism drew on the sacred

to consecrate an official ideology whose totalitarian aim was to destroy democratic diversity.

67. See Richman 1990:183–214 on the founding of the *Collège de sociologie* and the formation of a "sacred sociology." Also see Webster 1990:266–299 on the relation of the members of the *Collège de sociologie* to the Surrealist movement. See also Clifford 1981; Bürger [1974] 1984.

68. Even though Bataille saw how the sacred supported the rise of fascism when, in Germany and Italy, what he called the "right side" of the sacred became organized militarily, he thought that the "left side" of the sacred contained a source of power that would enhance, rather than suppress, freedom (see, e.g., Richman 1982). His theory of expenditure influenced in important ways the work of Jean Baudrillard (1972) and Sahlins (1972).

69. Benjamin [1955]1969:223.

70. See Heimonet 1988:129–148.

Chapter 2: Reconfiguring Exchange Theory

1. Edmund Leach (1957:127) called Malinowski an "obsessional empiricist" at once both a rebel against late nineteenth-century mechanistic thought but still a "child of his time," a victim of "those very epistemological windmills against which he charged so valiantly." See Weiner 1987 for another discussion of this problem in relation to Malinowski's Trobriand ethnography.

2. Malinowski 1922:89.

3. Ibid.

4. Ibid. But in the next sentence Malinowski writes: "With reverence he also would name them, and tell their history, and by whom and when they were worn, and how they changed hands, and how their temporary possession was a great sign of the importance and glory of the village."

5. Ibid.:512.

6. Ibid.:513.

7. Ibid.:513–514.

8. In an earlier essay, "Origines de la notion de monnaie" ([1914], 1969) Mauss already had surveyed Malaysian and Polynesian sources for information on property and sacred possessions.

9. There have been four major reanalyses of Mauss's views: Firth [1929] 1959; Johansen 1954; Lévi-Strauss [1950] 1987; and Sahlins 1968 with numerous replies and reanalyses, including Gathercole 1978; Guidieri 1984; and MacCormack 1982. Much of the data in this chapter are taken from my earlier essay published in *American Ethnologist* titled "Inalienable Wealth" (Weiner 1985a), but the theoretial scope has been expanded.

10. Sahlins 1972:160. In Weiner 1985a I present an extended discussion of Firth's critique of Mauss's analysis and Sahlins's reinterpretation of the hau, neither of which I elaborate on here.

11. Mauss [1925] 1954:41–42. In French medieval legal codes things *immeuble* include landed estates and other fixed property, whereas *meuble* designates personal property, chattel, and other things that can be alienated. Yet in the first English edition of *Essai sur le don* (ibid., 7) *immeuble* when used for Samoan fine mats is translated "indestructible property" and "real property" whereas in the second edition (Mauss [1925] 1990:9), the same references are translated "permanent paraphernalia" and "fixed property—immovable because of their destination" still obscuring for English-speaking readers the relevance of inalienable possessions. Later in that second edition, Mauss [1925] (ibid., 134, n. 245) notes that the Kwakiutl have two kinds of coppers: the more important ones that do not go out of the family and others that are of less value which in their circulation seem to be "satellites" for the first kind. See also Mauss ([1925] 1954:89, n. 17) on Samoan fine mats as "heirlooms."

12. In the first English edition, when Mauss ([1925] 1954:6) first refers to Samoan exchanges of *ie toga* and *oloa,* the terms are translated "masculine and feminine property," respectively. The French term for such exchange is *utérin.* See Weiner 1989:50–51 for a discussion of the problems surrounding the ethnographic reporting of Samoan exchanges of fine mats for oloa, as described in Shore 1982.

13. Mauss [1925] 1990:10.

14. In citing cognates Mauss ([1925] 1990:10) mentions other objects such as "precious articles, talismans, emblems, mats and sacred idols, sometimes even the traditions, cults, and magic rituals," thus confusing the issue. But in Tahitian, *taoa* means property or goods, and in ancient Tahiti, barkcloth was among the most valued wealth objects. In Tonga, *tooga* refers to fine mats, and in Mangareva, *toga* is the word for a cloak made from the paper mulberry tree. Among the Maori, *taonga* refer to nephrite objects and to woven cloaks, often called "mats" in the early literature; in a footnote on Maori taonga, Mauss is more precise: they include "the *pounamu,* the famous jades, the sacred property of the chiefs and the clans, usually the *tiki,* very rare, very personal, and very well carved; then there are various sorts of mats, one of which, doubtless emblazoned as in Samoa, bears the name *korowai*" (ibid., 91, n. 32).

15. Schneider and Weiner 1989:20–26; see also Lefferts 1983; March 1983; Cort 1989; Feeley-Harnik 1989; Gittinger 1979; Hoskins 1989; Messick 1987; Rubenstein 1986; J. Schneider 1987, 1989; Stone-Ferrier 1989.

16. Even with the economic value of Polynesian cloth and its political significance (Weiner 1982a, 1985a, 1989, and Weiner and Schneider 1989), not to mention women's centrality in its circulation, scholars (e.g., Goldman 1970; Kirch 1984; Ortner 1981; Sahlins 1958, 1972) continually overlook these objects as well as the women who make them in discussions of Polynesian political hierarchy. For descriptions of Polynesian cloth production see Buck 1924, 1964; Kooijman 1972, 1977; S. Mead 1969 on Maori cloaks; Gailey 1987 and Small 1987 on the economic implications of Tongan barkcloth production; Teckle 1984 on Fijian barkcloth production and exchange; and Rubenstein 1986 on Micronesian cloth production and its symbolic importance.

17. See Weiner and Schneider 1989 and J. Schneider 1987.

18. Mauss [1925] 1990:11.

19. Ibid. The text was first translated by Elsdon Best (1909:439) as it was told to him by his noted Maori informant, Tamati Ranapiri, and since then it has undergone many translations: Mauss's revised quotation of Best's translation (Mauss 1925), the first English translation of Mauss (1954), and the second as cited here as well as Professor Bruce Biggs's translation as quoted in Sahlins (1968 also 1972); it has also undergone innumerable critiques and reinterpretations. In the original Maori text, Ranapiri describes a series of exchanges in which the return for a valuable that passes from *A* to *B* to *C* would go from *C* through *B* and back to *A*. Note the similarity between this kind of exchange and Malinowski's description of Trobriand kula. Mauss was aware of these similarities when he wrote *The Gift* and this description, based on both Mauss and Malinowski, would later become Lévi-Strauss's ([1949] 1969) formulation of "generalized reciprocity."

20. Biggs in his translation of Ranapiri's text as cited in Sahlins (1968, 1972) used the word *valuable* each time Ranapiri referred to *taonga*.

21. Looking carefully at Best's translation, however, we immediately find a source of confusion because Best translated *taonga* with a variety of words such as "item," "article," "present," and "goods," indicating that he attached no significance to Ranapiri's use of *taonga*. Mauss must have recognized Best's inconsistency because in the middle of the text, he substituted *taonga* for Best's varied translation.

22. Pendergrast 1987:4.

23. Generically the flax is *Phormium tenax*. The Maori word base *kahu* is a reflex of the Proto-Polynesian term *kafu*, which means covering or cloth. See Best 1898b; Buck 1924; S. Mead 1969; Pendergrast 1987; Roth [1923] 1979 for discussions of production, styles, and weaving techniques.

24. Buck 1950:462; H. W. Williams [1844] 1975:84.

25. Best 1914, 1929b.

26. H. W. Williams [1844] 1975:84–85; Buck 1950:462.

27. Shortland 1882:107; Tregear 1891:113.

28. Best 1905/1906:12–15; Buck 1950:462–465; Shortland 1882:294. In ancient Hawaii, if a miscarriage occurred, the fetus acquired mana and became a deified spirit (Pukui 1942:378–379). In the Marquesas, even the first menstruation of a chiefly woman was attended with elaborate tapus that celebrated her potency (Thomas 1987:129).

29. Best states that "in Maori myth and belief the female sex is assigned an inferior position generally, and is spoken of as being connected with evil, misfortune, and death" (1924a:222). He notes, for example, that the spirit of the aborted fetus is thought to develop into a dangerous and malevolent spirit (*atua*). Yet in another source, Best reports these same spirits from miscarriages might be cultivated into war gods so that their power could be directed against powerful enemies (1905/1906:15). In Samoa, ancestral spirits (*aitu*) are believed to come into being from clots of blood and miscarriages (Cain 1971). See also the differences in two of Best's publications where he discusses the sacred and profane aspects of Maori women (1905/1906:16) and Maori men (1902:25).

30. The controversies over the meaning of mana have been especially

longlasting: e.g., Codrington 1891; Firth 1940; Hocart 1914, 1922; Hubert and Mauss [1898] 1964 (see Mauss 1975); Keesing 1984; Shore 1989; Valeri 1985. There has always been general agreement, however, that mana is associated with chiefly power—implicitly male chiefly power.

31. Valerio Valeri (1985:95–105) provides an extensive review of the major anthropological interpretations of mana and then relates them to his interpretation of how mana was used in ancient Hawaii.

32. Codrington 1891:51–52, 119–121.

33. Ibid.:57.

34. Hubert and Mauss [1898] 1964.

35. See, Firth 1940:483–484 on mana. Elsewhere Firth writes that "Mauss appears to have misinterpreted the Maori concept of the hau by ascribing to this 'vital essence' qualities with which it is not really endowed" ([1929] 1959:419).

36. Mauss 1975:121.

37. This same pragmatic meaning of mana has also been reported by, Firth (1940); Hocart (1922); and Hogbin (1935/1936).

38. Keesing 1984:152.

39. Gernet 1981:144. In writing about mana, Hubert and Mauss, following Durkheim's theory of the sacred, suggest that the quality of mana has a definite place in society in that it most often is considered to exist "outside the normal world and normal practices" (Mauss 1975:119). From a different perspective, Benjamin ([1955] 1969:221) emphasizes that works of art contain a "sensitive nucleus" that is "the essence of all that is transmissible from its beginning, ranging from its substantive duration to its testimony of the history which it has experienced."

40. Such importance associated with cloth as a conduit of ancestral power is found in many parts of the world. In the Yoruba Egungun cult in West Africa, where tailored cloth displays patrilineal solidarity, uncut cloth figures in the Efe–Gelede cult invokes the spiritual powers of elder women, female ancestors, and their deified spirits (Drewal 1979:197–198).

41. Aarne A. Koskinen (1972:104–105) argues that mana's primary meaning is procreative power, an interpretation described by other male scholars as male procreative power. See the same views espoused more recently by Sahlins (1981:15–17) and Valeri (1985:330–331).

42. Valeri 1985:104. Valeri argues that in ancient Hawaii only Hawaiian chiefs mediated between the "pure divine" and the human world whereas women occupied the "feminine destructive polluting pole" (ibid.: 113, 123–124). Sherry Ortner's essay on Polynesian gender and political hierarchy reveals how even feminist authors rely on misread classic interpretations. Ortner maintains that in Polynesia "negative ideology concerning women centers upon their sexual and reproductive activities" (1981:395). But Neil Gunson (1987:168) emphasizes that Polynesian "chiefly women, both sacred and secular, have obviously played an important role" and that studies that "do not give a prominent place to the political activities and social influence of women are likely to be in need of drastic revision." Discussing Marquesian gender and rank, Nicholas Thomas (1987) concludes that "women of higher rank were less

sharply distinguished from men than common women in respect of tapu rules and political action, as well as economically" (p. 138). See also Linnekin 1990 on Hawaiian women as sacred queens.

43. For references to mana and barkcloth see Valeri 1985:100, 290–295. On women as goddesses see Valeri 1985:101, 245, 274); and Linnekin 1990:24–28. And on reproduction see Valeri 1985:98, 270, 276, 287.

44. See Sahlins 1985:139–140 on Hawaii and the ancient Maori (ibid.: 55); but also see Weiner's(1985a:221–222) discussion of the gender implications of Sahlins's interpretation of the Maori hau.

45. Best 1898a:129; Buck 1924; S. Mead 1969. All weaving was done by women, except for certain kinds of dog-skin cloaks that were used in warfare and sometimes attended to by men. In many other societies, women's rituals of childbirth are similar to those practiced in cloth production. For example, among the Iban of Indonesia, women observe sacred taboos during childbirth, whereas Iban men follow the same sacred taboos during their headhunting attacks. Similar rituals were observed by women in the intricate preparation in which parts of bundles of unwoven fibers are first dyed to create aesthetic shadings of colors when the fibers are woven (Gittinger 1979:218–219).

46. Hanson and Hanson 1983:88–94.

47. T. W. Gudgeon describes the "truly great Ngatiporpu chieftainess, Hine Matiora" who ruled over hundreds of people and was known for her "beauty and wisdom" (1885:53). J. L. Nicholas (1817, 2:111) in an early account reports that women in the New Zealand Northland were permitted to speak on the *marae*, a council meeting place, as were women among East Coast tribes. Today, women are forbidden to speak publicly on the marae in other parts of the country (see Salmond 1975:149–152).

48. Heuer 1972:37. See also Best 1924b, 2:451.

49. S. Mead, personal communication.

50. Shortland 1882:29.

51. Best 1924a:158; Smith 1910:221.

52. Hanson and Hanson 1983:88–94; Weiner 1985a:221–223.

53. Best 1924a:10.

54. Shortland 1882:29.

55. Colenso 1868:355; Best 1905/1906:21. The stone used for chiefly weapons and ornaments is often identified as jade (see Watt 1986:157). I use nephrite throughout the text because, usually, the most valued taonga were made from this material.

56. According to Shortland (1851:37), the best quality stone used to cut the umbilical cord was called *Kahurangi,* the cloak of heaven.

57. See Best 1914, 1929a, 1929b. The ritual components differed from one geographical place to another, but the general ideologies were similar.

58. Best writes, "when presenting a cloak to a person, it would be laid outspread . . . so that the upper pan, the collar, would be next to him. When gifts were made in a house . . . a garment was deposited so that the neck [i.e., the collar] faced the window," which was a sacred pan of the house (1929b:35). *Whiri* is the Maori word for collar and the ancient term for plaiting mats (Best 1898b:652).

59. Best 1929a:248.

60. See the chants discussed in Best 1929a:250; also see S. Mead 1969:169; Taylor [1855] 1870. The gender differentiation between women and weaving and men and warfare is significant since both activities are tapu, but Maori women were not excluded from engaging in warfare.

61. Best 1929a:250.

62. Although Best made no mention of the bestowal of hau in the above discussion, in another publication he noted that in this ceremony the infant is endowed with "life, vigor . . . and the *hau-oro,* i.e., the hau of life or living hau" (1900/1901:93). See also Taylor [1855] 1870:76.

63. Gathercole (1978), pointing out the difficulty in relying completely on Best's work, referred to this early description by W. E. Gudgeon (1905).

64. W. E. Gudgeon 1905:127.

65. Tregear 1904:387. Best (1905/1906:165) describes a similar ritual among the Tuhoe in which the spirit of the deceased is believed to be sent on its way with flax about the mouth.

66. Best 1901:88.

67. Buck 1950:161.

68. Buck 1924.

69. Davidson 1984:74, 83–84; Golson 1959; Simmons 1968.

70. Of importance at this time were ornaments made from human bones, moa bones, whale ivory, and whale teeth.

71. Bellwood 1979:388. See Davidson 1984:83–84 for another description of human bones made into pendants.

72. Best 1924b, 2:54.

73. Polack 1838, 2:72.

74. Best 1914:160.

75. Palmer 1946:270.

76. Best 1929b, 2:55. The Hawaiian example in which chiefs worried about securing the highest secrecy for the burial of their bones in order to prevent rivals from making them into fishhooks addresses the same issue.

77. Firth [1929] 1959:389.

78. Taylor [1855] 1870:99–100.

79. Best 1924b:174. There is a similar connection here with the naming rituals in relation to the sacred window space and the sacred collars of cloaks.

80. S. Mead 1969:175.

81. Best 1912:175.

82. See Angas 1847, 1:335; Best 1903:62, 1912:215–216, 1924b:115, 1959:314–315; Firth [1929] 1959:354, n. 1; H. W. Williams [1844] 1975: 99; Yate 1835:151, for examples. Although each tribe had its own origin stories and genealogies of its most sacred taonga, what all taonga had in common "was their ability to act as a focus for ancestral power and talk" (Salmond 1984:118).

83. According to T. E. Donne ([1859] 1927:202), the parietal bone as well as whalebone were fashioned into hei-tiki neck pendants and "such a memento would be very much revered, and both the chief, whose head provided the

bone, and the wearer of the tiki would be honoured." Robin Watt (1986:158), however, dismisses the existing museum specimens as forgeries and questions whether the Maori did indeed have a tradition of fashioning hei-tiki from human parietal bones.

84. In fact, the many other objects carved from bones suggest that the hei-tiki may represent a transition from bone ornaments to nephrite weapons, as such weapons became prominent with expanding political factions. Donne ([1859] 1927:198–201) suggested that although the bones of the deceased were finally interred, the hei-tiki remained to circulate among the relatives of the deceased. The hei-tiki, he noted, "acquire some of the personality, actual identity, or spirit, of their owners, and thus . . . [they] become a virtual part of their living existence" (p. 198). Yate (1835:152) described the manner in which a hei-tiki would be wept and sung over in remembrance of the person to whom the ornament had once belonged.

85. S. Mead 1984:223.

86. Firth [1929] 1959:389, n. 3. In fact, the relation between Maori cloaks and land is clear in an example about the burial of the umbilical cord. When a child was born, the umbilical cord was buried on the land to which the child had rights and the cord was wrapped in a piece of "old garment"—a woven cloak (Colenso 1868:362).

87. Payments to religious experts for training others were also made in cloaks and nephrite possessions (Best 1914:156, 1924b:4).

88. Cruise in 1823 reported that a family wept over the cloak of their son as though it were the corpse (cited in S. Mead 1969:176). Tregear (1904:392) noted: "After the body was buried these mats [cloaks] were displayed and traditions connected with them were expounded by the elders." See also Buck 1950:420.

89. See, e.g., Angas 1847, 2:70; Buck 1950:420; Polack 1838, 2:72; Tregear 1904:390–391. For a time, Westernmade blankets replaced cloaks in these exchanges when Europeans and Americans engaged in a brisk flax trade, paying the Maori in guns and blankets (see K. Sinclair 1961:25–29). The Maori, anxious for both items, vigorously engaged in cash cropping until the British found that the flax was not strong enough for their needs. Firth cites several mid-nineteenth-century reports of exchanges where, in one case, "roast pigs, baskets [of] potatoes, and dried fish piled up, with [a] row of blankets intended as presents to friends exceeded a mile in length" and in another event, there were Witney blankets "nearly 400 yds. long . . . and 1,000 more besides as presents" ([1929] 1959:329). Yet with these changes, the importance of taonga as inalienable possessions did not die out.

90. Geary 1986:179.

91. The *New York Times* of October 14, 1988, reported that the shroud of Turin still was thought to be significant, "helping believers honor the holy person."

92. For the Iban, no man's honor was recognized until he had taken the head of an enemy; no woman was granted esteem until she wove a beautiful ikat cloth, whose designs had mythic origins. The laying out of the warps for

the loom was called the "warpath of women" and the heads of men's victims had to be wrapped in these sacred textiles before they could be stored in ceremonial houses (Gittinger 1979:218–219).

93. Firth [1929] 1959:355.

94. S. Mead, personal communication.

95. If a chief wanted to make a place sacred, he took a thread from his cloak and tied it to a pole in the ground (Taylor [1855] 1870:56). Palmer (1946: 270) notes that during the Hone Heke wars, the halting place of the army was decided upon when a leader deposited his cloak at the spot: "The mana of the recognized cloak was sufficient to halt the straggling column without a word or command."

96. Taylor [1855] 1870:56–58; S. P. Smith 1910:289. Best noted that if a well-born member of one tribe marries someone from another tribe, "he or she will act as a 'cord' [flax thread] to draw that tribe to our assistance in war" (1914:159).

97. For example, men were known to kill others just to obtain a particularly fine and well-known cloak (S. P. Smith 1910:193–194). In one account, the head of a chief could be returned to his clan only by the payment of a nephrite weapon, a cloak, or land (Best 1912:179).

98. Donne [1859] 1927:189–190.

99. S. Mead 1969:176; see also Best 1912:216.

100. Tregear 1904:393; see also S. Mead 1969:175.

101. Best 1912:216.

102. Trade in cloaks was as extensive as trade in nephrite adzes or traffic in bones (Polack 1838, 1:39; see also Best 1912:314; Colenso 1868:345–355; McNab 1908:375–376; Shortland 1851:36–37).

103. Metge 1976:260.

104. Quoted and translated by Salmond (1984:119). Salmond describes taonga as fixed points in the tribal network of names, histories, and relationships. They belonged to particular ancestors, are passed down particular descent lines, held their own stories, and were exchanged on certain memorable occasions. "Taonga captured history and showed it to the living, and they echoed patterns of the past from first creation to the present" (ibid.:118).

105. Angas (1847, 1:319), for example, described a feast in which the piles of food and gifts were over a mile long. Also see the list of such nineteenth-century exchanges in Firth ([1929] 1959:328–329).

106. Salmond (1975:2) writes that today the traditional territories that were controlled by the descent groups are largely symbolic since the land was sold or confiscated. Only the marae still exists as inalienable property as one man said, without the marae, "We are nothing."

107. S. Mead 1984:223. Mead also notes that sacred taonga adzes were set into carved handles. When a chief of the tribe died, the new handle was made and lashed to the blade: "Thus a new *ariki* [chief] was visibly proclaimed. During his lifetime it was the insignia of his rank; on his death the handle would be cut off and placed with his body" (ibid., 184).

108. Mauss [1925] 1990:91, n. 32.

109. S. Mead 1984:192.

Chapter 3: The Sibling Incest Taboo

1. For ease of reading, I am more narrowly using *sibling* to refer only to the relationship between sisters and brothers unless otherwise noted.

2. See n. 27 in the introduction and also n. 42 in chapter 2.

3. The debates have never ceased on the issues of sibling incest. See discussions of these debates and various conclusions in, Arens 1986; Goody 1956; D. Schneider 1976; also see de Heusch (1958) on the significance of sibling incest in African monarchies.

4. I recognize that Samoa and Hawaii each represent a different Polynesian cultural division and I am not suggesting any particular point of contact in the rise of political stratification. Samoa is part of Western Polynesia that includes other islands such as Pukapuka, Tonga, and the Tokelaus. Hawaii, in Eastern Polynesia, is culturally related to Tahiti, New Zealand, Easter Island, and the Marquesas. Burrows (1940) wrote a classic paper on these cultural and geographical divisions. See also Oliver 1989; Shore 1989.

5. Discriminations are made by elaborate physical and social taboos; Weiner 1976:49–50, 237–238.

6. Thomas (1989) also points out that the Melanesia–Polynesia division has been overdrawn. This dichotomy and the corresponding diagnostic features of "equality" and "hierarchy" have thereby inhibited a more comprehensive understanding of Pacific Island societies.

7. I thank Gyorgy Feher for directing me to this quotation as cited in Shell 1988:17.

8. Freud [1908] 1968:177.

9. Malinowski [1929] 1987:416.

10. Fortes 1953, 1958; but see Barnes 1973; and especially D. Schneider 1968a.

11. Lévi-Strauss [1949] 1969:25.

12. Fortes 1957; Leach 1957; D. Schneider 1968a; Spiro 1982.

13. Malinowski 1927:80–81. Melford Spiro (1982) argues that not only was Malinowski mistaken in his ethnographic interpretations but that the Trobrianders have a more severe Oedipal complex than is found in Western societies. See Weiner (1985b) for a different point of view.

14. Jones (1925) further showed that Trobriand conceptions of procreation in which the father was denied any role were unconscious expressions of the child's hostility toward his father, a view expanded by Robin Fox (1980) and Spiro (1982).

15. Parsons 1964; see Spiro 1982 for a traditional Freudian reinterpretation of Malinowski's assumptions about the Trobriand Oedipal complex.

16. Beidelman 1971:181–201. Ultimately he suggests that these incidents may be "a highly condensed way of describing the insoluble paradoxes or tensions centering upon the conflict between authority, age, and sexuality" (p. 196).

17. See Hopkins 1980 for many instances of brother–sister marriages in Roman Egypt.

18. In the Buganda monarchy of East Africa, a woman and her brother ruled together. Each had a separate palace, army, and retainers (Ray 1991).

19. Lévi-Strauss [1949] 1969; D. Schneider 1961.

20. Groves 1963:15–30.

21. All chiefly matrilineages are ranked vis-à-vis each other and only the chiefs from the highest-ranking ones are polygynous. But even these chiefs will not find wives unless they can demonstrate their political power (see Weiner 1976:44–50).

22. Malinowski also reports this: "The *waiwaia* [spirit child] is conveyed by a *baloma* [an ancestor] belonging to the same subclan as the woman, . . . the carrier is even as a rule some near *veiola* [matrilineal kin]" (1954:220). Some Trobrianders say a female relative brought the child, but others insist it must be a male relative, emphasizing the ambiguity. In the specific examples Malinowski gives, it is most often a man (ibid.:219). Even today, when most villagers are aware of Western biological explanations, many still point out how pregnancy began with dreams of male ancestors bringing the spirit child (see Weiner 1976:121–122, 1988:53–55 for other examples).

23. Malinowski 1922:177–180. Men also give their children food and other things. When children become adults they, in turn, support their fathers in economic ways that directly benefit their father and the members of his matrilineage. See Weiner 1976:121–167 for an in-depth discussion of the exchange relations that involve a man as father.

24. This controversy has had a long-standing history in anthropology (Delaney 1986; Franklin 1988; Leach 1966; D. Schneider 1968b; Spiro 1968, 1982; Weiner 1976, 1988).

25. Malinowski [1929] 1987:440.

26. Lévi-Strauss [1949] 1969:496. Lévi-Strauss goes on to show that the authority figures are men who reverse the disequilibrium created by giving a woman to another group of men whereas their children only serve to validate the perpetuation of these alliances through time.

27. See Weiner 1976, 1988 for details of these exchanges, which differ somewhat from Malinowski's descriptions.

28. Although this kind of marriage rarely occurs, most marriages are with a father's sister's daughter three generations removed (also called *tabu*) so that the rule of marriage given by Trobrianders is accurate in the majority of cases (Weiner 1979). Also see Fortes 1957; E. Leach 1958; Malinowski [1929] 1987 for earlier arguments about Trobriand kinship terms and father's sister's daughter's marriage.

29. See the same themes in Malinowski [1929] 1987:429–443 and Weiner 1987.

30. Feher (1990) points out these differences. The original text recorded and transcribed by Malinowski reads: "*Gala ikamkwamsi, gala imomomsi, u'ula ikarigasi*" ([1929] 1987:465) which means, "They do not eat, they do not drink, this is the reason they die." Malinowski's informant's commentary reads: "*Gala sitana ikamkwamsi, imomomsi, pela gala magisi, boge ivagi simwalisila, pela luleta ikaytasi*" (p. 472). This translation is: "They do not eat even a bit or

drink, they have no desire because of their shame, because they slept together" [translations mine].

31. The exact words of powerful magic spells state that the affected one will refuse all food and all drink. See an example of such magic in Weiner 1983:704.

32. It is as if all the elaborately ritualized intense sexuality that pervades so much of Trobriand adolescent life is another attempt, unsuccessful at the extreme, to disguise the power of sibling sexuality.

33. For ease of reading, I translate 'àiga as "descent group," but in actuality, the group at any one time or event may only be represented by certain branches rather than the entire unit. See Shore 1982 for an excellent discussion of Samoan kinship.

34. At its core, the members of this descent group trace their ancestry either to a founding woman whose descendants, both male and female, comprise the kin category known as *tamafafine,* or to a founding man, usually thought to be the brother of the female founder, whose descendants comprise the category, *tamatane;* Shore 1982:236.

35. The term *feagaiga* means "perpetual kinship" between the two; also "covenant" or "agreement"; as a verb, it means "to stand opposite" or "to face each other" (Milner 1966:8). A woman's sacred relationship to her brother and his children extends to the sacredness of her son, called *tamasā,* the sacred child, and to all those who stand as tamafafine to her brother.

36. Shore 1982:58. Also see pp. 58–97 and 221–283 for more extensive data on the complexity of Samoan chiefly organization.

37. See Shore 1982:91–95 for examples. See also Krämer ([1923] 1958) on the histories of high titles before Samoa was colonized.

38. Titleholders, both women and men, are selected by members of a descent group with the sacred sister's agreement. The highest titles usually are traced specifically to the founders of the original title. Titles of lower rank can be created at any time; one title can be split among several holders; some titles are even destroyed.

39. Krämer [1902] 1930, 1:54. Krämer gives an example on p. 20 of how a title became so powerful that the holder threatened to become dangerous even to his own descent group because the title was thought to have increased in power though the efforts of Nafannu, the goddess of war. Huntsman and Hooper (1975:424) point out that anthropologists emphasize the cursing power of the sacred sister whereas the other more beneficial powers in which sisters act as "spiritual" mothers to their brothers' children are ignored. Sacred power, as Beidelman (1986) has shown for ancient Greece and East Africa, is by its very nature ambiguous—at one turn subversive, evil, even mischievous, and at another turn, productive, generative, and imaginative.

40. Schoeffel (1981, 1987) shows that the cosmological justification for rank associated with mana depended upon mana being passed down through women; see also Krämer [1902] 1930. The sacred sister also receives the high-ranking *tapou* title at an early age. Similarly, her brother, who is destined to become a chief, was given the high-ranking *manaia* title, so that prior to their

marriages, brother and sister together officially represented the status, prestige, and potential of the descent group's main branches. Traditionally, they were the leaders, respectively, of the village organization of men and the village organization of women. See Shore 1982:101–105 on the men's *'aumàga* organization and the women's *aualuma* organization and the contemporary changes. See also Schoeffel 1977 on the origin and organization of women's community associations that replaced the aualuma when the missionaries reduced its importance.

41. Of course, the power of individual women varies; if a woman does not care to enforce and realize her rights, the rights disappear. See also Schoeffel 1981 for contemporary examples of women's decision-making authority.

42. Shore 1982:235. Only when a young woman is discovered sleeping with someone before marriage does her brother forget his proper role and become angry and often violent with her (ibid.). Further, although a girl and her brother should remain isolated from each other within the household, a man is expected to provide his sister with anything that she needs. Following her marriage, he also accords her husband the highest respect. See also Stuebel, cited in Krämer ([1902] 1930, 2:98).

43. Shore 1982:235.

44. Shore's informants told him that when "you think of their brothers, then you have love and pity for the girls, and you know that sex with them is bad" (1982:229).

45. In the literature this marriage ritual is spoken of as "defloweration," a highly sexist word that comes from stripping flowers off a plant, or the act of a flower shedding its pollen, and then was applied to the loss of virginity through ravishing. Despite the emphasis placed on virginity for high-ranking women at marriage, marriages of women who were not sacred sisters often took place by elopement, thereby avoiding the ritual.

46. Prior to the changes missionaries inflicted on these practices, elite women also practiced serial monogamy, securing the possibility of rights to various titles in more than one affinal descent group for their own natal kin groups.

47. Schoeffel 1987:188.

48. Cain 1971:174.

49. Schoeffel explains that such incestuous marriages produce a heightening and potentially dangerous concentration of mana, and therefore incest is deemed the origin of the highest-ranking titles. See especially the discussion of Malietoa La'auli, the son of a brother and sister union (Schoeffel 1987:186).

50. Beckwith 1932:195–198.

51. Valeri 1990.

52. Sahlins 1985:20.

53. Linnekin 1990:66–68. Reading chiefly genealogies in terms of the direction of marriage exchanges, Linnekin points out that a pattern emerges in which "lines of women [from brother–sister sibling sets], three to five generations long, give wives to lines of men" (p. 64).

54. Linnekin 1990:137–152.

55. Ibid.:154. Kamakau (1961:315) notes: "Women in those days were especially devoted to their brothers, and brothers to their sisters. It was common to see younger sisters sitting in their brothers' laps. Brothers chanted verses composed in honour of their sisters, and sisters of their brothers as a sign of devotion."

56. Malo 1951:54–55; Kamakau 1964:9.

57. Elbert 1956/1957:342. Further, Elbert (p. 346) states that Kenneth Emory in his lectures traced the record of marriages of close relatives from unpublished sources. He listed nine such marriages in the eighteenth and nineteenth centuries, beginning five generations before Kamehameha I. Since marriage and other claims could alter genealogical legitimacy of the most senior lines, in cases where marriage did not occur between true brothers and sisters, marriages between the children from two husbands of a high-ranking woman chief had the second priority with marriages of classificatory brothers and sisters of high-ranking women deemed the third most sacred (Goldman 1970:214). Even in those cases where outstanding abilities qualified a person for rulership, a noble had to trace a genealogical connection to at least one ancestor in the senior line within a ten-generation limit (Malo 1951:192).

58. M. Sinclair 1971:3–4.

59. Valeri 1985.

60. Tihi, a female god, was held in such great veneration by the people of Maui that she received the same veneration as the male god, Keoroeva (Ellis 1833, 4:72); further, both men and women priests officiated at certain temples. See n. 76 and examples from Ellis [1827] 1917:67; Kamakau 1964:20, 28, 67; Malo 1951:82, 178, n. 7. Compare Valeri (1985) who argues that only Hawaiian men stood in direct descent with gods (see chapter 2, nn. 42 and 43).

61. M. Sinclair 1971:6. Kamakau (1964:20, 28) shows that women had their own temples with their special gods and goddesses.

62. Malo 1951:191.

63. Hawaiian fine mat and tapa production reached an unparalleled development equaled in this part of the world only by the barkcloth made in Indonesia by the Toradja of central Celebes (Kooijman 1972:99). Unfortunately, descriptions of Hawaiian barkcloths and fine mats and the exact details of their circulation remain fragmentary because production and use of traditional cloth was discontinued by the mid-nineteenth century. At death, barkcloth was used for wrapping and burying the body, especially those of high rank (Green and Beckwith 1926:177–180; Malo 1951:97; Kamakau 1964:12). See also Linnekin 1990 for other examples of household use of barkcloth and mats.

64. Donald Rubenstein (1986:60) writes that in Micronesia, ritual fabrics "symbolically transform the wearer, tangibly imbuing him or her with spiritual force." Further, the art of weaving is highly esteemed because it is thought to be "a gift from the gods."

65. These skirts were called *pa'u* (Kooijman 1972:167) and this is also the word used for certain feather cloaks (see Brigham 1899:59). See Buck 1957:181. Linguistically, the connections between rank and biological reproduction extended to cloth. In Hawaii as well as Tahiti the word *matahiapo* is often used honorifically to refer to a distinguished chiefly title (Koskinen

1972:16). *Mata* means first, whereas *hiapo* refers to barkcloth, and according to Handy (1927:47), the term *makahiapo* was derived from the banyan tree, which provided the special barkcloths worn by the highest-ranking nobles. Further, when a woman died during the birth of her first child, it was said that the hiapo closed, the word referring to the woman's loin cloth and to her womb (Koskinen 1972:17).

66. See Kaeppler 1985.

67. Buck 1957; Linnekin 1990:47. Malo reports that a cloak made only of *mamo* bird feathers "was reserved exclusively for the king of a whole island, . . . it was his . . . battle cloak." Also, fine cloaks were used as the regalia of great chiefs and those of high rank and could not be worn by men of lesser rank (1951:77). Although Hawaiian women also ruled over entire islands, their possessions are rarely discussed.

68. See also Linnekin 1990:47–55.

69. Freycinet [1827–1839] 1978:85; Kamakau 1961:183. Brigham (1899) refers to the feather cloak worn by Princess Nakʻenaʻena and knew about the cloaks owned by Liliuokalani and Kapiʻolani; see Kent 1965:210 on Bishop's correspondence with Brigham.

70. Samwell 1967, 2, pt. 2:1,160. Malo notes that the carved whale tooth and the fly flap were both the "emblem and embellishment of royalty" (1951:77), but he only mentions kings.

71. Clerke 1967, 3, pt. 1:576–577.

72. Linnekin 1990:52–54.

73. Kaeppler 1985:111–116.

74. Ibid.:107. Malo states that the ancestry of high-ranking Hawaiians was recorded for each individual in long chants that, not surprisingly, were literally called "to weave a song" (1951:139, n. 5).

75. See Malo 1951:148; Kooijman 1972:165 for examples. The idea that cloth itself attracted and contained the gods and their powers is found elsewhere in Polynesia (see the Maori examples in chapter 2). Among the ancient Tahitians, when the finest barkcloths made by women were spread out, the spirits of the deceased ancestors and gods would enter the cloth and join in ritual events (Henry 1928:177). Further, special undecorated cloths made by women were wrapped in bales and hung from the ridgepoles and side beams of the sacred houses where the treasures and figures of the gods were kept (p. 153). See Rubenstein (1986) for Micronesian examples. In many other parts of the world, cloth is used in similar ways. See Feeley-Harnik's essay (1989) on Madagascar where among the Saklava, cloth was the agent for inducing spirit possession of former rulers; Gittinger 1979 on similar examples from Indonesia; Renne 1990 on the sacred properties of special kinds of Yoruba cloth.

76. The term *malo kea* referred to a white loin cloth and also was used as an epithet for a woman who enjoyed men's privileges. She was exempt from female taboos and could enter the temple sites at any time (Pukui and Elbert 1965:215).

77. Kamakau 1964:12. Many other details of this temple ritual demonstrate how closely it follows the rituals observed for the birth of a high-ranking child such as when braided coconut leaves were wrapped around the belly of

the wooden god figure and were called the "navel cord of its mother" (Malo 1951:173). When this was cut, the idol was then girded with fine cloth (Malo 1951:173–174; see also Valeri 1985:289–300).

78. In ancient Tahiti, when cloth was wound around a priest's arm, it indicated that a god had entered into the individual's body. See also E. S. C. Handy's (1927:149) similar accounts. See Mayer (1988) on the use of cloth on Hindu goddess figures which empowers male rulers. Shore (1989) presents a compelling discussion about the way tapu states were associated with protection and binding so that "to be tapu was to be empowered, but it was also to be immobilized. . . . to be bound to divine potency and was therefore a considerable burden" (p. 154). See, Cook's journals (Beaglehole 1967, 1:207–208) in which he describes how Tahitian men and women were wrapped in great quantities of barkcloth prior to the cloth's presentation (see also Ellis [1827] 1917:361). Compare the view of Valeri who, citing the instances when Hawaiian women also rolled themselves in masses of barkcloth, argues that the woman "represents a wild potentiality that has been tamed and made productive by her husband" (1985:301).

79. See Gunson 1987:171 for a list of Hawaiian women rulers.

80. See W. Ellis 1782:87; Rev. W. Ellis [1827] 1917:89, 312; 1833, 4:299; Fornander [1878–1885] 1969, 2:128, 130, 210, 269; and Kamakau 1964:10, 20 for specific references to women rulers in earlier centuries. Even after intensive Western contact enabled Kamehameha I to unify his dominance over all the islands, several of his wives and sisters became powerful regents and came to rule for many years (Kamakau 1961; Linnekin 1990).

81. See Allen 1982:162 on Liliuokalani's banking venture and Hammond 1987 on Hawaiian quilt making.

82. Mauss [1925] 1954:7. Margaret Mead (1930:73–75) briefly noted the economic importance of fine mats and how they gain value through the expertise of the women who make them.

83. Traditionally fine mats were also used as payments for all services. Today they are still essential, added to money for certain services, and huge amounts of fine mats are amassed for the opening of churches, schools, or government buildings. A new fine mat, never as valuable as an old one, sells for two hundred dollars or more in the Apia local market. Large sales of fine mats for American dollars are made to Samoans living in American Samoa because, although production had fallen off there, fine mats exchanges still are essential.

84. See Weiner 1989 for examples of these distributions. In Western Samoa, even though the fina mats sold in Apia's main market are extremely expensive, a new fine mat, regardless of the price paid, cannot replace the value of an old one, even if it is patched and faded brown with age. But in the hundreds of fine mats that circulate for an event, only those presented in certain categories, such as the fine mat of "farewell" when someone dies, are extremely valuable. Samoans deliberately hoard high-ranking fine mats for important occasions and the most ancient and valued ones remain stored away for generations, making them inalienable. So important are the strategies in keeping and giving that, at times, a person decides to hold his own funeral distributions of fine mats before he dies, thereby ensuring that the valuable ones are given to

the appropriate people. When he dies, even though it may be years later, he is buried without further exchanges.

85. At an event for a chief, each fine mat presented is a political message about the chief's support. See the examples of actual cases in Krämer ([1902] 1930, 2:50–57, 386–388). These distributions also demonstrate how kin relationships overlap and show the fluidity and boundaries of kin alliances.

86. Shore (1981) presents a different view of Samoan gender relations based on a structural analysis of dual oppositions in which he ranks women secondary to men. But he does not discuss the historical, economic, and political importance of women and fine mat production.

87. Just as chiefs select an orator to talk for them in political debates, so women also select an orator who will pronounce the name and giver of each presentation. At every major exchange event, a woman's brother first makes a formal presentation to her. Called a *sua*, it includes one of a kind of all major foods, such as a coconut, small pig, and a yam, plus an exceptionally valuable fine mat.

88. Stuebel, as quoted in Krämer ([1902] 1930, 1:100), notes that a chief tells his sons: "If one of our children takes a wife, the titi . . . [fine mat] of the bride is to be brought to my sister and her son. . . . Barkcloths and whatever you obtain you are to take first to my sister and her son!"

89. These exchanges from a man to his sister, like the sua, mark the care and dignity given to those who stand as tamafafine to those in the tamatane category. Similar associations of sisters with sexuality and reproduction are also expressed in the category names of other fine mat distributions. For example, *āfuafu* means to become pregnant and *'afu* is the name for fine mats presented from the groom's kin to the bride (Milner 1966:6). *Fa'atupu'* means the breaking of the hymen; the fine mat given as *fa'atupu'* also refers to the impending pregnancy of the women. This is also the name for the highest-ranking fine mat presented at a marriage and in cases of elopement, this fine mat is presented at the birth of the first child. See also Koskinen 1972:17.

90. Krämer [1902] 1930, 1:54. Ella writes that fine mats were "often retained in families as heirlooms, and many old *'ie* [fine mats] are well-known and more highly valued as having belonged to some celebrated family. On this account an old and ragged 'ie-toga would be more prized than a new and clean mat" (1899:169).

91. Ella notes that "the manufacture of the *'ie* [fine mat] is the work of women and confined to ladies of distinction, and common people dare not infringe the monopoly, which is *sā* (*tabu*, or sacred)" (1899:169).

92. In Samoa, the severing of the umbilicus was performed in a ritualized manner so that, for example, a Samoan girl's umbilical cord was cut on the board women used to make barkcloth whereas for a male infant, the umbilical cord was cut on a club so that he would become strong in warfare (Ella 1892:621; Turner 1884:175).

93. See Weiner 1989:53–54 for details of these exchanges and a discussion of the way exchanges of fine mats and oloa have been described in Shore 1982 as reciprocal exchange.

94. See Shore 1982:19–20 for a contemporary example; also see M. Mead

1930:43. Rubenstein (1986:62–63) notes that on Truk Island a man guilty of adultery or even of proposing adultery to another man's wife had to repay the crime with "a gift of loincloths," whereas on Faris Island, contemporary divorce payments to the dishonored spouse still include vast quantities of traditional fabric goods as well as store-bought blankets and cotton cloth.

95. See Krämer [1923] 1958. The bestowal of high-ranking titles necessitates approval from major branches of the descent group, measured in fine mats. In the last century, a contender for one of the highest titles defeated another, "lawful antagonist" because he had the support of two strong branches, "owing to their wealth in fine mats" (Krämer [1902] 1930, 1:26). Another account described how succession to one of the four highest titles only occurred when eight branches of the descent group came forward with huge piles of fine mats (ibid.:387). When the histories of these special fine mats are read, it becomes clear why certain descent groups and specific titles became so powerful over the last two hundred years (ibid.:57).

96. Gunson 1987; Schoeffel 1987.

97. Krämer [1902] 1930, 1:68–69. Ella notes that "failing a male heir, a daughter may be appointed to, or she may assume, the prerogative of chieftainship" (1892:631).

98. Untitled Samoan men and women are forbidden participation in village political events, just as they are unable to accumulate fine mats of distinction. As of 1981, untitled men were not even permitted to vote in the national elections.

99. Schoeffel 1977, 1981.

100. The Catholic church's insistence on serial monogamy also lessened the political advantages of women. Schoeffel claims that female statuses were redefined, and although today many more women hold titles than they did historically, the ritual authority of sisters is limited and a greater degree of patriarchal authority exists (1987:192). Elsewhere, Schoeffel (1981) makes a convincing case for the political importance of Samoan women before missionary influences. Also see Schoeffel 1987 and Gunson 1987 on the matrilineal transmission of rank.

101. See Linnekin 1991 for additional data on how Western administrators tried to make Samoans convert fine mats into monetary equivalences. Since even then there was much transporting of fine mats between Samoans living in American Samoa and Western Samoa, one administrative issue raised was whether the importing and exporting of fine mats should be subject to duty.

102. This support also includes those who are identified as tamafafine. Further, those who trace their genealogical connections through tamafafine links still are treated with the utmost respect by those who identify themselves as tamatane. Unless an individual holding a title, even one of the highest rank, receives the support of the members of his or her descent group, the title is "empty" and the chief has no power at all.

103. Since the introduction of cash and Western goods in the latter half of the nineteenth century, inflation has grown in the numbers of bundles and skirts women need. Today, this is even more intensified with the use of cloth and cash.

104. Weiner 1988:134–136.

105. These contemporary issues are explored in the film *The Trobriand Islanders of Papua New Guinea* (Wason 1990).

106. My argument differs somewhat from the case Irene Silverblatt (1987) describes. Whereas she argues that the establishment of the state transformed gender equality into gender hierarchy, I show that in Samoa, for example, gender hierarchy did not depend upon the emergence of the state.

Chapter 4: The Defeat of Hierarchy

1. Sahlins 1963; also see Earle 1977; Oliver 1974.

2. I take this chapter's title from Mitchell (1988), who with a reciprocity model, shows how the Wape men in the Torricelli Mountains of Papua New Guinea defeat the accumulation of wealth and the development of hierarchy by a system of rigorous traditional exchange supplemented with the Western infusion of money through gambling.

3. Dumont 1977:5.

4. Myers 1986, 1989; Spencer and Gillen [1899] 1968, 1927; Strehlow 1947.

5. Many anthropologists have described and theorized about the importance of The Dreaming in the constitution of Aboriginal social life: Durkheim [1912] 1965; Lévi-Strauss 1966; Munn 1970; Myers 1986; Róheim 1945; Stanner 1966, 1979.

6. See Myers 1986:47–70 for the most comprehensive and penetrating discussion of The Dreaming.

7. See Myers's (1986, 1989) excellent accounts of reproducing relatedness among the Pintupi.

8. Benjamin [1955] 1969:223.

9. Mauss calls attention to the importance of understanding that the person had to be seen in relation to the group and its ancestral validation when he wrote: "What is at stake . . . is more than the privilege and authority of the chief of the clan; it is the very existence both of the latter and of the ancestors" (1979:68–69). Kan notes that Tlingit ancestral names and titles are "tangibles placed on the living as clothing" (1986:199). The designs of the cloaks, often called blankets in the literature, document a person's historical rights to specific chiefly ranking and prerogatives (Jensen and Sargent 1986:81).

10. Among the Kwakiutl, when a valued copper had to be given to others, often only a piece was cut off and presented with the idea that at a later time, the original owner would be able to get it back at a later potlatch, making the original copper even more valuable when the piece was riveted back on (Boas 1897:349, 565). But Boas also noted that there are several kinds of coppers, one group that did not go out of the family and another group of less value that could circulate widely (ibid.:564, 579). Valued robes were sometimes cut apart and the pieces were highly valued (Emmons 1907).

11. The Zuni recently filed legal claims for the return of their sacred war-god statues that had been sold to museums and private collectors. Arguing in court that no individual Zuni ever had the right to give them away or sell them, the Zuni won their case. Also see the examples in Greenfield 1989.

12. Langer (1953:66) writes that "permanence of form, then, is the constant aim of living matter; not the final goal . . . but the thing that is perpetually being achieved, and that *is* always, at every moment, an achievement, because it depends entirely on the activity of 'living.' But 'living' itself is a process, a continuous change; if it stands still the form disintegrates—for *the permanence is a pattern of changes*. . . . What we call 'motion' in art . . . is *change made perceivable*, i.e., *imaginable*, in any way whatever."

13. This is a paraphrase of a Tlingit comment about wearing a valuable cloak that shows one's rank. Strategies are important and if the potlatch will not bring out important possessions, then a politically astute person will not wear a significant cloak. But when ranking is at stake then a person will wear the cloak that is most valuable: "When we wear our blankets, we show our face. We show who we are and where we come from" (Jensen and Sargent 1986:81). Even when button blankets came into vogue as the European trade in furs prohibited the Indians from using fur for their own robes, the designs in buttons indicated the rank of wearers (pp. 63–64).

14. See Poole's publications. My reinterpretation of Poole's data in part is based on an earlier essay (Weiner 1982b) which contains more extensive ethnographic data. I am very grateful to Poole, who generously provided me with additional information from his fieldwork. The interpretations I present here are of course my own.

15. See publications of A. J. Strathern and M. Strathern.

16. How we depend on an expert's authenticity is a topic that Hilary Putnam (1975:227–228) raises in questioning linguistic authenticity in relation to the reliability of "truth" or "meaning" in words. Putnam notes that although many people to whom gold is important know the word and recognize its meaning, only an expert can certify that a given piece of jewelry is actually gold. Irvine (1989:258) claims that the differentiation of authoritative statements from many other kinds of statements will arise only if the knowledge concerned is invested with social value that accrues with stability over time. What Irvine calls "chains of authenticity" occur when the expert's knowledge is given to others who, in turn, give it to others so that a kind of temporal reporting takes place.

17. Myers 1986:52.

18. Ibid.:53, 67.

19. These are the strategies that establish claims to land by building networks of relatedness with others (ibid.:127–158; Myers 1989).

20. Like a Trobriand chief passing on secret knowledge about land and other inalienable possessions to his successor, Pintupi restricted knowledge is inherently political. But whereas in the Trobriands, the value of land and other specific economic resources that follows with this knowledge (and the appropriate payments) enables a person to enhance his power through affinal and interclan alliances, Pintupi ownership of land consists of control over the

myths, ceremonies, and sacred objects that are associated with the ancestors of The Dreaming at a particular totemic–territorial place and this knowledge is only given to others at secret sites (Myers 1989:28). In discussing what the transmission of objects and designs that are part of The Dreaming means, Nancy Munn writes that what is being transmitted from one generation to the next is not only the objects but

a fundamental mode of orientation to objects in which experience of the self is firmly anchored in objective forms incorporating moral constraints. . . . But in another way, it is not merely a particular kind of object and meaning content which is being transmitted, but also a particular form of experiencing the world in which symbols of the collectivity are constantly recharged with intimations of the self (1970:157–158).

21. Myers (1989:28) further notes that by "learning about The Dreaming and seeing the rituals, one's very being is altered. People become, Pintupi say, 'different' and stronger." Munn (1970:157) states that what is being "inherited *via* ancestral transformations is not simply the moral order and authority structure itself, but also the *a priori* grounds upon which the possibilities of this order are built."

22. My use of the word *sphere* differs from Paul Bohannan's (1955) and Firth's ([1939] 1965) spheres or levels of exchange based on reciprocal returns where particular objects are exchangeable only for other kinds of objects.

23. Simmel 1950:332–333.

24. Like the Trobriands, the Aranda have played an important role in the history of anthropology, most especially in relation to theories of "primitive" religion. Durkheim relied on late nineteenth-century accounts of Aranda ceremonial life collected by Sir Baldwin Spencer and Francis Gillen for *The Elementary Forms of the Religious Life* ([1912] 1965). Extensive research among the Aranda was carried out by Carl Strehlow, a German missionary and linguist, and later his son, T. G. H. Strehlow. My citations of Strehlow refer only to T. G. H. Strehlow. Géza Róheim (1945) also wrote extensively on the Aranda.

25. Strehlow (1970:110–111) describes these "chiefs" in some detail and such leaders are also discussed in Spencer and Gillen ([1899] 1968:10–12).

26. Strehlow 1947:17. A person's own tjurunga is related to conception beliefs in which a spirit child is thought to enter a woman's body and at that moment, the tjurunga of the child is dropped onto the ground. At birth, the child's father goes to search for the dropped stone that will have the markings peculiar to the spirit child's totem. If none is found, then a wooden tjurunga is carved with the appropriate designs (Spencer and Gillen [1899] 1968:132). A famous Aranda male leader told Strehlow that he was the only man of his totem "within living memory . . . who has sprung into being from a visible tjurunga body at the storehouse. The others have been able to produce only man-made wooden objects as proof of their lineage" (1947:118). Conception sites vary in importance and sometimes a copy of a tjurunga is made when the original ancestral one cannot be found. According to Strehlow (p. 54), among the northern Aranda, humans are believed to be reincarnated from stone tjurunga and the wooden boards are only replicas of the original life-giving sacred stones. Spencer and Gillen ([1899] 1968:142) observed that wooden

boards can be as highly valued as stone ones, but their data are not as reliable as Strehlow's more precise information. Strehlow also notes that the word *tjurunga* has many meanings, all related to The Dreaming. He uses the word *tjurunga* to refer only to the sacred stone and wooden boards. I follow the same practice.

27. Spencer and Gillen [1899] 1968:132–134. Morton (1987:456) thinks that in some cases, the source of a tjurunga was an ancestor's phallus and others were the precondition for human procreation. But women, too, each receive a tjurunga when they are born (Strehlow 1947:93) and so the sexual symbolism is more complex.

28. Strehlow 1947:116.

29. Myers n.d. Munn (1970:142) writes that "any object created in any way by an ancestor is thought to contain something of himself [or herself] within it, and the various creative modes all imply a consubstantial relationship between the ancestor and his objectifications."

30. The most crucial knowledge of the tjurunga is a sacred chant whose verses give the tjurunga's ancestral name and the place of the ancestor's origin, i.e., which becomes a person's conception site (Strehlow 1947:118). According to Strehlow, only particular older men are taught the knowledge about the clan's ancestral tjurunga—the most valuable tjurunga of all (1947:122).

31. Spencer and Gillen [1899] 1968:158–159. These loans usually occur between two local groups ("estate groups" as W. E. H. Stanner [1965] calls them) who possess interlocking legends and the loan establishes peace between them. According to Spencer and Gillen, however, these lending groups need not be related to each other and the owners may even refuse a request.

32. Strehlow 1947:160–161. Spencer and Gillen ([1899] 1968:159) write that these loans are believed in some undefined way to bring good fortune. Lévi-Strauss (1966) notes that the exchange of tjurunga was like loaning out one's basic identity to the care of others. See also Myers 1989:35–38.

33. Strehlow 1947:122–123. In these affairs, decision-making authority that is more than momentarily constituted among a group of elders is vital not only to control the loans and other exchanges but because tjurunga are of such value to others that their proper inheritance must also be controlled.

34. Spencer and Gillen [1899] 1968:165. Therefore, the leader's secular power is also rooted in The Dreaming, because he becomes the focus of food production. Leaders are assured of a constant supply of food from younger men in response to their performance of ceremonies.

35. Myers 1989:35–37. These shifting constellations both genealogically and territorially comprise the ego-centered groups who come together for ceremonial events.

36. Myers, personal communication. Myers points out the difficulties in contemporary fieldwork in obtaining data about tjurunga or even in publishing such data. With future research, some of my conclusions no doubt will be revised but I emphasize how important these considerations are and how much we can understand from them about the constitution of authority.

37. Myers 1986:245.

38. R. M. Berndt 1965; Meggitt 1964; Strehlow 1970; compare Kolig 1981.

39. Kolig 1981: esp. 109–130, 131–149.

40. Myers 1986:219–255.

41. Strehlow (1947:92–93) notes that one of the Aranda's most sacred tjurunga belonged to a woman; ceremony after ceremony was given in her honor, but she could not witness any of these events. Yet he gives no information on the extent of power her authority invokes. Further, all references to the way men talk with contempt about women are about women as wives as they compare them to the power of their own female ancestors.

42. Strehlow writes that "there are, however, certain traditions and chant verses which are the exclusive property of native women, and of which the men are kept in ignorance. Far too little research has been made into this fascinating treasure of native folk-lore" (1947:93).

43. See Bell 1983, 1987; C. H. Berndt 1974; Goodale 1971; Hamilton 1980, 1981; Kaberry 1939.

44. Bell 1983.

45. See Bell 1987 for a discussion of how women are reasserting themselves in contemporary political matters.

46. One example often cited is that men inflict severe punishments upon women who intrude on the most sacred men's ritual events or who see certain objects of men's ritual paraphernalia. (See Merlan 1988 for a fuller discussion of this issue.)

47. See Bell 1983:239–244.

48. These issues also involve how men create a male gerontocracy. See, e.g., Bell 1987; Goodale 1971; Hiatt 1965; Kaberry 1939.

49. Merlan's (1986, 1988) argument revolves around the narrow way anthropologists have viewed sexuality. She believes that among Aborigines, sexuality is not perceived as an inherent part of an individual as it is in Western thought. Therefore, sexuality must be analyzed discreetly by locating the various points of asymmetries and interconnections between women and men.

50. Myers 1986:252–253.

51. Ibid.:251.

52. Merlan 1986:487.

53. Dussart 1988:187–188.

54. Glowczewski 1983a:225–239. Dussart (1988) says that women give men their hair after it is shaved following a death of a relative and then men weave the hair strings.

55. Technically, these clan lands are what Stanner calls an "estate," the "traditionally recognized locus ('country', 'home', 'ground', 'dreaming place') of some kind of patrilineal descent-group forming the core or nucleus of the territorial group" (1965:2).

56. Glowczewski 1983b.

57. Glowczewski 1983a:238.

58. Ibid.:236. This is an even closer connection between hair strings and cloth because traditionally, belts of hair strings provided the only Aboriginal clothes.

59. See Glowczewski's (1983a) discussion of hair strings and also Dussart 1988.

60. Myers 1986:229–230, 251, 307, n. 4; and personal communication.

61. Strehlow 1947:161.

62. Spencer and Gillen (1927:406) noted that hair strings (*gururknga*) are powerful, the word itself indicating a spiritual or sacred essence or substance.

63. Kaberry 1939:9.

64. This ritual work also involves men's initiation and fertility rituals that are necessary for giving birth. Poole notes that at one time women's initiation rituals were "longer and more complex than male initiation," but today girls only participate in special rituals at first menses (1984a:91). For men, it still takes from ten to fifteen years of various stages in initiation rituals to achieve the necessary growth that links them directly to a patrilineal ancestral line. See Poole (1982b) for details on male initiation; also see Barth (1987:59–60) on other Ok groups.

65. The biological and cosmological reproductive roles of husband and wife are extremely complex in detail, but in general, the physical, social, and cosmological form of a child (e.g., its "spirit" and "heart") is created out of female and male properties such as male and female blood, male semen, and female and male fertile fluids (Poole 1981b:124). Female fluids and substances are thought to produce anatomical features that are the first to decompose following death. Conversely, male properties create anatomical features that are "strong," "internal," and "hard," including bony structures, especially the skull (1981b:127). Also see Poole (1981b, 1982b, 1984b) on details of women as mothers.

66. Poole 1981b:122; see also Poole 1984b:196–197, 199.

67. Eating sacred taro is also an essential part of these rituals (Poole 1981b: 131).

68. Poole 1984a:91–92, n. 50.

69. Most of these sacred women, usually two in each clan, are members of senior lineages from which the male ritual leader is also selected (Poole 1981b:151). Also see Barth (1975:53, 65, 75, 87; 1987:65–66) for references to the significance of the neighboring Faiwolmin women's roles in men's initiation rituals.

70. This woman "removes, transforms, or embeds male and female substances in the bodies of female and males, respectively" (Poole 1981b:157).

71. See Poole (1981b) for more details.

72. Poole's own data indicate that a more inclusive concept of reproduction and production is necessary in order to understand Bimin-Kuskusmin gender relations, especially as practiced within Bimin-Kuskusmin ritual.

73. Ibid.:147.

74. These bones cannot be transferred from ossuaries to cult houses unless they are identified as those of either an initiated man or a woman who has had at least one child, for neither an uninitiated man nor a woman who has not given birth can become an ancestor (Poole, personal communication). Men are

thought to give birth as well and couvade is practiced. If a man has never "given birth," he, too, will be denied the right to become an ancestor (Poole 1982a).

75. Poole, personal communication; also see Poole 1981b:141–145.

76. According to Poole, all ritual leaders are associated with male and female fertile elements and substances.

77. Only the full incorporation of others into the group is possible, so that outsiders may become kin (Barth 1987:61–62).

78. Poole 1981b:155; also 1984a.

79. Poole 1981b:145.

80. According to Poole (1981b:145) over eighty percent of all marriages are intratribal and "fighting among affines is quite restricted" (ibid.). The women most feared for their poisoning and pollution are those from intertribal lineages where fighting with the Bimin-Kuskusmin is common.

81. Ibid.:148–149.

82. Unfortunately, we rarely have explicit data from any New Guinea society on the details of how compensation payments circulate (see Feil 1984:103–104; Josephides 1985:149–150; A. J. Strathern 1971:90, 192–193, 234–235). This is especially unfortunate because women are often directly involved in these payments both as givers and recipients.

83. Although Poole mentions that two other women are essential in these rituals, he does not explore their roles in relation to the older ritual leader. But see, Barth (1987:48–54) for comments on the use of female imagery and women's reproductive themes among Ok speaking peoples.

84. Poole 1981b:142. Elsewhere in a footnote Poole states that ". . . there is a recognized symbolic affinity between pre-menstruous maidens and post-menopausal women in certain mythic and ritual contexts" (1984a:91, n. 47).

85. If, however, female ritual leaders take on what appears to us as male powers, we must also recognize that men take on female powers at particular stages in their lives, for men are thought to give birth. Men as brothers also play a role in female initiation which occurs at a girl's first menses. The control of menstrual flow "is thought to be vested entirely in the ritual performance of male agnates" (Poole 1981b:143).

86. Harrison further notes that "they are investing, primarily, on one another's reproduction and trying to maintain permanent, exclusive claims in one another's female members' fertility against outsiders" (1988:329). Although Harrison does not discuss sibling intimacy, endogamy is practiced, resulting in close intersections between the relations of spouses and siblings.

87. Harrison explains that by restricting exchange, these things cannot be "alienated or re-used by the recipient (as movable wealth items can) to make independent transactions of his own" (ibid.:329).

88. There are cases where human bones do circulate in exchange, such as among the Kaulong of New Britain (see Goodale 1985). See also the many cases throughout human history discussed in Cantwell 1989.

89. Barth describes how a segment of the initiation ritual cycle ceased being done because a man lost the appropriate bone: "So the Baktaman must always

be unsure of the force of their images, and they are easily left adrift, robbed of their capacity to act—e.g., because a particular bone has been lost by a befuddled old man" (1987:61).

90. Briefly, moka, as described extensively by A. J. Strathern, involves a series of initiatory and main gifts transacted back and forth between two individuals who themselves are parts of chains of similar exchanges which link clans to each other and extend over the entire Melpa region (e.g., 1969, 1971, 1975, 1976, 1978). To the northwest of the Hagen region, the moka articulates with another elaborate exchange system: the *tee* of the Enga (Feil 1978, 1980, 1984; Meggitt 1972, 1974).

91. The authority of Melpa big men is created through their abilities to manipulate credit rather than control over the production of goods or food (A. J. Strathern 1969). Success does not "make his recipients or his rivals into his permanent subordinates" (A. J. Strathern 1971:13; A. J. Strathern 1982b:314).

92. Today, women do not retain full rights over their pigs although there are exceptions, but historical data on this point are not available; compare Feil 1984:111–112 and M. Strathern 1972.

93. Exactly when this occurred has not been clearly established (Hughes 1977).

94. A. J. Strathern 1979a:534.

95. Needing no further productive work, the pearl shells were directly appropriated by big men who came to hold a monopoly as they manipulated credit rather than production and channeled financial arrangements along the chains of exchanges (ibid.:532; see also 1971).

96. Pigs, however, continue to figure in moka, necessary for the initiatory exchanges, sacrificial offerings, and the moka feast itself.

97. Strathern and Strathern 1971:21.

98. Other tallies made from bamboo sticks were worn by moka players, indicating how many shell transactions a particular man had made. Each stick records that eight or ten pearl shells have been exchanged in initiatory exchanges that returned two shells and a pig. A man's sons, daughters, or wives may wear his tally (ibid.:185, n. 2). Throughout the highlands, shells were similarly important for compensation and bridewealth payments and throughout the region, men competed to get "their hands on them." Yet only among the Melpa did shells come to have the unique significance that led to the creation of these bamboo tallies (A. J. Strathern 1985:103).

99. A. J. Strathern 1983:73–88.

100. Georg F. Vicedom, a Lutheran missionary who lived in the Melpa area from 1934 to 1939, during the first disruptive years of pacification, noted that little towers made from cassowary feathers indicated how many shells a man had in circulation. Since a man's moka depended on the support of other members of his clan, these towers recorded the clan wealth or at least a man's particular power within the clan. Stands of ornamental bushes on the dancing ground also indicated how often a clan had held such a display of wealth. The

bushes could be very old and some belonged to previous generations (Vicedom and Tischner 1943–1948:822–823). Thus, some attempt to rank individuals and their clans was in evidence.

101. See Strathern and Strathern 1971:140. Unfortunately, there are few details available on how these pearl shells were exchanged or how long they could be kept out of circulation.

102. A. J. Strathern 1971:109.

103. Leahy and Crain 1937 as cited in Feil 1984:93. A. J. Strathern (1971:107–108) gives an illuminating account taken from an aged informant who discusses his surprise when he brought Taylor food and he was paid in shells. Prior to contact, only twenty-three men among two tribes had pearl shells in their possession (ibid.). But by 1938, with eight hundred Europeans resident in Mount Hagen, five to ten million pearl shells were airlifted into the town (Hughes 1977:315).

104. Women also obtained shells for their sexual services (A. J. Strathern 1979a:533), but it is unclear whether they had the freedom to decide on how these shells were to be used.

105. Pigs and pearl shells also constitute bridewealth and compensation payments, each of which can lead to later moka transactions (A. J. Strathern 1971:93–101). With inflation in pearl shells, bridewealth payments were similarly affected as big men to maintain their status had to give huge payments (ibid.:109–110). Other men, however, were able to find wives without the control of big men so that the very basis for kin and affinal relations was altered in terms of authority and control.

106. Strathern and Strathern 1971:21.

107. A. J. Strathern 1987:259.

108. By the 1970s, increased access to money through men's plantation work and cash-cropping coffee began to displace even the pearl shells; money now has become as competitive as pearl shells were in the colonial period. Big men as "capitalist entrepreneurs" try to impose their control over cash by referring to their earlier right to control pearl shells (A. J. Strathern 1982b:313; 1982c:148–149).

109. The subject of whether the Melpa once had ranking patrilineages with chiefs has been the subject of recent debate. Vicedom's account of Melpa society during the early 1930s describes an exploitative class society founded on racial domination with hereditary chiefs the apex of Melpa society and slaves at the bottom. Feil (1987:259) has argued that, prior to colonization, through the control of pearl shells by big men "inequality, stratification, and a system of ascribed leadership" took place. A. J. Strathern has sharply criticized both Vicedom and Feil arguing that Vicedom's depiction of chiefs and slaves made his book publishable in Germany during World War II. Against Feil's assumptions, he shows that even though these colonial changes grew in significance, they were not originally based on alterations "inside the clan." See also A. J. Strathern 1987:117.

110. A. J. Strathern 1970:575.

111. A. J. Strathern 1979b:48.

112. Ibid.:39–40; see also A. J. Strathern 1970.

113. A. J. Strathern 1979b:47–49.

114. M. Strathern writes that the husband–wife relationship

is a presumption of mutuality and hierarchy, providing a context for women's labor and effort; when women assist their husbands they are engaged in a 'social' enterprise. Wives are thus made out to be dependent upon men to give this value to their work. But a crucial second factor is the degree of influence actual men have over their spouses, and women's willingness to perceive things their way. (1981b:182)

In a later publication, she notes that "from the viewpoint of women, aspects of themselves are bound to their identification with their clan brothers" (M. Strathern 1984:167).

115. M. Strathern 1972.

116. According to M. Strathern: "Gender is the chief axis of the economic division of labor in Hagen . . . within the household between spouses" (1981b:181). Men depend upon their wives' efforts to produce surpluses of food to feed pigs, which enable them to accumulate more shells (now, money) and ultimately, more pigs. Women usually agree as to how their husbands should use the pigs; a man must acknowledge his wife's labor by insuring that she receives some of the returns on the particular transaction (M. Strathern 1984:167). But she emphasizes that through formal moka transactions, men influence others and thereby acquire public prestige, whereas vegetable foods "are not valuables and are not objects of public exchange." See also A. J. Strathern 1982b:309–310, 1982c:140, 1985:102.

117. Feil (1984:85–93) argues that this displacement of pigs by pearl shells did not occur in the tee. Consequently, the potential for big men to increase their power and influence through the control of a new, rare, and "mystical" wealth did not materialize.

118. Strathern and Strathern 1971:51–52.

119. Even today, when women are active in coffee production, men demand most of their earnings to develop further exchange networks. Women, who want to buy food and clothing for their children, are often accused by their husbands of "eating" money rather than "planting it" in moka (A. J. Strathern 1982c:149). The idea behind planting money is that it will grow and like fruit, can be harvested, although A. J. Strathern notes that recently some changes are noticeable with women investing their money in their own economic pursuits. M. Strathern (1981b:174) emphasizes that men often criticize women because they act for personal ends rather than for the wide social ends that men pursue. But A. J. Strathern points out that in a similar way to men, women criticize younger men's spending habits when they use money to buy beer, for gambling, and chasing young women (1982c:149). Men also take women's money to purchase expensive vehicles (A. J. Strathern 1979a, 1982b; M. Strathern 1981b, 1984).

120. LaFontaine 1973; L. L. Langness 1964; de Lepervanche 1967/1968; Salisbury 1964; Scheffler 1973; A. J. Strathern 1972.

121. Vicedom and Tischner 1943–1948:111–113. A. J. Strathern remarks that "pairs of groups which are closely allied and intermarried speak of themselves as *apa-pel,* 'mother's brothers, sister's sons, and cross-cousins,' to each

other" (1972:21). Further, the affiliation of married women to their natal clans is of great significance since, as A. J. Strathern points out, "many 'non-agnates' are persons 'brought back' by their mothers to their mothers' brothers' settlements, on widowhood, separation, or divorce from their husbands, or, in the past, as refugees of war" (1972:99).

122. A. J. Strathern 1972:18.

123. Vicedom and Tischner 1943–1948:48. A. J. Strathern (1972:124–128, 176–183) gives many examples of cases where controversies produced formal decisions about the future of children with their maternal kin. Strathern and Strathern 1971:159.

124. M. Strathern 1988:228–231.

125. M. Strathern 1981a.

126. A. J. Strathern 1972:98. Hagenders say that "a wife's people are at her back while she faces her husband" (Strathern and Strathern 1971:78).

127. A. J. Strathern 1972:18, 124–125, 179–181.

128. Ibid.:21. At her death or her children's deaths, payments are also made to her maternal kin (A. J. Strathern 1981:222).

129. If the payments are not made, the affines could bring sickness to the child or a man's wife may leave her husband with her children and return to stay with her natal kin (A. J. Strathern 1972:21).

130. Ibid.:125.

131. Weiner 1976. Although these net bags are exchanged between women, they never enter into men's exchanges, as they do at times elsewhere in New Guinea. Harrison (1985:123) reports that special net bags are made by Avatip female kin and these bags represent the material form of a man's spirit, animate and highly dangerous.

132. M. Strathern 1981a:683.

133. A. J. Strathern also notes that head hair is the seat of power and that the question of women's hair needs to be investigated further because "long 'manufactured', ringlets were in the past very popular with women of marriageable age" (1989:85, n. 6). As we have seen for Australia and Polynesia, the ritual and cosmological significance of hair, barkcloth, and netting is not unique to the Melpa but its importance is found throughout the Pacific.

134. Modjeska 1982:108. Modjeska also notes the error in assuming a direct connection between production and benefits accruing to the husband and his clan while ignoring future benefits to the woman's clan brothers.

135. In Polynesia, the Samoan sacred sister was feared by her own brother because she had the potential to be harmful to him and his children.

136. Nairn 1974 and A. J. Strathern 1976.

137. Schieffelin, personal communication.

Chapter 5: Kula

1. See Malinowski 1920, 1922. For other works on the kula see Firth 1957; Fortune 1932; Powell 1960; and J. P. S. Uberoi's (1962) reanalysis of Mali-

nowski's ethnography; see also Martha MacIntyre's (1983a) comprehensive bibliography. More recently, extensive fieldwork in the Northern Massim has led to further descriptions and analyses of kula in the Trobriands (Campbell 1983a, 1983b; Scoditti 1990; Scoditti and J. Leach 1983; Weiner 1983, 1988) and on other islands whose inhabitants participate in kula. See especially the essays in Leach and Leach 1983; also see Damon 1980; MacIntyre 1983b; Munn 1986, 1990.

2. Frederick Damon's (1980)) essay on kula was followed by a debate over whether or not kula shells were inalienable and therefore, classifiable as gifts or alienable like "commodities" (Damon 1982; Feil 1982; Gregory 1982; A. J. Strathern 1982a). The underlying problem with this debate is its grounding in the simple opposition between gift and commodity. Munn points out (1986:298, n. 41) that Damon's classification obscures the fundamental unity of a shell's movements in kula in relation to the fact that the shell is a personal possession, controlled by its owner. Arjun Appadurai (1986) argues that the general categorical separation between gift and commodity should be eliminated. But as I pointed out in chapters 1 and 2, inalienable possessions attain absolute value that is subjectively constituted and distinct from the exchange value of commodities or the abstract value of money.

3. For example, Beidelman (1989:231) points out that in the Homeric epics, fame can be bestowed only by others and is a prize of such magnitude that Odysseus and Achilles risk everything to gain it.

4. Braudy 1986:29–43. See Munn's important discussion of the theoretical significance of fame in kula (1977, 1983, 1986:116–117).

5. In fact, as Beidelman (1989:228) points out, Mauss ([1921] 1969) appears to have gotten his first insights about agonistic exchange behavior from his reading on the ancient Greeks. Unfortunately, despite his insights into the agonistic exchange among the Northwest Coast Indians and the Trobrianders' kula voyages, in his theoretical model Mauss ([1925] 1990) made reciprocal gift giving, like Durkheim's sacred domain, unambiguous. Beidelman discusses at some length that Simmel, writing twenty years before Mauss, attains a far more complex analysis of exchange in which economic exchange always involves both sacrifice and resistance.

6. On Muyuw Island, for example, Damon (1980:275) notes that the two men of importance in local affairs control 50 percent of the shells coming into Muyuw.

7. Today, kula exchanges continue to provide villagers with access to fame at a supralocal level, even in campaigns for national public office. In 1964, when the first national elections were held, Lepani Watson, a Trobriand candidate for the House of Assembly, campaigned in the D'Entrecasteaux Islands, a major part of his voting district. Even though at the time Watson was not a significant figure in kula, having gone to mission school and having lived in Port Moresby for thirteen years prior to the election, his association with kula—especially his father's earlier kula fame—enabled him to win the seat (Fink 1965:195–197; J. W. Leach 1976).

8. See Herman 1987 on ritualized friendship in ancient Greece. Although most Greek scholars discuss these gifts as examples of reciprocity, the renown

of possessions such as suits of armor indicates that these gifts had individual histories. To give away such a possession, like the Pintupi tjurunga designs, was an extension of kinship and many of these objects became inalienable.

9. For example, in judging the value of an armshell, a kula player feels the weight of the shell, counts the number of cowrie shells attached to its widest part, studies the shell's circumference and then looks for the red striations that mark the shell's age. With a necklace, the length is measured, the speed with which a person's hand slips along the full length of the necklace suggests the fineness of grinding, and the color and dimensions of each individual shell are calculated (Campbell 1983b:230). In addition, Campbell gives details on how each part of the valuable is ranked. She notes that overall there are five major named categories for armshells and six for necklaces.

10. As MacIntyre points out, "the 'name' of a particular valuable is said to be built or created by the lives of its successive owners" (1983b:148).

11. Missionaries, entrepreneurs, and adventurers settled in the Massim in the mid-nineteenth century and used newly made shells as payment to local workers (see A. J. Strathern 1983 for a comparison between moka and kula).

12. When Seligman made his Massim survey in 1904, he noted the ancestry of stone axe blades (Seligman 1910:514, 518). See also Campbell 1983b:237 and Malinowski 1922:504.

13. Grimshaw 1911:302. In 1959, Charles Julius, a government anthropologist visiting the Trobriands, reported that when he tried to purchase a stone axe blade for the museum in Port Moresby, he was told by a villager not to buy the axe offered to him because it was of little value since it had no name. Julius was told that "any really good and important axe, worthy of a prominent part in kula exchanges, would have its traditional name" (1960:63).

14. While Malinowski (1922) recognized that certain armshells and necklaces could be diverted to another man rather than given to the intended partner, he did not perceive that some valuables operated as the property of their owners (see Weiner 1976:180–181, 1988:149–154). From more recent research we now know that kitomu are found in all kula districts throughout the Massim. For other discussions see Campbell 1983a:206; Damon 1980:281–282, 1983:323–327; Munn 1986:151–155; and MacIntyre 1983b:373–376.

15. Campbell reports that although initially a new large white armshell may be classed with other high-ranking shells, when a red patina resulting from continual handling of the shell over many years appears on the shell's surface, its value becomes even greater or when a necklace becomes so worn from use that with additional grinding the string can slip through a person's hand like "a very fine fishing line" (1983b:230).

16. See Weiner 1988 for a more detailed description of these exchanges.

17. A. J. Strathern (1986:86–88) writes that investment of personal identities in shells does not occur with the Melpa today, since money is so much more important, although prior to the European inflation of Melpa shells, this identification did occur.

18. See Beidelman 1989. Even in societies without rank, such as on Gawa Island, precise discriminations are made between kula players. Munn (1986:51) reports that a Gawan man considered strong in kula is figuratively contrasted

with the weakness of "a man who eats." Similarly, in the Trobriands, women who do not work hard at producing bundles are criticized as other women complain: "You only want to eat."

19. A few years ago, when an important Kiriwina chief suddenly became ill and died on his return flight from Port Moresby, many rumors quickly circulated that a kula partner he met in the capital had poisoned him. Fortune noted the continual controversies over each kula transaction (1932:214–218) and he, too, was told by a Dobuan informant: "Many men died because of [kula shells]" (p. 210). See Munn 1986 and especially 1990 on how Gawans link the subversive agency of the witch (resulting in illness and death) with the desires of a kula recipient (resulting in fame).

20. In Kiriwina, some lesser-ranking kula men who are related to chiefs will participate with chiefs but still they only have access to lower-ranking shells.

21. Munn (1986:107–109) further concludes that the "ranking scale [of shells] depicts the process of becoming known, as one of increasing uniqueness, an increasing capacity to be identified and spoken of in one's specificness. . . . The shell model of the process of becoming famous or climbing is thus an icon of the same process for men" (1986:107–109). Munn points out that "although men and youths of all Gawan dala participate in kula (their common participation itself being a part of contemporary Gawan egalitarianism), kula provides a medium for defining hierarchical differences between men" (ibid., p. 42).

22. Even in past decades, when objects, such as stone axe blades, shell belts, and boars' tusks, were included as important parts of kula, only the most valued articles had individual names and histories. These alternate valuables are rarely used now, largely because the technology for their manufacture has been lost (Seligman and Strong 1906:235–242; Seligman 1910:531).

23. Seligman (1910) noted the presence of Trobriand chiefs when he traveled in 1904 in the Massim. Malinowski referred to the head of the Tabalu clan as "paramount chief," a term introduced in Seligman's discussion (see also Firth 1975). Since then, whether the Trobriands have chiefs has been a subject debated both by anthropologists (Bradfield 1964; Brunton 1975; Fortune 1964; Groves 1956; Powell 1960; Watson 1956) and by the Australian Administration (Julius 1960), in large part because throughout Papua New Guinea, societies with hereditary ranking lineages and chiefs are rare.

24. On Gawa, villagers often commented to Munn about how different their own egalitarian ways were from the Trobriands, as they explained to her how one Trobriand chief is higher than all others (1986:70). Much like every leader in the Massim, however, the power of Trobriand chiefs is not without limits for if a chief is too coercive or exercises too much autonomy, eventually through sorcery, he becomes his own victim. See Young's (1983) perceptive account of power and sorcery on Goodenough Island.

25. Historically, there has always been competition between chiefly matri-lineages. For example, prior to colonization, Omarakana village, the seat of the Tabalu, was burned to the ground by an opposing chiefly group and the Tabalu were forced to live elsewhere for a period of time. But the origin stories that comprise the "deed" to land document the arrival of the Tabalu in Omarakana

after staying a brief time in the northern part of the island and their subsequent control of land in this area. See Weiner 1976:46–52 for more details.

26. These limitations affect all Trobriand chiefs, even those who are members of the highest-ranking matrilineage. See Weiner 1976:204–207, 1988: 97–110 for details about the histories and competition between chiefs.

27. On Vakuta Island, women produce and exchange skirts (Campbell 1989), but these skirts never circulate as a limited currency as do Kiriwina bundles. In the southern Massim, Battaglia (1990) reports exchanges of women's "bulk wealth" that consist of mats, fiber capes, and today, articles of clothing purchased in stores.

28. Kiriwina women occasionally may engage in kula transactions in certain circumstances when their sons are young, securing their partners until the sons are old enough to engage in kula themselves. But these women never go on overseas kula. See Scoditti and Leach 1983 for references to a Kitava woman who today is an outstanding kula player. See also MacIntyre 1983b on Tubetube women who began to do kula in the early part of this century.

29. See J. W. Leach 1983:141–143 for a discussion of who participates in Kiriwina kula. Although Damon (1980:275) notes that Muyuw villagers believe that everyone participates in kula, he says only a small number of people "handle" most of the shells.

30. Men who live on the island of Kaleuna, to the west of Kiriwina, manufacture kitomu shells.

31. See the discussions of Damon 1980 and Munn 1983, 1986.

32. Compare A. J. Strathern 1983. This view differs from Damon's discussion of kula in which he argues that the ownership of kitomu is based on who actually produces them so that kitomu are "congealed labour." This enables him to equate kitomu with "a kind of 'capital,' in the restricted sense of something used to make something else" (1980:285).

33. According to Munn, members of a matrilineage may also decide to withdraw the kitomu at some future time, but Munn does not give information on how the withdrawal takes place. A woman may figure significantly in these discussions, as she can convince her husband to give a kitomu shell to her brother in order to increase her brother's chance for kula fame (1986:126–127). Damon (1980:281–282) also mentions briefly that on Muyuw, kitomu may be owned either by a single person or the group, but he gives no further information.

34. See Weiner 1976:180–183 for a description of these axe blades and their importance. See also J. Williams 1988 on the danger and fear that the axes represent and their importance to chiefs. The stone was quarried on Muyuw Island, but work ceased in the last century (Seligman 1910:531). Damon (1980:291, n. 21) notes that Muyuw kitomu are linked to the kinship system through exchange the way stone axe blades function in Kiriwina.

35. Only on an important occasion, such as the death of a chief or for compensation payments of a high-ranking person, will kitomu shells enter these internal exchanges. In the last century, however, kitomu were used in compensation payments following warfare. At that time, pearlers in the area often paid workers with kitomu shells and some kitomu necklaces were manufactured in

the southern village of Sinaketa, although, as noted earlier, these necklaces were not of high quality.

36. Campbell 1983a; Munn 1986.

37. When the leading young Kiriwina radical, John Kasaipwalova, the nephew of a high-ranking chief, rose to fame in the 1970s, he was able to engage in kula with great success (especially for a young man) because his political opposition to the highest-ranking Trobriand chiefs already had made his name known to others. See Weiner 1988:17–24 for details on the history of John Kasaipwalova and his opposition group.

38. Campbell 1983b:238.

39. However, when villagers are seeking large kitomu shells, this rigid circulation does not apply.

40. Damon (1980:278) reports that Muyuw villagers accuse everyone in kula of lying.

41. Bambi Schieffelin (1990) uses this imagery of "layers" of exchanges in her excellent discussion of the way Kaluli children are socialized into learning the proper way to give things without returns to others.

42. See also Damon 1980; Campbell 1983a; and Munn 1986 for examples of *vaga* shell transactions.

43. At this stage, there are many ploys that can be used, both by him and by those who want the shell, especially if it is large and fine. Players bring him food and other valuables, even money. They give him other kula shells to interest him in themselves. When they come to his village for kula, they have long conversations with him and his wife, hoping to convince his wife of their strength and sincerity so she will influence her husband. An owner of a kitomu often keeps several men on the line, deciding on one while making another man think he will win the shell. Of course, if too many players are played off against each other, some become angry.

44. The same seductive techniques such as giving food and other gifts and speaking knowledgeably that heighten a man's chances to interest a kitomu owner also apply to the first time a man sees a woman with whom he wants to sleep. Then he tries to become "good friends" with her by giving her gifts of tobacco and betel and may even resort to magical spells to "turn her mind" toward him. See Munn 1986:51–61, 109–118 on kula speech, hospitality, and seductive techniques among Gawan kula players. See also Guidieri 1973 for an analysis of kula fame and seduction.

45. See Weiner 1988:139–158 for details of these transactions.

46. Through successful control over material resources and relationships and through the work of continually attending to one's kula partners, strong players attract others, both as partners and younger supporters.

47. This happened recently in northern Kiriwina where a high-ranking chief had angered many of his kula partners to the extent that when he died, his partners refused to send his successor important "chiefly" shells.

48. Today, with more availability of motor boats and cash, some players now can bypass the dependency on close partners and travel by themselves to more distant places, making their own contacts as well as getting large kitomu without waiting out the years of intermediate shell transfers. Some players who

have the opportunity to travel by air take trips to Port Moresby where they now have partners. See Damon 1980:274 for another example of such shortcuts.

49. Narayan 1952.

50. Within a local village, players may have kin ties to each other and even be on the same kula paths. On Kiriwina Island, there are villages to the south where players have kula partners with villagers who live in the north, but these partners are usually related through chiefly alliances rather than descent or marriage.

51. See Munn (1986:153, 155). For both Gawa and the Trobriands, the histories of high-ranking kitomu are called by the same term as the important histories of land. As a Gawan man told Munn, "One can refer to kitomu as *kiyay* (heirlooms): 'We leliyu kitomu' (i.e., discuss their long past travels). Similarly, he said, one can 'leliyu' land, referring to matrilineal ancestors (tabu)" (1986:153). See Weiner 1976:44–50 for a discussion of land claims and the importance of these origin stories.

52. See also Munn 1977:46.

53. One Dobu woman has kept an extraordinarily famous shell for thirty years and finally the news was circulating in 1990 that she was ready to give it in the next kula exchange. All the important kula players were vying for it.

54. Malinowski 1922:83.

55. Beidelman 1989.

56. What Munn calls the "grounding of self-definition in the appraisal of the other" is the essential validation for the realization of ranking that must be authenticated by others (1986:51).

57. Munn, too, recognizes a conflict between keeping and giving: "The relative autonomy entailed in the kitomu principle enables a man to circulate his kitomu within kula, continually *separating it from himself,* while at the same time *keeping his kitomu for himself* (as represented, for instance, in his right to withdraw it from circulation)" (ibid.:153).

58. See Weiner 1976:49–50 for examples of such conflict.

Bibliography

Allen, Helena G. 1982. *The Betrayal of Liliuokalani: The Last Queen of Hawaii 1838–1917.* Glendale, Calif.: Arthur H. Clark.

Angas, George French. 1847. *Savage Life and Scenes in Australia and New Zealand.* 2 vols. London: Smith, Elder and Co.

Appadurai, Arjun. 1986. "Introduction: Commodities and the Politics of Value." In *The Social Life of Things: Commodities in Cultural Perspective,* ed. Arjun Appadurai, 3–63. Cambridge: Cambridge University Press.

Arens, William. 1986. *The Original Sin.* New York: Oxford University Press.

Arens, William, and Ivan Karp. 1989. "Introduction." In *Creativity of Power,* ed. William Arens and Ivan Karp, xi–xxix. Washington, D.C.: Smithsonian Institution Press.

Atkinson, Jane M. 1982. "Review Essay: Anthropology." *Signs* 8(2):236–258.

Baldwin, John W. 1970. *Masters, Princes, and Merchants: The Social Views of Peter the Chanter and His Circle.* Princeton, N.J.: Princeton University Press.

Barnes, John A. 1973. "Genetrix: Genitor :: Nature: Culture." In *The Character of Kinship,* ed. J. Goody, 61–74. Cambridge: Cambridge University Press.

Barth, Fredrik. 1975. *Ritual Knowledge Among the Baktaman of New Guinea.* New Haven, Conn.: Yale University Press.

———. 1987. *Cosmologies in the Making: A Generative Approach to Cultural Variation in Inner New Guinea.* Cambridge: Cambridge University Press.

Basso, Keith. 1984. "'Stalking with Stories': Names, Places and Moral Narratives." In *Text, Play, and Story: The Construction and Reconstruction of Self and Society,* ed. Edward Bruner, 19–55. Proceedings of the American Ethnological Society. Washington, D.C.

Bateson, Gregory. [1936] 1958. *Naven.* 2d ed. Stanford: Stanford University Press.

Battaglia, Debbora. 1990. *On the Bones of the Serpent: Person, Memory, and Mortality in Sabarl Island Society.* Chicago: University of Chicago Press.

Baudrillard, Jean. 1972. *Pour une critique de l'économie politique du signe*. Paris: Gallimard.

Beaglehole, John C., ed. 1967. *The Journals of Captain James Cook on His Voyage of Discovery*. Vol. 3, *The Voyage of the Resolution and Discovery 1776–1780*. Parts 1 and 2. Cambridge: Cambridge University Press (for the Hakluyt Society).

Bean, Susan S. 1989. "Ghandhi and Khadi, the Fabric of Indian Independence." In *Cloth and Human Experience*, ed. Annette B. Weiner and Jane Schneider, 355–376. Washington, D.C.: Smithsonian Institution Press.

Becker, Ernest. 1973. *The Denial of Death*. New York: Free Press.

Beckwith, Martha W. 1932. *Kepelino's Traditions of Hawaii*. Bernice P. Bishop Museum Bulletin 95. Honolulu: Bernice P. Bishop Museum.

Beidelman, Thomas O. 1966. "Swazi Royal Ritual." *Africa* 36(4):373–405.

———. 1971. "Some Kaguru Notions about Incest and Other Sexual Prohibitions." In *Rethinking Kinship and Marriage*, ed. Rodney Needham, 181–202. London: Tavistock Publications.

———. 1986. *The Moral Imagination in Kaguru Modes of Thought*. Bloomington: Indiana University Press.

———. 1989. "Agonistic Exchange: Homeric Reciprocity and the Heritage of Simmel and Mauss." *Cultural Anthropology* 4:227–259.

Bell, Diane. 1983. *Daughters of the Dreaming*. Melbourne: McPhee Gribble.

———. 1987. "The Politics of Separation." In *Dealing with Inequality: Analyzing Gender Relations in Melanesia and Beyond*, ed. Marilyn Strathern, 112–129. Cambridge: Cambridge University Press.

Bellwood, Peter. 1979. *Man's Conquest of the Pacific*. New York: Oxford University Press.

Benjamin, Walter. [1955] 1969. *Illuminations: Essays and Reflections*, ed. Hannah Arendt. New York: Schocken Books.

Bennett, Lynn. 1983. *Dangerous Wives and Sacred Sisters: Social and Symbolic Roles of High-Caste Women in Nepal*. New York: Columbia University Press.

Benveniste, Emile. [1969] 1973. *Indo-European Language and Society*, trans. Elizabeth Palmer. Miami Linguistics Series 12. Coral Gables, Fla.: University of Miami Press.

Berndt, Catherine H. 1974. "Digging Sticks and Spears, or, the Two-Sex Model." In *Woman's Role in Aboriginal Society*, 2d ed., ed. Fay Gale, 64–80. Canberra: Australian Institute of Aboriginal Studies.

Berndt, Ronald M. 1965. "Law and Order in Aboriginal Australia." In *Aboriginal Man in Australia*, ed. R. M. Berndt and C. H. Berndt, 167–206. Sydney: Angus and Robertson.

Best, Elsdon. 1898a. "Omens and Superstitious Beliefs of the Maori." *Journal of the Polynesian Society* 7:119–136, 233–243.

———. 1898b. "The Act of the Whare Pora: Clothing of the Ancient Maori." *Transactions of the New Zealand Institute* 31:625–658.

———. 1900/1901. "Spiritual Concepts of the Maori." *Journal of the Polynesian Society* 9:173–199; 10:1–20.

———. 1901. "Maori Magic." *Transactions of the New Zealand Institute* 34:69–98.

———. 1902. "Notes on the Art of War as Conducted by the Maori of New Zealand." *Journal of the Polynesian Society* 11:11–41, 47–75, 127–162, 219–246.

———. 1903. "Maori Marriage Customs." *Transactions of the New Zealand Institute* 36:14–67.

———. 1905/1906. "The Lore of the Whare-Kohanga." *Journal of the Polynesian Society* 14:205–215; 15:1–26, 147–162, 183–192; 16:1–12.

———. 1909. "Maori Forest Lore." *Transactions of the New Zealand Institute* 42:433–481.

———. 1912. *The Stone Implements of the Maori*. Dominion Museum Bulletin 4. Wellington: Government Printer.

———. 1914. "Ceremonial Performances Pertaining to Birth." *Journal of the Royal Anthropological Institute* 44:127–162.

———. 1924a. *Maori Religion and Mythology*. Dominion Museum Bulletin 10. Wellington: Government Printer.

———. 1924b. *The Maori*. 2 vols. Wellington: Memoirs of the Polynesian Society. Vol. 5.

———. 1929a. "Maori Custom Pertaining to Birth and Baptism." *Journal of the Polynesian Society* 38:241–269.

———. 1929b. *The Whare Kohanga (The 'Nest House') and Its Lore*. Dominion Museum Bulletin 13. Wellington: Government Printer.

———. 1959. *Maori School of Learning*. Wellington: Government Printer.

Bloch, Marc. 1961. *Feudal Society*, trans. L. A. Manyon. Chicago: University of Chicago Press.

Boas, Franz. 1897. "The Social Organization and the Secret Societies of the Kwakiutl Indians." *Report of the U.S. National Museum (1894–95)*:311–738.

Bohannan, Paul. 1955. "Some Principles of Exchange and Investment Among the Tiv." *American Anthropologist* 57:60–70.

Bourdieu, Pierre. 1976. "Marriage Strategies as Strategies of Social Reproduction." In *Family and Society*, trans. Elberg Forster and Patricia M. Ranum, ed. Robert Forster and Orest Ranum, 117–144. Baltimore: Johns Hopkins University Press.

Bradfield, Richard M. 1964. "Malinowski and 'The Chief'." *Man* 64:224–225.

Braudy, Leo. 1986. *The Frenzy of Renown: Fame and Its History*. Oxford: Oxford University Press.

Brigham, William T. 1899. "Hawaiian Feather Work." *Memoirs of the Bernice P. Bishop Museum* 1(1):1–86. Honolulu.

Brunton, Ron. 1975. "Why Do the Trobriands Have Chiefs?" *Man* (n.s.) 10:544–558.

Buck, Peter (Te Rangi Hiroa). 1924. "The Evolution of Maori Clothing." *Journal of the Polynesian Society* 33:25–47.

———. 1950. *The Coming of the Maori*. 2d ed. Wellington: Whitcombe and Tombs.

———. 1957. *Arts and Crafts of Hawaii*. Bernice Bishop Museum Bulletin 45. Honolulu: Bishop Museum Press.

Bürger, Peter. [1974] 1984. *Theory of the Avant Garde*. Manchester: Manchester University Press.

Burrows, Edwin G. 1940. "Culture Areas in Polynesia." *Journal of the Polynesian Society* 49:349–363.

Cain, Horst. 1971. "The Sacred Child and the Origins of Spirit in Samoa." *Anthropos* 66:173–181.

Campbell, Shirley F. 1983a. "Kula in Vakuta: The Mechanics of Keda." In *The Kula: New Perspectives on Massim Exchange,* ed. Jerry W. Leach and Edmund Leach, 210–227. Cambridge: Cambridge University Press.

———. 1983b. "Attaining Rank: A Classification of Kula Shell Valuables." In *The Kula: New Perspectives on Massim Exchange,* ed. Jerry W. Leach and Edmund Leach, 229–248.

———. 1989. "A Vakutan Mortuary Cycle." In *Death Rituals and Life in the Societies of the Kula Ring,* ed. Frederick Damon and Roy Wagner, 46–72. Dekalb: Northern Illinois University Press.

Cantwell, Ann Marie. 1989. *The Fate of His Bones, the Oracle of His Ashes: The Use of Relics in the Construction of Society.* Paper presented at the World Archaeological Congress, Vermillion, South Dakota.

Carruthers, Mary. 1990. *The Book of Memory: A Study of Memory in Medieval Culture.* Cambridge: Cambridge University Press.

Clark, Grahame. 1986. *Symbols of Excellence.* Cambridge: Cambridge University Press.

Clerke, Charles. 1967. *Journal.* See Beaglehole, 1967.

Clifford, James. 1981. "On Ethnographic Surrealism." *Comparative Studies in Society and History* 23:539–564.

Codrington, R. H. 1891. *The Melanesians: Studies in Their Anthropology and Folklore.* Oxford: Clarendon Press.

Cohn, Bernard S. 1989. "Cloth, Clothes, and Colonialism: India in the Nineteenth Century." In *Cloth and Human Experience,* ed. Annette B. Weiner and Jane Schneider, 303–354. Washington, D.C.: Smithsonian Institution Press.

Colenso, William. 1868. "On the Maori Races of New Zealand." *Transactions of the New Zealand Institute* 1:339–424.

Cort, Louise A. 1989. "The Changing Fortunes of Three Archaic Japanese Textiles." In *Cloth and Human Experience,* ed. Annette B. Weiner and Jane Schneider, 377–414. Washington, D.C.: Smithsonian Institution Press.

Damon, Frederick H. 1980. "The Kula and Generalised Exchange: Considering Some Unconsidered Aspects of 'The Elementary Structures of Kinship.'" *Man* (n.s.) 15:267–292.

———. 1982. "Alienating the Inalienable." Correspondence, *Man* (n.s.) 17:342–343.

———. 1983. "What Moves the Kula: Opening and Closing Gifts on Woodlark Island." In *The Kula: New Perspectives on Massim Exchange,* ed. Jerry W. Leach and Edmund Leach, 309–342. Cambridge: Cambridge University Press.

Davidson, Janet. 1984. *The Prehistory of New Zealand.* Auckland: Longman Paul.

Delaney, Carol. 1986. "The Meaning of Paternity and the Virgin Birth Debate." *Man* (n.s.) 21:494–513.

Donne, T. E. [1859] 1927. *The Maori Past and Present*. London: Seeley Service.

Drewal, Henry John. 1979. "Pageantry and Power in Yoruba Costuming." In *The Fabrics of Culture*, ed. Justine M. Cordwell and Ronald A. Schwarz, 189–230. The Hague: Mouton.

Duby, Georges. 1980. *The Chivalrous Society*. Berkeley, Los Angeles, London: University of California Press.

Dumont, Louis. 1977. *From Mandeville to Marx: The Genesis and Triumph of Economic Ideology*. Chicago: University of Chicago Press.

Dunlop, Ian (producer, director). 1972. *Toward Baruya Manhood*. (With Maurice Godelier, anthropologist.) Port Moresby: Institute for Papua New Guinea Studies.

Durkheim, Emile. [1893] 1984. *The Division of Labor in Society*, trans. W. D. Halls. New York: Free Press.

———. [1912] 1965. *The Elementary Forms of the Religious Life*, trans. J. Swain. New York: Free Press.

Dussart, Françoise. 1988. "Warlpiri Women Yawulyu Ceremonies." Ph.D. diss., Australian National University, Canberra.

Earle, Timothy K. 1977. "A Reappraisal of Redistribution: Complex Hawaiian Chiefdoms." In *Exchange Systems in Prehistory*, ed. T. K. Earle, 213–229. New York: Academic Press.

Elbert, Samuel H. 1956/1957. "The Chief in Hawaiian Mythology." *Journal of American Folklore* 64:99–113, 341–355; 70:264–276, 306–322.

Ella, Reverend Samuel. 1892. *Samoa*. Report of the Fourth Meeting of the Australian Association for the Advancement of Science, 620–644. Sydney: Australian Association for the Advancement of Science.

———. 1899. "Polynesian Native Clothing." *Journal of the Polynesian Society* 8:165–170.

Ellis, William. 1782. *An Authentic Narrative of a Voyage Performed by Captain Cook*. 2 vols. London: Goulding.

Ellis, Rev. William. 1833. *Polynesian Researches During a Residence of Nearly Eight Years in the Society and Sandwich Islands*. 4 vols. New York: J. & J. Harper.

———. [1827] 1917. *A Narrative of a Tour Through Hawaii, or Owhyhee; with Remarks on the History, Traditions, Manners, Customs, and Language of the Inhabitants of the Sandwich Islands*. Honolulu: Hawaiian Gazette.

Emmons, George T. 1907. "The Chilkat Blanket." *Memoirs of the American Museum of Natural History* 3:329–409.

Engels, Friedrich. [1884] 1972. *The Origin of the Family, Private Property, and the State*. New York: International Publishers.

Feeley-Harnik, Gillian. 1989. "Cloth and the Creation of Ancestors." In *Cloth and Human Experience*, ed. Annette B. Weiner and Jane Schneider, 73–116. Washington, D.C.: Smithsonian Institution Press.

Feher, Gyorgy. 1990. "A Cultural Interpretation of the Trobriand Sibling Incest Taboo." M.A. thesis, New York University.

Feil, Daryl K. 1978. "Women and Men in the Enga 'Tee'." *American Ethnologist* 5:263–279.

———. 1980. "Symmetry and Complementarity: Patterns of Competition and Exchange in the Enga 'Tee'." *Oceania* 51:20–39.

———. 1982. "Alienating the Inalienable." Correspondence, *Man* (n.s.) 17: 340–342.

———. 1984. *Ways of Exchange*. St. Lucia: University of Queensland Press.

———. 1987. *The Evolution of Highland Papua New Guinea Societies*. Cambridge: Cambridge University Press.

Fink, Ruth A. 1965. "The Esa'ala-Losuia Open Electorate." In *The Papua New Guinea Elections 1964*, ed. David G. Bettison, Colin A. Hughes, and Paul W. van der Veur, 284–298. Canberra: Australian National University Press.

Firth, Raymond. 1940. "The Analysis of Mana: An Empirical Approach." *Journal of the Polynesian Society* 49:483–512.

———. 1951. *Elements of Social Organization*. New York: Philosophical Library.

———. 1957. "The Place of Malinowski in the History of Economic Anthropology." In *Man and Culture: An Evaluation of the Work of Bronislaw Malinowski*, ed. Raymond Firth, 209–228. London: Routledge and Kegan Paul.

———. [1929] 1959. *Economics of the New Zealand Maori*. Wellington: Government Printer.

———. [1939] 1965. Primitive Polynesian Economy, 2d ed. London: Routledge and Kegan Paul.

———. 1975. "Seligman's Contributions to Oceanic Anthropology." *Oceania* 45:272–282.

Fornander, Abraham. [1878–1885] 1969. *An Account of the Polynesian Race*. 3 vols. Rutland, Vt.: Charles E. Tuttle.

Fortes, Meyer. 1953. "The Structure of Unilineal Descent Groups." *American Anthropologist* 55:17–41.

———. 1957. "Malinowski and the Study of Kinship." In *Man and Culture: An Evaluation of the Work of Bronislaw Malinowski*, ed. Raymond Firth, 157–188. London: Routledge and Kegan Paul.

———. 1958. "Introduction." In *The Developmental Cycle in Domestic Groups*, ed. Jack Goody, 1–14. Cambridge: Cambridge University Press.

Fortune, Reo F. 1932. *Sorcerers of Dobu*. New York: E. P. Dutton.

———. 1964. "Malinowski and 'The Chief'." *Man* (n.s.) 64:102–103.

Fox, Robin. 1980. *The Red Lamp of Incest*. New York: E. P. Dutton.

Franklin, Sarah B. 1988. "The Virgin Birth Debates: Biology and Culture Revisited." M.A. thesis, New York University.

Freud, Sigmund. [1908] 1968. "Family Romances." In *The Standard Edition of the Complete Psychological Works of Sigmund Freud*, ed. James Strachey, vol. 9. London: Hogarth Press.

Freycinet, Louis Claude deSaulses de. [1827–1839] 1978. *Hawaii in 1819: A Narrative Account by Louis Claude deSaulses de Freycinet*, trans. Ella W. Wiswell, ed. Marion Kelly. Pacific Anthropological Records 26. Honolulu: Bishop Museum Press.

Gailey, Christine. 1987. *Kinship to Kingship: Gender Hierarchy and State Formation in the Tongan Islands.* Austin: University of Texas Press.

Gathercole, Peter. 1978. "'Hau', 'Mauri', and 'Utu'." *Mankind* 11:334–340.

Geary, Patrick. 1986. "Sacred Commodities: The Circulation of Medieval Relics." In *The Social Life of Things: Commodities in Cultural Perspective,* ed. Arjun Appadurai, 169–191. Cambridge: Cambridge University Press.

Gernet, L. 1981. "'Value' in Greek Myth." In *Myth, Religion, and Society,* ed. R. L. Gordon, 111–146. Cambridge: Cambridge University Press.

Ginsburg, Faye D. 1989. *Contested Lives: The Abortion Debate in an American Community.* Berkeley, Los Angeles, London: University of California Press.

Ginsburg, Faye D., and Rayna Rapp. In press. "The Politics of Reproduction." *Annual Review of Anthropology.*

Gittinger, M. 1979. *Splendid Symbols: Textiles and Tradition in Indonesia.* Washington, D.C.: Textile Museum.

Glowczewski, Barbara. 1983a. "Death, Women, and 'Value Production': The Circulation of Hair Strings among the Walpiri of the Central Australian Desert." *Ethnology* 22:225–239.

———. 1983b. "Viol et inviolabilité: un mythe territorial en Australie centrale." In *Cahiers de Littérature Orale* 14:125–150.

Godelier, Maurice. 1986. *The Making of Great Men: Male Domination and Power among the New Guinea Baruya.* Cambridge: Cambridge University Press.

Goldman, Irving. 1970. *Ancient Polynesian Society.* Chicago: University of Chicago Press.

Golson, Jack. 1959. "Culture Change in Prehistoric New Zealand." In *Anthropology in the South Seas,* ed. J. D. Freeman and W. R. Geddes, 29–74. New Plymouth, New Zealand: Thomas Avery and Sons.

Goodale, Jane. 1971. *Tiwi Wives.* Seattle: University of Washington Press.

———. 1985. "Pig's Teeth and Skull Cycles: Both Sides of the Face of Humanity." *American Ethnologist* 12:228–244.

Goody, Jack. 1956. "A Comparative Approach to Incest and Adultery." *British Journal of Sociology* 7:286–305.

Green, Laura C., and Martha W. Beckwith. 1926. "Hawaiian Customs and Beliefs Relating to Sickness and Death." *American Anthropologist* 28:176–208.

Greenfield, Jeanette. 1989. *The Return of Cultural Treasures.* Cambridge: Cambridge University Press.

Gregory, Chris A. 1982. "Alienating the Inalienable." Correspondence, *Man* (n.s.) 17:343–345.

Grimshaw, Beatrice Ethel. 1911. *The New New Guinea.* Philadelphia: J. B. Lippincott.

Groves, Murray. 1956. "Trobriand Islands and Chiefs." *Man* 56:190.

———. 1963. "Western Motu Descent Groups." *Ethnology* 2:15–30.

Gudgeon, Thomas Wayth. 1885. *The History and Doings of the Maoris.* Auckland: H. Brett.

Gudgeon, W. E. 1905. "Maori Religion." *Journal of the Polynesian Society* 14:107–130.

Guidieri, Remo. 1973. "Il Kula: ovvero della truffa. Una reinterpretazione dei pratiche simboliche dell isol Trobriand." *Rassegna italiana de sociologia* 14(4):559–594.

———. 1984. *L'Abondance des pauvres: six aperçus critiques sur l'anthropologie.* Paris: Edition de Seuil.

Gunson, Neil. 1987. "Sacred Women Chiefs and Female 'Headmen' in Polynesian History." *Journal of Pacific History* 22:139–171.

Hamilton, Annette. 1980. "Dual Social Systems: Technology, Labour, and Women's Secret Rites in the Eastern Western Desert of Australia." *Oceania* 51:4–19.

———. 1981. "A Complex Strategical Situation: Gender and Power in Aboriginal Australia." In *Australian Women: Feminist Perspectives,* ed. N. Grieve and P. Grimshaw, 69–85. Melbourne: Oxford University Press.

Hammond, Joyce C. 1986. *Tifaifai and Quilts of Polynesia.* Honolulu: University of Hawaii Press.

Handy, E. S. C. 1927. *Polynesian Religion.* Bernice P. Bishop Museum Bulletin 34. Honolulu: Bishop Museum Press.

Hanson, F. Allan, and Louise Hanson. 1983. *Counterpoint in Maori Culture.* Boston: Routledge and Kegan Paul.

Harrison, Simon. 1985. "Ritual Hierarchy and Secular Equality in a Sepik River Village." *American Ethnologist* 12:413–426.

———. 1988. "Magical Exchange of the Preconditions of Production in a Sepik River Village." *Man* (n.s.), 23:319–333.

Hayden, Ilse. 1987. *Symbol and Privilege: The Ritual Context of British Royalty.* Tucson: University of Arizona Press.

Heimonet, Jean-Michel. 1988. "From Bataille to Derrida: *Différence* and Heterology." *Stanford French Review* 12(1):129–148.

Henry, Teuira. 1928. *Ancient Tahiti.* Bernice P. Bishop Museum Bulletin 48. Honolulu: Bishop Museum Press.

Herman, Gabriel. 1987. *Ritualized Friendship and the Greek City.* Cambridge: Cambridge University Press.

Herzfeld, Michael. 1980. "The Dowry in Greece: Terminological Usage and Historical Reconstruction." *Ethnohistory* 27(3):225–241.

Heuer, Berys. 1972. *Maori Women.* Wellington: A. H. and A. W. Reed.

Heusch, Luc de. 1958. *Essais sur le symbolisme de l'inceste royal en Afrique.* Brussels: Université Libre de Bruxelles.

Hiatt, L. 1965. *Kinship and Conflict.* Canberra: Australian National University.

Hirschman, Albert O. 1977. *The Passions and the Interests: Political Arguments for Capitalism Before Its Triumph.* Princeton, N.J.: Princeton University Press.

Hocart, Arthur M. 1914. "Mana." *Man* 14:97–101.

———. 1922. "Mana Again." *Man* 22:11–13.

Hogbin, H. Ian. 1935/1936. "Mana." *Oceania* 6:241–274.

Hopkins, Keith. 1980. "Brother–Sister Marriage in Roman Egypt." *Comparative Studies in Society and History* 22:303–354.

Hoskins, Janet. 1989. "Why Do Ladies Sing the Blues? Indigo Dyeing, Cloth Production, and Gender Symbolism in Kodi." In *Cloth and Human Experi-*

ence, ed. Annette B. Weiner and Jane Schneider, 141–173. Washington, D.C.: Smithsonian Institution Press.

Hubert, Henry, and Marcel Mauss. [1898] 1964. *Sacrifice: Its Nature and Function,* trans. W. D. Halls. Chicago: University of Chicago Press.

Hughes, Ian. 1977. *New Guinea Stone Age Trade: The Geography and Ecology of Traffic in the Interior.* Terra Australis 3. Canberra: Department of Prehistory, Research School of Pacific Studies, Australian National University.

Huntsman, Judith, and Antony Hooper. 1975. "Male and Female in Tokelau Culture." *Journal of the Polynesian Society* 84:415–430.

Irvine, Judith T. 1989. "When Talk Isn't Cheap: Language and Political Economy." *American Ethnologist* 16:248–267.

Jensen, Doreen, and Polly Sargent. 1986. "Robes of Power: Totem Poles on Cloth." Museum Notes 17. Vancouver: University of British Columbia Press.

Johansen, J. Prytz. 1954. *The Maori and His Religion in Its Non-Ritualistic Aspects.* Copenhagen: I Kommission Hos Ejnar Munksgaard.

Jones, E. 1925. "Mother-Right and the Sexual Ignorance of Savages." *International Journal of Psychoanalysis* 6:109–130.

Jordanova, Ludmilla. 1980. "Natural Facts: A Historical Perspective on Science and Sexuality." In *Nature, Culture, Gender,* ed. Carol MacCormack and Marilyn Strathern, 42–69. Cambridge: Cambridge University Press.

Josephides, Lisette. 1985. *The Production of Inequality: Gender and Exchange among the Kewa.* London: Tavistock.

Julius, Charles. 1960. "Malinowski's Trobriand Islands." *Journal of the Public Service of the Territory of Papua and New Guinea* 2:1–2.

Kaberry, Phyllis. 1939. *Aboriginal Woman, Sacred and Profane.* London: Routledge and Kegan Paul.

Kaeppler, Adrienne L. 1985. "Hawaiian Art and Society: Traditions and Transformations." In *Transformations of Polynesian Culture,* ed. Anthony Hooper and Judith Huntsman, 105–131. Auckland: The Polynesian Society.

Kahn, Miriam. 1986. *Always Hungry, Never Greedy: Food and the Expression of Gender Relations in a Melanesian Society.* Cambridge: Cambridge University Press.

Kamakau, Samuel Manaiakalani. 1961. *Ruling Chiefs of Hawaii.* Honolulu: Kamehameha Schools Press.

———. 1964. *Ka Poe Kahiko: The People of Old,* ed. Dorothy Barrere. Honolulu: Bernice P. Bishop Museum.

Kan, Sergei. 1986. "The 19th-Century Tlingit Potlatch: A New Perspective." *American Ethnologist* 13:191–212.

Kent, Harold Winfield. 1965. *Charles Reed Bishop: Man of Hawaii.* Palo Alto, Calif.: Pacific Books.

Keesing, Roger M. 1984. "Rethinking *Mana.*" *Journal of Anthropological Research* 40(2):137–156.

Kettering, Sharon. 1988. "Gift-giving and Patronage in Early Modern France." *French History* 2(2):131–151.

Kirch, Patrick Vinton. 1984. *The Evolution of the Polynesian Chieftains*. Cambridge: Cambridge University Press.

Kolig, Erich. 1981. *The Silent Revolution: The Effects of Modernization on Australian Aboriginal Religion*. Philadelphia: Institute for the Study of Human Issues.

Kooijman, Simon. 1972. *Tapa in Polynesia*. Bernice P. Bishop Museum Bulletin 234. Honolulu: Bishop Museum Press.

———. 1977. *Tapa on Moce Island Fiji: A Traditional Handicraft in a Changing Society*. Leiden: E. J. Brill.

Koskinen, Aarne A. 1972. *Ariki the First Born: An Analysis of a Polynesian Chieftain Title*. Helsinki: Academia Scientiarum Fennica.

Krämer, Augustin. [1902] 1930. *The Samoan Islands*. 2 vols., trans. D. H. and M. DeBeer. Stuttgart: E. Schweizerbart.

———. [1923] 1958. *Salamasina*, trans. the Association of Marist Brothers. Stuttgart: E. Schweizerbart.

LaFontaine, Jean. 1973. "Descent in New Guinea: An Africanist View." In *The Character of Kinship*, ed. Jack Goody, 35–52. London: Cambridge University Press.

Langer, Susanne. 1953. *Feeling and Form: A Theory of Art*. New York: Charles Scribner's Sons.

Langness, Lewis L. 1964. "Some Problems in the Conceptualization of Highlands Social Structure." In *New Guinea: The Central Highlands*, ed. James B. Watson. *American Anthropologist* 66:162–182.

Laslett, Peter. 1963. "Introduction." In John Locke, *Two Treatises of Government*, 2d ed., 15–135. Cambridge: Cambridge University Press.

Leach, Edmund R. 1957. "The Epistemological Background to Malinowski's Empiricism." In *Man and Culture: An Evaluation of the Work of Bronislaw Malinowski*, ed. R. Firth, 119–138. London: Routledge and Kegan Paul.

———. 1958. "Concerning Trobriand Clans and the Kinship Category *Tabu*." In *The Developmental Cycle in Domestic Groups*, ed. Jack Goody, 120–145. London: Cambridge University Press.

———. 1966. "Virgin Birth." *Proceedings of the Royal Anthropological Institute*: 39–49.

———. 1968. "Virgin Birth." Correspondence, *Man* (n.s.) 3:651–656.

Leach, Jerry W. 1976. "The 1972 Elections in the Kula Open." In *Prelude to Self-Government*, ed. D. Stone, 469–491. Canberra: Australian National University Press.

———. 1983. "Trobriand Territorial Categories and the Problem of Who Is Not in the Kula." In *The Kula: New Perspectives on Massim Exchange*, ed. Jerry W. Leach and Edmund Leach, 121–146. Cambridge: Cambridge University Press.

Leach, Jerry W., and Edmund Leach, eds. 1983. *The Kula: New Perspectives on Massim Exchange*. Cambridge: Cambridge University Press.

Leacock, Eleanor Burke. 1972. "Introduction." In *The Origin of the Family, Private Property, and the State* by Frederick Engels, 7–68. New York: International Publishers.

———. 1981. *Myths of Male Dominance*. New York: Monthly Review Press.

Leahy, M., and M. Crain. 1937. *The Land That Time Forgot*. London: Hurst and Blackett.

Lepervanche, Marie de. 1967/1968. "Descent, Residence, and Leadership in the New Guinea Highlands." *Oceania* 38:134–158, 163–189.

Lefferts, Leedon H., Jr. 1983. "Textiles, Buddhism, and Society in Northeast Thailand." Paper presented at the Wenner-Gren Conference on Cloth and Human Experience, Troutbeck, N.Y.

Lévi-Strauss, Claude. [1949] 1969. *The Elementary Structures of Kinship*. Boston: Beacon Press.

———. [1950] 1987. *Introduction to the Work of Marcel Mauss*, trans. Barbara Freeman. London: Routledge and Kegan Paul.

———. 1966. *The Savage Mind*. Chicago: University of Chicago Press.

Linnekin, Jocelyn. 1990. *Sacred Queens and Women of Consequence: Rank, Gender, and Colonialism in the Hawaiian Islands*. Ann Arbor: University of Michigan Press.

———. 1991. "Fine Mats and Money: Contending Exchange Paradigms in Colonial Samoa." *Anthropological Quarterly* 64(1):1–13.

Little, Lester K. 1978. *Religious Poverty and the Profit Economy in Medieval Europe*. Ithaca, N.Y.: Cornell University Press.

Locke, John. [1690] 1963. *Two Treatises of Government*, 2d ed., ed. P. Laslett. Cambridge: Cambridge University Press.

MacCormack, G. 1982. "Mauss and the 'Spirit' of the Gift." *Oceania* 52:286–293.

MacCormack, Carol H., and Marilyn Strathern, eds. 1980. *Nature, Culture, and Gender*. Cambridge: Cambridge University Press.

MacIntyre, Martha. 1983a. *The Kula: A Bibliography*. Cambridge: Cambridge University Press.

———. 1983b. "Changing Paths: An Historical Ethnography of the Traders of Tubetube." Ph.D. diss. Australian National University, Canberra.

Maine, Henry Sumner. 1875. *Ancient Law*. New York: Henry Holt.

Malinowski, Bronislaw. 1920. "Kula: The Circulating Exchange of Valuables in the Archipelagoes of Eastern New Guinea." *Man* 20:97–105.

———. 1922. *Argonauts of the Western Pacific*. London: Routledge and Kegan Paul.

———. 1926. *Crime and Custom in Savage Society*. New York and London: International Library of Psychology, Philosophy, and Scientific Method.

———. 1927. *Sex and Repression in Savage Society*. New York: Harcourt Brace and World.

———. [1929] 1987. *The Sexual Life of Savages*. Boston: Beacon Press.

———. 1935. *Coral Gardens and Their Magic*. 2 vols. New York: American Book Company.

———. 1954. *Magic, Science, and Religion and Other Essays*. New York: Doubleday.

Malo, David. 1951. *Hawaiian Antiquities (Moolelo Hawaii)*, trans. Nathaniel Emerson. Honolulu: Bernice P. Bishop Museum.

March, Katherine. 1983. "Weaving, Writing, and Gender." *Man* (n.s.) 18: 729–744.

Marx, Karl. [1867] 1976. *Capital: A Critique of Political Economy*, trans. Ben Fowkes. Vol. 1. London: Penguin Books.

Mauss, Marcel. 1925. "Essai sur le don: Forme et raison de l'échange dans les sociétés archaïques." *L'Année sociologique* Nouvelle Serie 1:30–186.

———. 1950. *Sociologie et anthropologie*. Paris: Presses Universitaires de France.

———. [1925] 1954. *The Gift*, trans. Ian Cunnison. Glencoe: Free Press.

———. [1914] 1969. "Origines de la notion de monnaie." In *Oeuvres* vol. 2, 106–112. Paris: Editions de minuit.

———. [1921] 1969. "Une forme ancienne de contrat chez les thraces." In *Oeuvres* vol. 3, 35–43. Paris: Editions de minuit.

———. 1975. *A General Theory of Magic*, trans. Robert Brain. New York: W. W. Norton.

———. 1979. *Sociology and Psychology*. London: Routledge and Kegan Paul.

———. [1925] 1990. *The Gift*, trans. W. D. Halls. New York: W. W. Norton.

Mayer, Adrian. 1988. "Ruleship and Divinity: The Case of the Modern Indian Prince and Beyond." Paper presented at the Conference on Divine Rule, New York University.

McNab, R. 1908. *Historical Records of New Zealand*. 2 vols. Wellington: A. R. Shearer.

Mead, Margaret. 1930. *The Social Organization of Manu'a*. Bernice P. Bishop Museum Bulletin 76. Honolulu: Bishop Museum Press.

Mead, Sidney M. 1969. *Traditional Maori Clothing*. Wellington: A. H. and A. W. Reed.

———, ed. 1984. *Te Maori: Maori Art from New Zealand Collections*. New York: Harry N. Abrams.

Meek, Ronald L. 1967. *Economics and Ideology and Other Essays*. London: Chapman Hall.

Meggitt, Mervyn J. 1964. "Indigenous Forms of Government Among the Australian Aboriginal." *Bijdragen tot de Taal* 120:163–180.

———. 1972. "System and Subsystem: The Te Exchange Cycle Among the Mae Enga." *Human Ecology* 1:111–123.

———. 1974. "Pigs Are Our Hearts: The Te Exchange Cycle Among the Mae Enga of New Guinea." *Oceania* 44:165–203.

Merlan, Francesca. 1982. "A Mangarrayi Representational System: Environment and Cultural Symbolization in Northern Australia." *American Ethnologist* 9:145–166.

———. 1986. "Australian Aboriginal Conception Beliefs Revisited." *Man* (n.s.) 21:474–493.

———. 1988. "Gender in Aboriginal Social Life: A Review." In *Social Anthropology and Australian Aboriginal Studies*, ed. Ronald M. Berndt and Robert Tonkinson, 15–76. Canberra: Aboriginal Studies Press.

Messick, Brinkley. 1987. "Subordinate Discourse: Women, Weaving and Gender Relations in North Africa." *American Ethnologist* 14:210–226.

Metge, A. Joan. 1976. *The Maoris of New Zealand: Rautahi*. London: Routledge and Kegan Paul.

Milner, George Bertram. 1966. *Samoan Dictionary*. London: Oxford University Press.

Mitchell, William E. 1987. *The Bamboo Fire: Field Work with the New Guinea Wape*, 2d ed. Prospect Heights, Ill.: Waveland Press.

———. 1988. "The Defeat of Hierarchy: Gambling as Exchange in a Sepik Society." *American Ethnologist* 15(4):638–657.

Modjeska, Nicholas. 1982. "Production and Inequality: Perspectives from Central New Guinea." In *Inequality in New Guinea Highlands Societies,* ed. Andrew Strathern, 50–108. Cambridge: Cambridge University Press.

Morton, John. 1987. "The Effectiveness of Totemism: 'Increase Ritual' and Resource Control in Central Australia." *Man* (n.s.) 22:453–474.

Munn, Nancy. 1970. "The Transformation of Subjects into Objects in Walbiri and Pitjantjara Myth." In *Australian Aboriginal Anthropology,* ed. Ronald Berndt, 141–163. Nedlands: University of Western Australia Press.

———. 1973. *Walbiri Iconography: Graphic Representation and Cultural Symbolism in a Central Australian Society.* Ithaca, N.Y.: Cornell University Press.

———. 1977. "The Spatiotemporal Transformation of Gawa Canoes." *Journal de la Société des Océanistes* 54–55:39–53.

———. 1983."Gawan Kula: Spatiotemporal Control and the Symbolism of Influence." In *The Kula: New Perspectives on Massim Exchange,* ed. Jerry W. Leach and Edmund Leach, 277–308. Cambridge: Cambridge University Press.

———. 1986. *The Fame of Gawa: A Symbolic Study of Value Transformation in a Massim (Papua New Guinea) Society.* Cambridge: Cambridge University Press.

———. 1990. "Constructing Regional Worlds in Experience: Kula Exchange, Witchcraft and Gawan Local Events." *Man* (n.s.) 25(1):1–17.

Murra, John V. 1989. "Cloth and Its Function in the Inka State." In *Cloth and Human Experience,* ed. Annette B. Weiner and Jane Schneider, 275–302. Washington, D.C.: Smithsonian Institution Press.

Myers, Fred R. 1986. *Pintupi Country, Pintupi Self: Sentiment, Place, and Politics among Western Desert Aborigines.* Washington, D.C.: Smithsonian Institution Press. Reprinted 1991. Berkeley, Los Angeles, London: University of California Press.

———. 1989. "Burning the Truck and Holding the Country: Pintupi Forms of Property and Identity." In *We Are Here: Politics of Aboriginal Land Tenure,* ed. Edwin N. Wilmsen, 15–42. Berkeley, Los Angeles, London: University of California Press.

———. n.d. "Place, Identity, and Exchange: Nurturance as the Process of Social Reproduction in a Kin-Based Society." Unpublished MS.

Nairn, Charlie (producer, director). 1974. *The Kawelka—Ongka's Big Moka.* (With Andrew J. Strathern, anthropologist.) Disappearing World Film Series. Manchester: Granada Television of England.

Narayan, R. K. 1952. *The Financial Expert.* Chicago: University of Chicago Press.

Nicholas, J. L. 1817. *Narrative of a Voyage to New Zealand in the Years 1814 and 15.* 2 vols. London: James Black & Son.

O'Brien, Mary. 1981. *The Politics of Reproduction.* London: Routledge and Kegan Paul.

Oliver, Douglas L. 1974. *Ancient Tahitian Society*. 3 vols. Honolulu: University of Hawaii Press.

———. 1989. *The Pacific Islands*. 3d ed. Honolulu: University of Hawaii Press.

Ortner, Sherry B. 1974. "Is Female to Male as Nature Is to Culture?" In *Woman, Culture, and Society*, ed. Michelle Zimbalist Rosaldo and Louise Lamphere, 67–87. Stanford, Calif.: Stanford University Press.

———. 1981. "Gender and Sexuality in Hierarchical Societies: The Case of Polynesia and Some Comparative Implications." In *Sexual Meanings: The Cultural Construction of Gender and Sexuality*, ed. Sherry Ortner and Harriet Whitehead, 359–409. Cambridge: Cambridge University Press.

Palmer, Blake. 1946. "Mana—Some Christian and Moslem Parallels." *Journal of the Polynesian Society* 55:263–275.

Parsons, Anne. 1964. "Is the Oedipus Complex Universal: The Jones–Malinowski Debate Revisited and a South Italian 'Nuclear Complex'." *The Psychoanalytic Study of Society* 3:278–328.

Pendergrast, Mick. 1987. TE AHO TAPU: *The Sacred Thread*. Honolulu: University of Hawaii Press.

Polack, Joel S. 1838. *New Zealand: Being a Narrative of Travels and Adventure . . . between 1831 and 1837*. 2 vols. London: Richard Bentley.

Poole, Fitz John Porter. 1981a. "Tanam: Ideological and Sociological Configurations of Witchcraft among Bimin-Kuskusmin." *Social Analysis* 8:58–76.

———. 1981b. "Transforming 'Natural' Woman: Female Ritual Leaders and Gender Ideology among Bimin-Kuskusmin." In *Sexual Meanings*, ed. Sherry B. Ortner and Harriet Whitehead, 116–165. Cambridge: Cambridge University Press.

———. 1982a. "Couvade and Clinic in a New Guinea Society: Birth among the Bimin-Kuskusmin." In *The Use and Abuse of Medicine*, ed. M. W. de Vries, R. L. Berg, and M. Lipkin, Jr., 54–95. New York: Praeger.

———. 1982b. "The Ritual Forging of Identity: Aspects of Person and Self in Bimin-Kuskusmin Male Initiation." In *Rituals of Manhood*, ed. Gilbert H. Herdt, 99–154. Berkeley, Los Angeles, London: University of California Press.

———. 1984a. "Cultural Images of Women as Mothers: Motherhood Among the Bimin-Kuskusmin of Papua New Guinea." *Social Analysis* 15:73–93.

———. 1984b. "Symbols of Substance: Bimin-Kuskusmin Models of Procreation, Death, and Personhood." *Mankind* 14:191–216.

———. 1987. "Ritual Rank, the Self, and Ancestral Power: Liturgy and Substance in a Papua New Guinea Society." In *Drugs in Western Pacific Societies: Relations of Substance*, ed. Lamont Lindstrom, 149–196. Lanham: University Press of America.

Powell, H. A. 1960. "Competitive Leadership in Trobriand Political Organization." *Journal of the Royal Anthropological Institute* 90 (1):118–148.

Pukui, Mary Kawena. 1942. "Hawaiian Beliefs and Customs During Birth, Infancy, and Childhood." In *Occasional Papers of Bernice P. Bishop Museum*, 357–381. Honolulu: Bishop Museum Press.

Pukui, Mary Kawena, and Samuel H. Elbert. 1965. *Hawaiian Dictionary*.

Honolulu: University of Hawaii Press.

Putnam, Hilary. 1975. "The Meaning of Meaning." In *Mind, Language, and Reality*: Philosophical Papers 2, ed. Hilary Putnam, 215–271. Cambridge: Cambridge University Press.

Radin, Margaret Jane. 1982. "Property and Personhood." *Stanford Law Review* 34:956–1015.

Rapp, Rayna. 1987. "Reproduction and Gender Hierarchy: Amniocentesis in Contemporary America." Paper presented at the Wenner-Gren Conference on Gender Hierarchies. Mijas, Spain.

Ray, Benjamin C. 1991. *Myth, Ritual, and Kingship in Buganda*. Oxford: Oxford University Press.

Renne, Elishe. 1990. "Wives, Chiefs, and Weavers: Gender Relations in Bunu Yoruba Society." Ph.D. diss. New York University.

Richman, Michèle H. 1982. *Reading Georges Bataille: Beyond the Gift*. Baltimore: Johns Hopkins University Press.

———. 1990. "Anthropology and Modernism in France: From Durkheim to the Collège du Sociologie." In *Modernist Anthropology: From Fieldwork to Text*, ed. Marc Manganaro, 183–214. Princeton, N.J.: Princeton University Press.

Rogers, Garth. 1977. "'The Father's Sister Is Black': A Consideration of Female Rank and Power in Tonga." *Journal of the Polynesian Society* 86(2):157–182.

Róheim, Géza. 1945. *The Eternal Ones of the Dream*. New York: International Universities Press.

Roth, Henry Ling. [1923] 1979. *The Maori Mantle*. Carlton, England: Ruth Bean.

Rousseau, Jean Jacques. [1762] 1966. *Emile*. New York: Dutton.

Rubenstein, Donald H. 1986. "Fabric Arts and Traditions." In *The Art of Micronesia*, ed. Jerome Feldman and Donald H. Rubenstein, 45–69. Honolulu: University of Hawaii Press.

Rubin, Gayle. 1975. "The Traffic in Women: Notes on the 'Political Economy' of Sex." In *Toward an Anthropology of Women*, ed. Rayna Reiter, 157–210. New York: Monthly Review Press.

Rubin, Miri. 1987. *Charity and Community in Medieval Cambridge*. Cambridge: Cambridge University Press.

Sacks, Karen. 1979. *Sisters and Wives: The Past and Future of Sexual Equality*. Westport, Conn.: Greenwood Press.

Sahlins, Marshall D. 1958. *Social Stratification in Polynesia*. Seattle: University of Washington Press.

———. 1963. "Poor Man, Rich Man, Big Man, Chief: Political Types in Melanesia and Polynesia." *Comparative Studies in Society and History* 5:285–303.

———. 1968. "Philosophie politique de 'l'essai sur le don'." *L'Homme* 8:5–17.

———. 1972. *Stone Age Economics*. Chicago: Aldine-Atherton.

———. 1976. *Culture and Practical Reason*. Chicago: University of Chicago Press.

————. 1981. *Historical Metaphors and Mythical Realities: Structure in the Early History of the Sandwich Island Kingdom.* Association for Social Anthropology in Oceania Special Publication 1. Ann Arbor: University of Michigan Press.

————. 1985. *Islands of History.* Chicago: University of Chicago Press.

Salisbury, Richard F. 1964. "New Guinea Highlands Models and Descent Theory." *Man* 64:168–171.

Salmond, Anne. 1975. HUI: *A Study of Maori Ceremonial Gatherings.* Auckland: Reed Methuen.

————. 1984. "Nga Huarahi O Te Ao Maori." In Te Maori, *Maori Art from New Zealand Collections,* ed. Sidney M. Mead, 109–137. New York: Harry N. Abrams.

Samwell, David. 1967. *Journal.* See Beaglehole, 1967.

Scheffler, Harold W. 1973. "Kinship, Descent, and Alliance." In *Handbook of Social and Cultural Anthropology,* ed. J. J. Honigmann, 747–793. Chicago: Rand McNally.

Schieffelin, Bambi. 1990. *The Give and Take of Everyday Life: Language Socialization of Kaluli Children.* Cambridge: Cambridge University Press.

Schneider, David. 1961. "Introduction: The Distinctive Features of Matrilineal Descent Groups." In *Matrilineal Kinship,* ed. David Schneider and Kathleen Gough, 1–29. Berkeley, Los Angeles: University of California Press.

————. 1968a. "What Is Kinship All About?" In *Kinship Studies in the Morgan Centennial Year,* ed. Priscilla Reining, 32–63. Washington, D.C.: Anthropological Society of Washington.

————. 1968b. "Virgin Birth." (correspondence) *Man* (n.s.) 3:126–129.

————. 1976. "The Meaning of Incest." *The Journal of the Polynesian Society* 85:149–169.

Schneider, Jane. 1987. "The Anthropology of Cloth." *Annual Review of Anthropology* 16:409–448.

————. 1989. "Rumplestiltskin's Bargain: Folklore and the Merchant Capitalist Intensification of Linen Manufacture in Early Modern Europe." In *Cloth and Human Experience,* ed. Annette B. Weiner and Jane Schneider, 177–213. Washington, D.C.: Smithsonian Institution Press.

Schneider, Jane, and Annette B. Weiner. 1989. "Introduction." In *Cloth and Human Experience,* ed. Annette B. Weiner and Jane Schneider, 1–29. Washington, D.C.: Smithsonian Institution Press.

Schoeffel, Penelope. 1977. "The Origin and Development of Women's Associations in Western Samoa, 1830–1977." *Journal of Pacific Studies* 3:1–21.

————. 1981. "Daughters of Sina, A Study of Gender, Status, and Power in Western Samoa." Ph.D. diss. Australian National University, Canberra.

————. 1987. "Rank, Gender, and Politics in Ancient Samoa." *The Journal of Pacific History* 23(3–4):175–193.

Scoditti, Giancarlo M. G. 1990. *Kitava: A Linguistic and Aesthetic Analysis of Visual Art in Melanesia.* Berlin: Mouton de Gruyter.

Scoditti, Giancarlo M. G., and Jerry W. Leach. 1983. "Kula on Kitava." In *The Kula: New Perspectives on Massim Exchange,* ed. Jerry W. Leach and Edmund Leach, 249–273. Cambridge: Cambridge University Press.

Seligman, C. G. 1910. *The Melanesians of British New Guinea.* Cambridge:

Cambridge University Press.

Seligman, C. G., and W. M. Strong. 1906. "Anthropological Investigations in British New Guinea." *The Geographical Journal* 27(3):347–369.

Shell, Marc. 1988. *'Measure for Measure,' Incest, and the Ideal of Universal Siblinghood*. Stanford, Calif.: Stanford University Press.

Shore, Bradd. 1981. "Sexuality and Gender in Samoa: Conceptions and Missed Conceptions." In *Sexual Meanings*, ed. Sherry B. Ortner and Harriet Whitehead, 192–215. Cambridge: Cambridge University Press.

———. 1982. *Sala'ilua: A Samoan Mystery*. New York: Columbia University Press.

———. 1989. "Mana and Tapu." In *Developments in Polynesian Ethnology*, ed. Alan Howard and Robert Borofsky, 137–173. Honolulu: University of Hawaii Press.

Shortland, Edward. 1851. *Southern Districts of New Zealand*. London: Longman Brown.

———. 1882. *Maori Religion and Mythology*. London: Longmans Green and Co.

Simmel, Georg. 1950. *The Sociology of Georg Simmel*, trans. and ed. K. Wolff. New York: Free Press.

———. [1907] 1978. *The Philosophy of Money*, trans. Tom Bottomore. London: Routledge and Kegan Paul.

Simmons, D. R. 1968. "The Lake Hauroko Burial and the Evolution of Maori Clothing." *Records of the Otago Museum* 5:1–40.

Sinclair, Keith. 1961. *A History of New Zealand*. London: Oxford University Press.

Sinclair, Marjorie. 1971. "The Sacred Wife of Kamehameha I: Keopuolani." *The Hawaiian Journal of History* 5:3–23.

Silverblatt, Irene. 1987. *Moon, Sun, and Witches: Gender Ideologies and Class in Inca and Colonial Peru*. Princeton, N.J.: Princeton University Press.

Small, Cathy A. 1987. "Women's Associations and Their Pursuit of Wealth in Tonga: A Study in Social Change." Ph.D. diss. University of Pennsylvania, Philadelphia.

Smith, Adam [1776] 1937. *The Wealth of Nations*, ed. E. Cannan. New York: Modern Library.

———. [1790] 1976. *The Theory of Moral Sentiments*, ed. D. D. Raphael and A. L. Macfie. Oxford: Clarendon Press.

Smith, S. Percy. 1910. "History and Traditions of the Taranaki Coast." Wellington: *Memoir of the Polynesian Society*, Vol. I.

Soddy, Frederick. 1933. *Wealth, Virtual Wealth and Debt; the Solution of the Economic Paradox*. New York: E. P. Dutton.

Spencer, Baldwin, and F. J. Gillen. 1927. *The Arunta*. 2 vols. London: Macmillan.

———. [1899] 1968. *The Native Tribes of Central Australia*. London: Macmillan.

Spiro, Melford E. 1968. "Virgin Birth, Parthenogenesis, and Physiological Paternity: An Essay in Cultural Interpretation." *Man* (n.s.) 3:242–261.

———. 1982. *Oedipus in the Trobriands*. Chicago: University of Chicago Press.

Stanner, W. E. H. 1965. "Aboriginal Territorial Organization: Estate, Range, Domain, and Regime." *Oceania* 36(1):1–26.

———. 1966. *On Aboriginal Religion*. Oceania Monograph 11. Sydney: University of Sydney Press.

———. 1979. *White Man Got No Dreaming*. Canberra: Australian National University Press.

Stone-Ferrier, Linda. 1989. "Spun Virtue, the Lacework of Folly, and the World Wound Upside Down: Seventeenth-Century Dutch Depictions of Female Handwork." In *Cloth and Human Experience,* ed. Annette B. Weiner and Jane Schneider, 215–242. Washington, D.C.: Smithsonian Institution Press.

Strathern, Andrew J. 1969. "Finance and Production: Two Strategies in New Guinea Highlands Exchange Systems." *Oceania* 40:42–67.

———. 1970. "The Female and Male Spirit Cults in Mount Hagen." *Man* (n.s.) 5:571–585.

———. 1971. *The Rope of Moka*. Cambridge: Cambridge University Press.

———. 1972. *One Father, One Blood*. London: Tavistock.

———. 1975. "By Toil or by Guile? The Use of Coils and Crescents by Tolai and Hagen Big-Men." *Journal de la Société des Océanistes* 31:363–378.

———. 1976. "Transactional Continuity in Mount Hagen." In *Transaction and Meaning,* ed. Bruce Kapferer, 277–287. Philadelphia: Institute for the Study of Human Issues.

———. 1978. "'Finance and Production' Revisited: In Pursuit of a Comparison." In *Research in Economic Anthropology,* Vol. 1, ed. George Dalton, 73–104. Greenwich, Eng.: JAI Press.

———. 1979a. "Gender, Ideology, and Money in Mount Hagen." *Man* (n.s.) 14:530–548.

———. 1979b. "Men's House, Women's House: The Efficacy of Opposition, Reversal, and Pairing in the Melpa 'Amb Kor' Cult." *Journal of the Polynesian Society* 88:37–51.

———. 1981. "Death as Exchange: Two Melanesian Cases." In *Mortality and Immortality,* ed. Sally Humphreys and Helen King, 205–223. New York: Academic Press.

———. 1982a. "Alienating the Inalienable." Correspondence, *Man* (n.s.) 17:548–551.

———. 1982b. "The Division of Labor and Processes of Social Change in Mount Hagen." *American Ethnologist* 9:307–319.

———. 1982c. "Tribesmen or Peasants?" In *Inequality in New Guinea Highland Societies,* ed. Andrew Strathern, 137–157. Cambridge: Cambridge University Press.

———. 1983. "The Kula in Comparative Perspective." In *The Kula: New Perspectives on Massim Exchange,* ed. Jerry W. Leach and Edmund Leach, 73–88. Cambridge: Cambridge University Press.

———. 1985. "Lineages and Big-Men: Comments on an Ancient Paradox." *Mankind* 15:101–109.

———. 1987. "Social Classes in Mount Hagen? The Early Evidence." *Ethnology* 26:245–260.

————. 1989. "Flutes, Birds and Hair in Hagen (PNG)." *Anthropos* 84(1–3): 81–87.

Strathern, Andrew J., and Marilyn Strathern. 1971. *Self-Decoration in Mount Hagen*. London: Gerald Duckworth.

Strathern, Marilyn. 1972. *Women in Between*. London: Seminar Press.

————. 1981a. "Culture Is a Netbag: The Manufacture of a Subdiscipline in Anthropology." *Man* (n.s.) 16:665–688.

————. 1981b. "Self-Interest and the Social Good: Some Implications of Hagen Gender Imagery." In *Sexual Meanings,* ed. Sherry B. Ortner and Harriet Whitehead, 166–191. Cambridge: Cambridge University Press.

————. 1984. "Subject or Object? Women and the Circulation of Valuables in Highlands New Guinea." In *Women and Property, Women as Property,* ed. Renée Hirschon, 158–175. New York: St. Martin's Press.

————. 1988. *The Gender of the Gift*. Berkeley, Los Angeles, London: University of California Press.

Strehlow, Theodor Georg Heinrich. 1947. *Aranda Traditions*. Melbourne: University of Melbourne Press.

————. 1970. "Geography and the Totemic Landscape in Central Australia: A Functional Study." In *Australian Aboriginal Anthropology,* ed. Ronald Berndt, 92–140. Nedlands: University of Western Australia Press.

Tambiah, Stanley. 1982. "Famous Buddha Images and the Legitimation of Kings." *Res* 4:5–20.

————. 1984. *The Buddhist Saints of the Forest of the Cult of the Amulets*. Cambridge: Cambridge University Press.

Taylor, Richard. [1855] 1870. Te Ika a Maui or *New Zealand and Its Inhabitants*. London: Wertheim and McIntosh.

Teckle, Belainesh. 1984. "The Position of Women in Fiji: Vatulele, A Case Study." Ph.D. diss. University of Sydney.

Thomas, Nicholas. 1987. "Unstable Categories: *Tapu* and Gender in the Marquesas." *Journal of Pacific History* 22:123–138.

————. 1989. "The Force of Ethnology: Origins and Significance of the Melanesia/Polynesia Division." *Current Anthropology* 30:27–41.

Tregear, E. 1891. *Maori–Polynesia Comparative Dictionary*. Wellington: Lyon and Blair.

————. 1904. *The Maori Race*. Wanganui, New Zealand: A. D. Willis.

Turner, Reverend G. A. 1884. *Samoa, A Hundred Years Ago and Long Before*. London: Macmillan.

Uberoi, J. P. Singh. 1962. *Politics of the Kula Ring: An Analysis of the Findings of Bronislaw Malinowski*. Manchester: Manchester University Press.

Unamuno y Jugo, Miguel de. [1921] 1954. *Tragic Sense of Life,* trans. J. E. Crawford Flitch. New York: Dover Publications.

Valeri, Valerio. 1985. *Kingship and Sacrifice: Ritual and Society in Ancient Hawaii*. Chicago: University of Chicago Press.

————. 1990. "Constitutive History: Genealogy and Narrative in the Legitimation of Hawaiian Kingship." In *Culture Through Time: Anthropological Approaches,* ed. Emiko Ohnuki-Tierney, 154–192. Stanford: Stanford University Press.

Veblen, Thorstein. 1899. *The Theory of the Leisure Class*. New York: Macmillan.

Vicedom, Georg F., and H. Tischner. 1943–1948. *Die Mbowamb*. 3 vols. Trans. F. E. Rheinstein and E. Klestadt. Hamburg: Cram, de Guyter and Co.

Wason, David (producer, director). 1990. *The Trobriand Islanders of Papua New Guinea* (with Annette B. Weiner, anthropologist). Disappearing World Film Series. Manchester: Granada Television of England.

Watson, Lepani. 1956. "Trobriand Island Clans and Chiefs." *Man* 56:164.

Watt, Robin J. 1986. "On 'Inalienable Wealth'." *American Ethnologist* 13:157–158.

Webster, Steven. 1990. "Historical Materialist Critique." In *Modernist Anthropology: From Fieldwork to Text*, ed. Marc Manganaro, 266–299. Princeton, N.J.: Princeton University Press.

Wechsler, Howard J. 1985. *Offerings of Jade and Silk: Ritual and Symbol in the Legitimation of the T'ang Dynasty*. New Haven, Conn.: Yale University Press.

Weiner, Annette B. 1976. *Women of Value, Men of Renown: New Perspectives in Trobriand Exchange*. Austin: University of Texas Press.

———. 1979. "Trobriand Kinship from Another View: The Reproductive Power of Women and Men." *Man* (n.s.) 14:328–348.

———. 1980. "Reproduction: A Replacement for Reciprocity." *American Ethnologist* 7(1):71–85.

———. 1982a. "Plus Précieux que l'or: Relations et échanges entre hommes et femmes dans les sociétés d'Océanie." *Annales* 37(2):222–245.

———. 1982b. "Sexuality among the Anthropologists, Reproduction among the Informants." *Social Analysis* 12:52–65.

———. 1983. "From Words to Objects to Magic: Hard Words and the Boundaries of Social Interaction." *Man* 18:690–709.

———. 1985a. "Inalienable Wealth." *American Ethnologist* 12:52–65.

———. 1985b. "Oedipus and Ancestors." *American Ethnologist* 12:758–762.

———. 1987. "Introduction." In *The Sexual Life of Savages in North-Western Melanesia*, by Bronislaw K. Malinowski [1929], xiii–xlix. Boston: Beacon Press.

———. 1988. *The Trobrianders of Papua New Guinea*. New York: Holt, Rinehart & Winston.

———. 1989. "Why Cloth? Wealth, Gender, and Power in Oceania." In *Cloth and Human Experience*, ed. Annette B. Weiner and Jane Schneider, 33–72. Washington, D.C.: Smithsonian Institution Press.

Weiner, Annette B., and Jane Schneider, eds. 1989. *Cloth and Human Experience*. Washington, D.C.: Smithsonian Institution Press.

White, Stephen D. 1988. *Custom, Kinship and Gifts to Saints: The Laudatio Parentum in Western France, 1050–1150*. Chapel Hill: University of North Carolina Press.

Williams, H. W. [1844] 1975. *A Dictionary of the Maori Language*. Wellington: Government Printer.

Williams, Jason. 1988. "Sorcery and Power in the Trobriands: The Political Economy of Fear." M.A. thesis. New York University.

Yate, William. 1835. *An Account of New Zealand*. London: R. B. Seeley and W. Burnside.

Young, Michael W. 1971. *Fighting with Food; Leadership, Values, and Social Control in a Massim Society*. Cambridge: Cambridge University Press.

———. 1983. *Magicians of Manumanua: Living Myth in Kalauna*. Berkeley, Los Angeles, London: University of California Press.

Index

value of, 112–113. *See also* Inalienable
possessions
Potlatch, 41, 59, 180 n. 10
Pounamu, 164 n. 10
Power: barkcloth and, 86–87; cosmology
and, 5; defined, 157 n. 2; difference
and, 150–151; exchanges and, 102,
151–155; of female ritual leaders, 186
n. 85; gender and, 95–97; missionary
impact on women and, 91; polygamy
and, 172 n. 21; ramifications of, 3;
reciprocity and, 43; of ritual leaders,
116; sacred, 173 n. 39; of sisters, 72.
See also Authority
Pregnancy: father and, 73–74; rituals of,
13; tapu state of, 53; Trobriander explanation of, 172 n. 22
Premarital sexuality, 74, 79. *See also*
Sexuality
"Primitive" societies: beliefs regarding, 2,
154; compared to Western economy,
31–32; early accounts of, 30; exchange in, 40–41; on sacred formalization, 40
Production: capitalism and need for, 41;
cosmology and, 4; food, 183 n. 34.
See also Cloth
Property: body parts as, 161 n. 42; bones
as, 58–60, 73, 103–104, 113–116;
clan lands, 184 n. 55; immovable, 32;
inalienable and alienable, 160; landed,
34–35, 38–39, 61–63, 181 nn. 19,
20, 184 n. 55; marae as inalienable,
36–40, 51–52, 170 n. 106; in medieval legal codes, 164 n. 11; movable,
32; Pintupi, 181 n. 20; private, 28,
34–35; value of, 162 n. 59; Western
history of, 160 n. 35. *See also* Inalienable possessions
Protection, 28, 90
Public/domestic boundaries, 4
"Pure gifts," 25

Quilts, Hawaiian, 88

Ranapiri, Tamati, 54, 63
Ranking: authentication of, 196 n. 51;
biological reproduction and, 64;
change and, 9; debate over Melpa,
188 n. 109; difference between, 94–
95; Hawaiian, 81–82, 86; kula and,
139–140, 144–145; mana and, 64,

173 n. 40; mats and, 88, 179 n. 95;
moka and, 119–120, 144–145; political significance of, 83; recreation of,
96; Samoan, 77–78, 90; selected by
sacred sisters, 173 n. 38; serial monogamy and, 174 n. 46; of shells, 193
n. 21; shown by cloak, 181 n. 13;
through matrilineage line, 73. *See also*
Chiefs; Hierarchy
Reciprocity: comparison of, 98–99; development of urban ideology, 29; fine-
mat distributions and, 89–90; hierarchy and, 42; kinship and, 66–67;
kula, 140–144; Malinowski's description of, 31–32; marketplace and, 28–
33; marriage and, 14, 27; as outer
manifestation, 64; possessions and,
41–42; power and, 43; as regulatory
mechanism, 2; returns during, 46;
sibling incest taboo and, 70–73; social
cohesiveness and, 31; totality of, 41–
42. *See also* Exchange
Replacement, defined, 159 n. 2
Reproduction: Aranda rituals of, 106–
107; Bimin-Kuskusmin rituals of,
117; "birth" of shells, 143; change as
threat to, 9; control over, 14, 96, 186
n. 86; cultural, 67, 91, 147; denial of
father's role, 171 n. 14; gender and,
12–17; of kin, 11; kula and female,
144–145; matrilineal, 74, 76–77;
Maori women and, 49–50, 52–54;
Melpa women and, 125; political intensity of, 97; role of male and female,
166 nn. 41, 44, 185 n. 65; sibling
roles in, 72–73, 83, 151; social practice of, 13; of social relations, 4;
symbolism of net bags and, 129; symbolism of tjurunga, 106–107; Trobriand women and, 73–74. *See also*
Biological reproduction; Cultural
reproduction
Restricted knowledge. *See* Secret
knowledge
The Return of Cultural Treasures (Greenfield), 161 n. 45
Rituals: Aboriginal sex-segregated, 109;
bones and, 57, 103, 117; childbirth,
167 n. 45; of clan identities, 101;
communal integration and, 41; of defloweration, 174 n. 45; of first menstruation, 165 n. 28; hair-string belts

Designer:	U.C. Press Staff
Compositor:	Prestige Typography
Text:	10/13 Galliard
Display:	Galliard
Printer:	Maple-Vail Book Manufacturing Group
Binder:	Maple-Vail Book Manufacturing Group